C000243747

THE LIBRARY

OF THE

NEW YORK STATE SCHOOL

OF

INDUSTRIAL AND LABOR

RELATIONS

AT

CORNELL UNIVERSITY

Carnegie Endowment for International Peace

DIVISION OF ECONOMICS AND HISTORY

John Bates Clark, LL.D., Director

ECONOMIC AND SOCIAL HISTORY

OF THE WORLD WAR

(*BRITISH SERIES*)

JAMES T. SHOTWELL, Ph.D.

GENERAL EDITOR

WITH THE COLLABORATION OF THE BRITISH
EDITORIAL BOARD

OXFORD
AT THE CLARENDON PRESS

ECONOMIC AND SOCIAL HISTORY OF THE WORLD WAR

BRITISH EDITORIAL BOARD

Sir William H. Beveridge, K.C.B., M.A., B.C.L. (Chairman).
H. W. C. Davis, C.B.E., M.A.
Professor E. C. K. Gonner, C.B.E., M.A., Litt.D.
F. W. Hirst, Esq.
Thomas Jones, M.A.
J. M. Keynes, C.B., M.A.
Professor W. R. Scott, D.Phil., Litt.D., LL.D., F.B.A.
Professor J. T. Shotwell, Ph.D. (*ex officio*).

For List of other Editors and the plan of the Series see end of this volume.

PRICES AND WAGES

IN THE

UNITED KINGDOM, 1914–1920

BY

ARTHUR L. BOWLEY, Sc.D.

PROFESSOR OF STATISTICS, UNIVERSITY OF LONDON

OXFORD: AT THE CLARENDON PRESS

London, Edinburgh, New York, Toronto, Melbourne and Bombay

HUMPHREY MILFORD

1921

PRINTED IN ENGLAND
AT THE OXFORD UNIVERSITY PRESS

EDITOR'S PREFACE

In the autumn of 1914 when the scientific study of the effects of war upon modern life passed suddenly from theory to history, the Division of Economics and History of the Carnegie Endowment for International Peace proposed to adjust the programme of its researches to the new and altered problems which the War presented. The existing programme, which had been prepared as the result of a conference of economists held at Berne in 1911, and which dealt with the facts then at hand, had just begun to show the quality of its contributions ; but for many reasons it could no longer be followed out. A plan was therefore drawn up at the request of the Director of the Division, in which it was proposed by means of an historical survey, to attempt to measure the economic cost of the War and the displacement which it was causing in the processes of civilization. Such an ' Economic and Social History of the World War ', it was felt, if undertaken by men of judicial temper and adequate training, might ultimately, by reason of its scientific obligations to truth, furnish data for the forming of sound public opinion, and thus contribute fundamentally toward the aims of an institution dedicated to the cause of international peace.

The need for such an analysis, conceived and executed in the spirit of historical research, was increasingly obvious as the War developed, releasing complex forces of national life not only for the vast process of destruction but also for the stimulation of new capacities for production. This new economic activity, which under normal conditions of peace might have been a gain to society, and the surprising capacity exhibited by the belligerent nations for enduring long and increasing loss—often while presenting the outward semblance of new prosperity—made necessary a reconsideration of the whole field of war economics. A double obligation was therefore placed upon the Division of Economics and History. It was obliged to concentrate its work upon the problem thus presented, and to study it as a whole; in other words, to apply to it the tests and disciplines of history. Just as the War itself was a single event, though penetrating by seemingly unconnected ways to the remotest parts of the world, so the analysis of it must be developed according to a plan at once all embracing and yet adjustable to the practical limits of the available data.

During the actual progress of the War, however, the execution of this plan for a scientific and objective study of war economics proved impossible in any large and authoritative way. Incidental studies and surveys of portions of the field could be made and were made under the direction of the Division, but it was impossible to undertake a general history for obvious reasons. In the first place, an authoritative statement of the resources of belligerents bore directly on the conduct of armies in the field. The result was to remove as far as possible from scrutiny those data of the economic life of the countries at war which would ordinarily, in time of peace, be readily available for investigation. In addition to this difficulty of consulting documents, collaborators competent to deal with them were for the most part called into national service in the belligerent countries and so were unavailable for research. The plan for a war history was therefore postponed until conditions should arise which would make possible not only access to essential documents but also the co-operation of economists, historians, and men of affairs in the nations chiefly concerned, whose joint work would not be misunderstood either in purpose or in content.

Upon the termination of the War the Endowment once more took up the original plan, and it was found with but slight modification to be applicable to the situation. Work was begun in the summer and autumn of 1919. In the first place a final conference of the Advisory Board of Economists of the Division of Economics and History was held in Paris, which limited itself to planning a series of short preliminary surveys of special fields. Since, however, the purely preliminary character of such studies was further emphasized by the fact that they were directed more especially towards those problems which were then fronting Europe as questions of urgency, it was considered best not to treat them as part of the general survey but rather as of contemporary value in the period of war settlement. It was clear that not only could no general programme be laid down *a priori* by this conference as a whole, but that a new and more highly specialized research organization than that already existing would be needed to undertake the Economic and Social History of the War, one based more upon national grounds in the first instance and less upon purely international co-operation. Until the facts of national history could be ascertained, it would be impossible to proceed with comparative analysis ; and the different national histories were themselves of almost baffling intricacy and variety. Consequently the former European Committee of Research was dissolved, and in its place it was decided to erect an Editorial Board in each of the larger countries and to nominate special editors in the smaller ones, who should concentrate, for the present at least, upon their own economic and social war history.

The nomination of these boards by the General Editor was the first step taken in every country where the work has begun. And if any justification was needed for the plan of the Endowment, it at once may be found in the lists of those, distinguished in scholarship or in public affairs, who have accepted the responsibility of editorship. This responsibility is by no means light, involving, as it does, the adaptation of the general editorial plan to the varying demands of national circumstances or methods of work ; and the measure of success attained is due to the generous and earnest co-operation of those in charge in each country.

Once the editorial organization was established there could be little doubt as to the first step which should be taken in each instance toward the actual preparation of the history. Without documents there can be no history. The essential records of the War, local as well as central, have therefore to be preserved and to be made available for research in so far as is compatible with public interest. But this archival task is a very great one, belonging of right to the governments and other owners of historical sources and not to the historian or economist who proposes to use them. It is an obligation of ownership ; for all such documents are public trust. The collaborators on this section of the war history, therefore, working within their own field as researchers, could only survey the situation as they found it and report their findings in the form of guides or manuals ; and perhaps by stimulating a comparison of methods, help to further the adoption of those found to be most practical. In every country, therefore, this was the point of departure for actual work ; although special monographs have not been written in every instance.

This first stage of the work upon the war history, dealing with little more than the externals of archives, seemed for a while to exhaust the possibilities of research. And had the plan of the history been limited to research based upon official documents, little more could have been done, for once documents have been labelled ' secret ' few government officials can be found with sufficient courage or initiative to break open the seal. Thus vast masses of source material essential for the historian were effectively placed beyond his reach, although much of it was quite harmless from any point of view. While war conditions thus continued to hamper research, and were likely to do so for many years to come, some alternative had to be found.

Fortunately such an alternative was at hand in the narrative, amply supported by documentary evidence, of those who had played some part in the conduct of affairs during the war, or who, as close observers in privileged positions, were able to record from first or at least second-hand knowledge the economic history of different phases of the great war, and of its effect upon society. Thus a series of monographs was planned consisting for the most part of unofficial yet authoritative statements, descriptive or historical, which may best be described as about half way between memoirs and blue-books. These monographs make up the main body of the work assigned so far. They are not limited to contemporary, war-time studies ; for the economic history of the war must deal with a longer period than that of the actual fighting. It must cover the years of ' deflation ' as well, at least sufficiently to secure some fairer measure of the economic displacement than is possible in purely contemporary judgments.

With this phase of the work, the editorial problems assumed a new aspect. The series of monographs had to be planned primarily with regard to the availability of contributors, rather than of source material as in the case of most histories ; for the contributors themselves controlled the sources. This in turn involved a new attitude towards those two ideals which historians have sought to emphasize, consistency and objectivity. In order to bring out the chief contribution of each writer it was impossible to keep within narrowly logical outlines ; facts would have to be repeated in different settings and seen from different angles, and sections included which do not lie within the strict limits of history ; and absolute objectivity could not be obtained in every part. Under the stress of controversy or apology, partial views would here and there find their expression. But these views are in some instances an intrinsic part of the history itself, contemporary measurements of facts as significant as the facts with which they deal. Moreover, the work as a whole is planned to furnish its own corrective ; and where it does not, others will.

In addition to this monographic treatment of source material, a number of studies by specialists is already in preparation, dealing with technical or limited subjects, historical or statistical. These monographs also partake to some extent of the nature of first-hand material, registering as they do the data of history close enough to the source to permit verification in ways impossible later. But they also belong to that constructive process by which history passes from analysis to synthesis. The process is a long and difficult one, however, and work upon it has only just begun. To quote an apt characterization, in the first stages of a history like this one is only ' picking cotton '. The tangled threads of events have still to be woven into the pattern of history ; and for this creative and constructive work different plans and organizations may be needed.

In a work which is the product of so complex and varied co-operation as this, it is impossible to indicate in any but a most general way the apportionment of responsibility of editors and authors for the contents of the different monographs. For the plan of the History as a whole and its effective execution the General Editor is responsible; but the arrangement of the detailed programmes of study has been largely the work of the different Editorial Boards and divisional Editors, who have also read the manuscripts prepared under their direction. The acceptance of a monograph in this series, however, does not commit the editors to the opinions or conclusions of the authors. Like other editors, they are asked to vouch for the scientific merit, the appropriateness and usefulness of the volumes admitted to the series; but the authors are naturally free to make their individual contributions in their own way. In like manner the publication of the monographs does not commit the Endowment to agreement with any specific conclusions which may be expressed therein. The responsibility of the Endowment is to History itself—an obligation not to avoid but to secure and preserve variant narratives and points of view, in so far as they are essential for the understanding of the War as a whole.

J. T. S.

TABLE OF CONTENTS

TABLE OF CONTENTS

PART II. WAGES

LIST OF TABLES AND DIAGRAMS

TABLES

PART I

PART II

DIAGRAMS

INTRODUCTION AND SUMMARY

THE purpose of this book is to give an account of the principal movements in prices and rates of wages in the United Kingdom from the beginning of the War to the summer of 1920.

Neither prices nor wages were left to the unfettered play of supply and demand, and their changes are closely related to changes in administration and control; but the work of the Government Departments is the subject of other volumes in this series, and therefore the reasons for particular regulations and the methods of administration are not here discussed or described, and dates relating to them are only given where they seem necessary for the understanding of the nature of the changes. This volume deals with results, not with causes.

The upward movement of wholesale and retail prices which began at the outbreak of the War, and of wages which began in 1915, continued with little interruption till the spring of 1920 in the case of wholesale prices, while in the autumn of 1920 the level of retail prices was still rising, and wages of miners had just advanced, while no wages had fallen. There is then no obvious date at which this history should end and the records have in fact been carried up to July or August 1920, the most recent dates for which they were generally available at the time of writing.[1] It was obvious that the levels of the summer and autumn of 1920 could not be permanent; the forces which disturbed the relations between prices and wages were not yet spent, and the demand for and supply of goods and labour were not in equilibrium. It has now become clear, however, that the date of the close of the present record was that of the

---

[1] Some tables have been completed to a later date.

turning-point, and that the prices and money wages of the . third quarter or fourth quarter of 1920 were at the maximum reached in the sequel to the War. The date of the conclusion is then well chosen, and the story of one phase of price movement is finished. Since, however, the European demand for goods is not yet effective and currency is still unstable, no forecast can be made with any confidence of the probable extent of the fall of prices that commenced in the winter of 1920-1 and its effect on wages.

No minutely accurate measurement can be made of the movement of average wages or the change in the purchasing power of money in general, for the ordinary methods of measurement of prices are not valid in times of catastrophic change, and the relations between rates of wages and earnings were altered and the personnel of the labour force changed ; but there is no doubt about the general course of prices and wages.

The growths of wholesale and of retail prices in general are shown in Diagrams I and II (pp. 11 and 22). In both cases a nearly uniform growth took place year by year (if not month by month) in the first three years of the War, that of wholesale prices being more rapid than that of retail prices. In both cases the extension of control and the fixing of prices or the granting of subsidies checked the growth from the summer of 1917 till the date of the Armistice, and at the same time the general measurements become almost meaningless since goods could no longer be freely purchased. After the Armistice there was a tendency to fall, but as control was removed the ordinary action of supply and demand resulted in prices at which in fact goods could be bought, and from May 1919 the upward movement again became marked till a maximum of wholesale prices was reached in the spring of 1920. Retail prices and the cost of living advanced till a later month as restrictions and subsidies were successively abolished and as the increase in wages cost per unit of production made itself felt.

It is not so easy to give a graphic record or a simple account of the movement of wages. After a few months of unsettlement the demand for war materials and the withdrawal of men to the army resulted in very plentiful employment. The opportunity of increased family earnings at former rates of pay together with an active patriotic spirit prevented for some time demands for increased wages. As food became scarce and prices rose, however, earnings became insufficient in some cases to meet the reasonable needs of efficient subsistence, and bonuses and war wages were given, while the great demand for labour had its natural effect in raising rates of wages. From 1917 workmen were more inclined to press for the full market value of their work and patriotic fervour was damped by the dearth and dearness of commodities, and wages were continuously forced up till the Armistice. So far as a generalization is possible, we may state that the growth of *rates of wages* generally lagged behind that of prices, but *earnings*, in those very numerous cases where piece rates or overtime gave facilities for additional work and pay, increased more rapidly than prices from the outbreak of War to the Armistice. In the early part of 1919 the war-rates continued though earnings probably tended to fall ; and the working classes, fairly content with existing rates in view of the slight fall in prices, devoted their attention to reduction of hours, so that in fact the normal working week was generally reduced by some 10 per cent., while the same money was received for the shorter week as formerly for the longer. When the rise of prices set in again there were continued further upward movements of wages, and at the same time several of the more powerful trade unions made definite efforts to secure a higher standard of living than before the War, while the principle of a minimum wage, intended to be sufficient to allow a livelihood more liberal than had been customary, was widely applied. The result was that during 1919 and 1920 there was a race between wages and prices; it was possible because of the elasticity of the currency to obtain higher money wages, but it was not possible to obtain higher real wages for less work unless in exceptional cases. Such data as are available for comparing the growth of wages with the increase in the cost of living are discussed in detail in the latter part of this book. There can be no doubt that some sections (especially the worst paid) of the working classes were better off in the summer of 1920 than before the War, and it is probable that other sections were worse off. It is not possible to decide whether the average of all wages, measured in purchasing power, had risen or fallen. It is, however, clear that the position is unstable; rates of wages beyond the equilibrium point are only temporarily possible, and must result in unemployment unless they fall.[1] Many involved questions have to be settled in political, financial, and industrial spheres, before the world situation is definite and production and distribution stable, and it will be a long time before a steady equilibrium is obtained. Till then it will not be possible to decide how the War ultimately affected the working-class standard of living.

In Chapter I will be found a summary of the change in wholesale prices, in Chapter IV of the increase in retail prices and in the cost of living, and in Chapter VII the relative movements of wages and of prices are compared.

---

[1] This was written before the commencement of the great wave of unemployment in the winter 1920–1.

PART I. PRICES

CHAPTER I

GENERAL MOVEMENT OF WHOLESALE PRICES

Difficulty of measurement in War circumstances. The method of index-numbers.
Index-numbers of the *Statist*, the *Economist*, and the Board of Trade. The regular
increase 1914 to 1917. The check in 1918 and subsequent rise. *Note*. Detailed
analysis of the three index-numbers.

THE movement of prices in a general sense is not a quite
simple conception. We observe that prices of many commodities
are rising, while others are stationary and a few are falling, and
there is no obvious way in which these various changes can be
combined so as to give a single measurement. The problem is
an old one, and great attention has been given to it by economists and statisticians for more than half a century. The method
adopted has been to make a systematic average of the different
movements ; the price of each commodity is conceived as
influenced by two sets of factors, the first of which arises from
the conditions of supply and demand peculiar to the commodity, the second is due to causes influencing fundamentally
all prices alike and connected with the amount of money and
its circulation. The process of averaging tends to eliminate the
variations in the first set of factors and to leave as a residuum
the resultant of the second set, thus affording a measurement
of the effect of the universal or common causes. The resulting
measurements are thrown into the form of percentage changes,
and the series of numbers so obtained are called index-numbers.
Thus the index-number for wholesale prices in the United
Kingdom, according to one reckoning in 1912, was 114 as compared with 100 in 1900. This increase of 14 per cent. is the
average of the increases in the prices of a number of selected
commodities.

B

The method of index-numbers is now generally used in all developed countries for measuring the general movement not only of wholesale prices but also of retail prices, of wages, and of other phenomena where a general change is masked by individual variations.

Such a measurement of the general movement of prices, in a period when the changes are rapid and in which the ordinary conditions of demand and supply are replaced by controls and combinations, presents problems of great difficulty. This method of index-numbers, which is sufficient for most purposes in ordinary times, requires re-examination, and the conception of a change in the general level of prices calls for a fresh analysis in the altered circumstances.

We will confine ourselves for the present to wholesale prices, that is, to prices of goods as bought by the manufacturer or the merchant, and postpone the question of the movement of retail prices and its reciprocal, viz. the change in the purchasing power of money in the hands of the consumer, to a later chapter.

A general rise of prices is usually conceived in its relation to a fall in the value of currency, and the measurement of the former as an indirect or inverse way of obtaining a measurement of the latter. There are kindred problems which in ordinary times can be handled by the same mechanism, such as the value that a given aggregate of goods (e.g. goods exported from the United Kingdom) would have reached if prices had remained stationary at the levels of an earlier year ; but it cannot be assumed that methods valid in ordinary times are appropriate for the period 1914 to 1919, and it is well to restrict the investigation to the measurement of the fall in the value of currency.

The price which is generally considered is the market price, where buyers (and usually sellers) are in competition with each other, and where there is no restriction externally imposed on the amount that any buyer can purchase. Such prices are determined by the interaction of supply and demand, and in the long run are the result of the balance of the various economic forces influencing production and distribution, whose nature and action form the subject-matter of ordinary economic analysis. In such circumstances a statement that 1 oz. of gold, 60 lb. of wool, 12 cwt. of steel, and 8 cwt. of flour have all the same value has an intelligible meaning. But if the Government buys the whole supply of wool, fixes the price of steel, and rations the consumption of flour, the whole analysis which leads to the meaning of the phrase, ' value in exchange ', breaks down. When a maximum price or maximum consumption is fixed, we can no longer know what is the relative value of the commodities affected. If a law was passed now (in 1920) that no goods should be sold at a price more than twice that of July 1914, and was successfully enforced, the value of money to would-be purchasers would fall heavily, for they would not be able to obtain at all many of the goods they desired ; a price has no meaning unless goods can be sold and bought.

A second difficulty encountered by compilers of index-numbers is of a less theoretical nature. It is typified by the case of beet-sugar, whose price forms one of the items both of the *Economist's* and of the *Statist's* numbers ; German sugar was not purchasable after the declaration of war, and some numbers had to be interpolated to fill the gap ; it is not at all clear on what principle the interpolation was made. In other cases also the price quotation used prior to the War became at one date or another unavailable ; thus flour, town house-holds or town-made white, had to be replaced by G.R.[1] flour, which was of a variable quality. The *Economist* index-number is made up of 44 entries ; of these the quality appears to have been changed[2] during the War in the cases of flour, beef, tea, sugar (two kinds), iron bars, jute, silk, wool (English and Australian), cotton (Egyptian), leather, and timber (two kinds), and there was no market quotation for many months in the cases of imported wheats, coffee, butter, lead, flax, seal-oil, rape

---

[1] That is, Government Regulation flour as authorized by the Ministry of Food.

[2] It is very unfortunate that the compilers of the *Economist* and of the *Statist* index-numbers have never made clear how they have met the difficulties of obtaining comparable quotations in the years 1914–20, and that consequently readers have to depend entirely on the judgement of the compilers. It may be that part of their methods has been misinterpreted in this book.

seed, steam coal ; in at least three other cases the price was
fixed by Government, and there remain at the most 19 items
out of 44 which represent market prices of unchanged grades.
Similar difficulties must be concealed in the *Statist* index-
number, where unfortunately the details published do not
allow one to learn how the obstacles were overcome.

The index-numbers of the *Statist* and of the *Economist* are
both compiled from market quotations of selected commodities,
and (as can be seen by the note on pp. 12–17) on so nearly
the same basis that from the known principles of weighted
averages they should show nearly identical results ; their
apparently remarkable agreement during the War is due to
this commonness of origin, while the minor divergencies point
to differences in the methods adopted for meeting the difficulties
indicated above. If they were independent their agreement
would afford strong evidence that they were adequate measurements of some definite quantity ; as it is, it may only
indicate that the arithmetical operations have been correctly
performed.

The Board of Trade index-number of wholesale prices,
though it covers very nearly the same group of commodities
(see note, p. 15), differs markedly in structure and method
from those already named. In most cases the prices used are
the average prices of commodities exported or imported, the
averages being obtained by dividing the declared values of the
goods at the time of importation or exportation by their
quantities. None of the commodities have dropped out of
trade, and, therefore, there has been no need for interpolation
or other doctoring of the figures, and though there have no
doubt been some changes in quality (e. g. in the cases of bacon
and of tea), on the whole these can have slight influence. Most
of the prices are to a great extent independent of any Government regulations, but British wheat, potatoes, beef, mutton,
milk, and bricks, whose joint importance amounts to about
one-third of the aggregate, are valued at the home prices. This
index-number then affords a better measurement of the movement of prices in the open market, so far as one existed, and

its precision might be expected to be considerable even in abnormal conditions. Unfortunately, however, it appears not to be sufficiently sensitive during 1918 and 1919, when the movement of prices varied greatly among the important commodities.

It is necessary to consider briefly the mechanism and theory of index-numbers, in order to determine how far the measurement they afford is dependable in abnormal periods, it being assumed that we have decided their general purpose. The mechanism is, as is well known, as follows. A number of commodities is selected, all of which are important in manufacture or consumption, and for all of which a market quotation for the price of a well-defined quality is available. The obvious necessity that the quality should be unchanged [1] during any period under review limits the selection in practice to raw materials or to goods in an elementary stage of manufacture (as pig-iron, refined sugar, &c.); the most advanced stage included is found in cotton cloth, which is one of the commodities contained in the index-number of the *Economist*. These conditions limit the number of possible items to such an extent that in practice, when all are included, we have only about fifty independent quotations. A base year or period is then chosen, and the price of each commodity in each year is expressed as a percentage or ratio of its price in the base period. The average (weighted or unweighted) of these ratios or percentages in a particular year gives the index-number for that year.[2] Given the commodities and their price-ratios, it can be shown that the choice of different base periods and of different weights (or relative importance to be given to the ratios) has very little effect on the index-number obtained when prices are on the whole rising or falling at nearly the same rates one with another, and if the number of commodities whose movements are not

---

[1] It is a weakness of the Board of Trade index-number that the average prices of some of the commodities included (e.g. wool) are based on a wide range of qualities, whose relative amounts may change.

[2] The method of using totals instead of averages, adopted especially in America, does not affect the essentials of the problem, but only amounts to a particular way of using weights.

directly dependent one on another (as flour and wheat or steel and pig-iron and coal) is fairly considerable ; perhaps 40 is sufficient under normal conditions. But when we find that the price-ratios of such important goods as wheat, cotton yarn, petroleum, and rubber show such divergent ratios as 2·34, 4·18, 2·12, and 0·81 when October 1919 is compared with the average of January and April 1914, it is evident that the index-number must be significantly affected by the relative importance given to them. The price quotations selected should be regarded as samples of the prices of all wholesale (unmanufactured) goods, and the method of sampling has evidently not sufficient precision if different reasonable choices give divergent results.

Now it is impossible to determine a unique logical system of weights in this case, and if it was determined we could not find the prices of unchanged qualities of many of the commodities which we ought to include, for reasons already stated. We may admit the statement that where the three index-numbers before us show nearly the same movements, that the true movement whose measurement we seek is described with fair accuracy by any of the three ; but, at the same time, when the numbers are divergent, the true measurement is not known at all precisely. The following table and accompanying diagram show that the numbers agree remarkably well from 1914 up to some month in 1918, in fact the index-numbers for the *average* of the year 1918 are 233, 234, 235, respectively, when the level in January to July 1914 is taken as 100. For the first four years of the War we have, therefore, a reasonably precise measurement, so far as one can be obtained from a small number of raw materials. But during the latter part of 1918 and subsequently to the end of the diagram and table the Board of Trade index differs considerably from those of the *Economist* and the *Statist*, and these latter are not in close agreement with each other. These differences can be traced in detail, and appear to result to a great extent from the heavier weight given by the Board of Trade to seeds, bricks, and hides, and the less to rubber, indigo, and crystals than by the *Economist* ; the first-named group rose in price considerably after 1917, the latter fell. We have then no very definite measurement of prices in general during this recent period.

TABLE I

INCREASES PER CENT. IN SHORT PERIODS OF WHOLESALE PRICES AS SHOWN
BY INDEX-NUMBERS

		Statist	Econo-mist	Board of Trade
Average for 1915 compared with January–July 1914		+ 31	+ 28	+ 27
,, 1916 ,, ,, average for 1915		+ 27	+ 30	+ 29
,, 1917 ,, ,, ,, 1916		+ 29	+ 27	+ 30
,, 1918 ,, ,, ,, 1917		+ 10	+ 10	+ 10
,, 1919 ,, ,, ,, 1918		+ 7	+ 4	+ 11
,, November 1918 compared with January–July 1914		+137	+140	+153
,, April 1919 ,, ,, November 1918		− 5	− 7	+ 2
,, March 1920 ,, ,, April 1919		+ 42	+ 45	+ 28
,, March 1920 ,, ,, January–July 1914		+218	+223	+230

From the beginning of the War to the end of 1917 prices rose nearly regularly 27 per cent. per annum, which is equivalent to a cumulative 2 per cent. monthly.

TABLE II

THE STATIST INDEX-NUMBERS COMPARED WITH NUMBERS SHOWING UNIFORM
INCREASE

	1914		1915		1916		1917	
	Statist	Uniform rise [1]	Statist	Uniform rise	Statist	Uniform rise	Statist	Uniform rise
January			117	113	150	143	193	181
February			122	115	154	146	199	185
March			126	117	158	149	205	189
April	100	100	128	120	163	152	209	192
May			130	122	164	155	212	196
June			129	125	159	158	218	200
July			129	127	158	161	214	204
August	106	102	130	129	163	164	213	208
September	108	104	131	132	163	168	214	212
October	109	106	133	135	173	171	219	217
November	108	108	137	137	183	174	222	221
December	111	110	143	140	187	178	225	225

[1] To nearest integer.

It will be seen from this table (or from the diagram in which a straight line represents a uniform rate of increase) that the rise was accelerated during the winter months, and retarded or completely neutralized in the middle of each year.

The customary rise did not take place after December 1917 ; prices crept up very slowly till the Armistice, rising only 6½ per cent. in ten months.   In the following six months they fell, till in March and April 1919 they had returned to the level of December 1918.   From April or May 1919 onwards there was a considerable rise, but, as the tables given show, its extent is open to conjecture.   It is at the period of relatively stationary prices that those of many articles were controlled, and as a preliminary generalization it may be suggested that control checked the rise of prices effectively, whatever its effect on supply, while on its removal an increase at least as rapid as during the early years of the War took place.   This effect will be examined in more detail in respect of various prices in a subsequent chapter.   But it has already been pointed out that the control of prices tends to destroy the meaning of an index-number, so that we cannot expect to be able to measure the general change during 1918 and 1919.   When the index-numbers again show agreement as to the whole rise since December 1917, we shall probably again be on safe ground ; but the time has arrived to recast the choice of commodities and of market quotations, and when that task is undertaken it should be possible to make an adequate measurement for the doubtful period as a whole.

TABLE III

INDEX-NUMBERS OF WHOLESALE PRICES.   MONTHLY AVERAGE OF JANUARY
TO JULY 1914 TAKEN AS 100

Date	Statist [1]	Economist [1]	Board of Trade [2]
1914			
August . .	106	104	—
September .	108	107	—
October . .	109	106	—
November .	108	107	—
December .	111	108	—

[1] At end of month.   [2] Average for month

TABLE III (*continued*)—INDEX-NUMBERS OF WHOLESALE PRICES. MONTHLY
AVERAGE OF JANUARY TO JULY 1914 TAKEN AS 100

Date	Statist [1]	Economist [1]	Board of Trade [2]
1915			
January . .	117	116	—
February .	122	121	—
March . .	126	128	—
April . .	128	129	—
May . .	130	129	—
June . .	129	126	—
July . .	129	127	—
August . .	130	127	—
September .	131	129	—
October . .	133	130	—
November .	137	135	—
December .	143	140	—
Average for year .	131	128	127
1916			
January	150	148	—
February	154	155	—
March	158	155	—
April	163	162	—
May	164	167	—
June	159	163	—
July	158	162	—
August	163	169	—
September	163	171	—
October	173	177	—
November	183	185	—
December	187	190	—
Average for year	165	167	164
1917			
January . .	193	191	—
February .	199	196	—
March . .	205	205	—
April . .	209	208	—
May . .	212	209	—
June . .	218	218	—
July . .	214	216	—
August . .	213	219	—
September .	214	218	—
October . .	219	220	—
November .	222	223	—
December .	225	226	—
Average for year .	212	212	214

[1] At end of month.   [2] Average for month.

TABLE III (*continued*)—INDEX-NUMBERS OF WHOLESALE PRICES. MONTHLY
AVERAGE OF JANUARY TO JULY 1914 TAKEN AS 100

Date	Statist [1]	Economist [1]	Board of Trade [2]
1918			
January . .	225	224	—
February .	227	225	—
March . .	228	227	—
April . .	230	230	—
May . .	231	232	—
June . .	233	236	—
July . .	233	236	—
August . .	237	242	—
September .	239	241	—
October . .	239	240	254
November .	237	240	253
December .	237	235	263
Average for year .	233	234	235
1919			
January . .	233	226	254
February .	227	224	255
March . .	224	220	262
April . .	224	223	258
May . .	235	231	242
June . .	242	239	245
July . .	250	249	248
August . .	258	251	264
September .	260	254	272
October . .	272	262	282
November .	280	270	296
December .	285	284	304
Average for year .	249	244	261
1920			
January . .	297	300	314
February .	316	315	325
March . .	318	323	330
April . .	323	318	329
May . .	315	317	327
June . .	310	303	347
July . .	308	304	356
August . .	307	299	334
September .	301	295	339
October . .	290	277	332
November .	271	255	321
December .	251	229	310
Average for year .	301	298	327

[1] At end of month.   [2] Average for month.

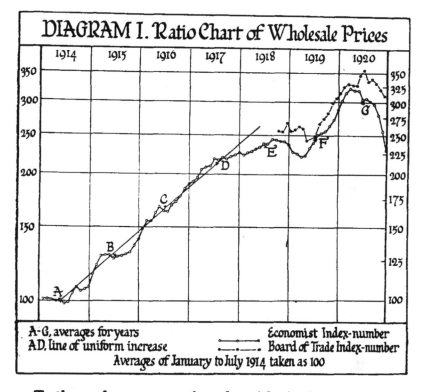

DIAGRAM I. Ratio Chart of Wholesale Prices

A-G, averages for years
AD, line of uniform increase
Economist Index-number
Board of Trade Index-number
Averages of January to July 1914 taken as 100

To those who can use ratio or logarithmic charts—a method of presentation which is now being popularized—the accompanying diagram shows these movements very clearly. On these charts a given vertical distance shows a definite ratio movement (say an increase of 2 per cent. or the ratio 1·02); a straight line (at any angle) shows a uniform rate of increase. Thus a straight line drawn from A to D on the diagram indicates a rise of 2 per cent. per month or 27 per cent. per annum ; and it passes very nearly through the points B and C; here A, B, C, D indicate the average price levels of January to July 1914, and of 1915, 1916, and 1917, on the reckoning of the *Statist*. The same line passes above the point E, the average level for 1918, and shows a slackening in the rate of increase. The more rapid final increase is indicated by the steepness of the line after April 1918.

Note on the Index-numbers of the Board of Trade, the
' Statist ', and the ' Economist '

The genesis of the *Board of Trade Index-number* of wholesale
prices is shown in the House of Commons Paper (No. 321 of
1903), ' Wholesale and Retail Prices '.   The average import
prices (obtained by dividing the declared value of the imports
of each commodity for the year by the quantity imported and
stated annually in *The Statistical Abstract for the United Kingdom*) are used in the cases of copper regulus, crude zinc, block
tin, pig and sheet lead, raw cotton, foreign sheep and lamb's
wool, jute, flax, silk, foreign wheat, barley and oats, maize,
hops, rice, bacon, eggs, refined sugar, tea, coffee, cocoa, rum,
wine, unmanufactured tobacco, cottonseed, linseed, olive oil,
palm oil, paraffin, petroleum, hewn fir, caoutchouc, and hides.
Export prices, computed in a similar way from the statistics
of exports, are used for coal, pig-iron, British wool, and herrings.
The *Gazette* average prices are used for British wheat, barley,
and oats ; the prices of first-class live meat at the Metropolitan
Cattle Market for beef and mutton ; the prices paid at one or
two of the London hospitals for potatoes and milk, and in the
case of bricks the price of stocks at Glasgow (*loc. cit.*, pp. xxxv–
xxxvii).

The year 1871 was taken as base in the first instance, but
this has been changed to the year 1900, the price in which was
equated to 100 in the case of each article.

The weights allotted to the price-ratios were ' the estimated
value in millions sterling of the annual consumption of the
article, the period selected being, as far as possible, the years
1881–1890 ' (p. 442), and the same weights have been used even
though the base year was changed.   The value of the milk
consumed included that used in butter and cheese till 1912 ;
since then separate calculations have been made for milk,
butter and margarine, and cheese, and the number of entries
raised from 45 to 47.   The accompanying table (pp. 16–17)
shows the weights for the various articles, merging the home and
foreign supplies.

The figures are to be found in the *Board of Trade Journal*, in the January numbers of the *Labour Gazette*, and in the *Monthly Bulletin of Statistics* issued on behalf of the Supreme Economic Council.

The *Economist Index-number* (published monthly in the *Economist*, London) depends on market quotations of the prices of 44 commodities ' mainly in London and Manchester '. Prior to the War the quotations taken were : *Wheat*, North Manitoba No. 1 and British Gazette ; *Flour*, town households * ; *Barley* and *Oats*, British Gazette ; *Potatoes*, good English ; *Rice*, Rangoon ; *Beef*, inferior middling to prime large * ; *Mutton*, inferior middling to prime * ; *Pork* ; *Tea*, mean of Congou, mid.-com. to med. gd. * ; *Coffee*, Jamaica ord. to fine ord. * ; *Sugar*, cane, West India Syrops crop,* and *Beet*, German * ; *Butter*, Danish ; *Tobacco*, Virginia leaf in bond ; *Pig-iron*, Middlesbro' good marked bars ; *Steel*, heavy rails ; *Iron Bars*, Welsh port * ; *Coal*, best steam Newcastle * and best Yorks. silkstone house ; *Lead*, English pig ; *Tin*, English bars ; *Copper*, standard ; *Silk*, blue elephant ; *Hemp*, Manila ; *Flax*, Riga Z.K. ; *Jute*, native firsts* ; *Wool*, English * and good Victoria * ; *Cotton*, middling American, and Egypt good fair brown * ; *Cotton yarn*, 32's twist ; *Cotton cloth*, 16 × 15, 39 in. shirting ; *Timber*,* Dantzig and Memel ; *Leather*, mixed tannings, butts or bends * ; *Petroleum*, waterwhite ; *Oil*, mean of seal pale * and Palm Lagos ; *Seeds*, mean of linseed and English rape ; *Tallow*, town ; *Indigo*, Bengal good red violet ; *Crystals*, soda bicarbonate ; *India-rubber*, Para fine hard. Those marked * appear to have been replaced by other grades at various dates or for them no quotations were available ; it is not clear how these changes were worked into the index-number.[1]

The average of each quotation in 1901–5 was equated to 50, each of the 44 commodities being given equal importance at that period.

The *Statist Index-number* (formerly Sauerbeck's) published in the *Statist*, London, is calculated from similar data, 60 price

---

[1] See note 2 on p. 37, and see also the *Economist* of February 19, 1921, pp. 407 seq., where the difficulties are still concealed.

quotations being used, some of which are averaged together so as to give only 45 price-ratios. The details can be found in any volume (generally in the March number) of the *Journal of the Royal Statistical Society* in years earlier than 1919 and in the July number of 1920. There appears to be no clear statement available about the procedure followed when war conditions necessitated a change of quotation.

The average price for the period 1867–77 is equated to 100, so that each of the 45 commodities was given equal importance at that period.

The choice of the base period affects the relative importance given to the price-ratios when two subsequent years are compared with each other. The following example (from the *Statist* compilation) shows the nature of the process :

	1867–77	1913	1917	Price-ratio, 1913–17
Flour . . .	100	66	127	$1{\cdot}924 = r_1$
Sugar . . .	100	38	115	$3{\cdot}026 = r_2$
Tea . . .	100	48	117	$2{\cdot}437 = r_3$
Sum of 3 . .	300	152	359	
Mean of 3 . .	100	50·7	119·7	

Now the method of index-numbers may be thus stated. We have a number of ratios, r_1, r_2, r_3 . . ., each expressing the ratio of a price in the year under consideration (1917) to the price in the year with which we wish to make comparison (1913, or the first seven months of 1914). Weights, depending on the relative importance, based on the presumed value of the amount consumed or on some other computation, are assigned to the ratios, say w_1, w_2, w_3 . . ., and the average taken, viz. :

$$\frac{w_1 \times r_1 + w_2 \times r_2 + w_3 \times r_3 + \ldots}{w_1 + w_2 + w_3 + \ldots}$$

This average of the ratios, multiplied by 100, gives the required index-number.

In the example above the ratio of the index-number in 1917 to that in 1913 is $119{\cdot}7 : 50{\cdot}7 = 2{\cdot}36$ approx. What are the weights given to the different ratios ?

We have $2\cdot36 = \dfrac{119\cdot7}{50\cdot7} = \dfrac{359}{152} = \dfrac{127 + 115 + 117}{66 + 38 + 48}$

$$= \dfrac{66 \times \dfrac{127}{66} + 38 \times \dfrac{115}{38} + 48 \times \dfrac{117}{48}}{66 + 38 + 48}$$

$$= \dfrac{66r_1 + 38r_2 + 48r_3}{66 + 38 + 48} = 0\cdot43r_1 + 0\cdot25r_2 + 0\cdot32r_3.$$

In the comparison of 1917 with 1913, flour, sugar, and tea are no longer of equal importance, but flour is given greater weight than tea and much greater than sugar.

When many items are averaged, this movement of weights has little effect in ordinary times, and the choice of weights and of the base year is not of very great importance; but as shown above (pp. 6–7) we cannot ignore the difficulty since 1914.

The following table shows approximately the effective relative weights given to price-ratios when subsequent years are compared with the period immediately before the War; these are computed as nearly as possible by the method indicated in the numerical example just given.

TABLE IV

RELATIVE IMPORTANCE OF SIX GROUPS IN THE THREE INDEX-NUMBERS

	Statist	Economist	Board of Trade
Date of comparison	1913	January to July 1914	January to July 1914
Vegetable food	14·4 }	21·9 }	66·0
Animal food	18·2 }		
Tropical food, drink, and tobacco .	5·6	13·5 }	
Minerals	20·3	24·2	8·9
Textiles	17·5	18·7	17·1
Miscellaneous	24·0	21·7	8·0
Total of weights	100·0	100·0	100·0

It is evident that the Board of Trade weights differ radically from the other two systems, and that these are not in close accordance with each other. When the Board of Trade number is used, twice as much importance is given to food as to materials; with the others the proportions are nearly reversed. The results of this difference in weighting in the four main groups (food, minerals, textiles, and miscellaneous) above is to give 324 for the Board of Trade and 318 for each of the others when the second quarter of 1920 is compared with the second quarter of 1914 taken as 100.

The following table shows in more detail the relative importance given to the various commodities at the most recent dates for which complete information is readily available. There was little change up to 1914 in the proportions.

TABLE V

RELATIVE WEIGHTS OF ALL COMMODITIES IN THE THREE INDEX-NUMBERS [1]

	Statist, 1913		Economist, 1901–5		Board of Trade, 1900	
Wheat and flour . .	50		68		93	
Barley	18		23		44	
Oats	19		23		32	
Maize	19		0		16	
Potatoes . . .	17		23		65	
Rice	21		23		2	
Hops	0		0		8	
Vegetable food . .		144		159		259
Beef	50		23		103	
Mutton . . .	53		23		61	
Pork	27		23		0	
Bacon	27		0		42	
Butter	25		23		24 [2]	
Milk	0		0		57	
Cheese	0		0		8	
Eggs	0		0		10	
Herrings . . .	0		0		14	
Animal food . .		182		91		318
Sugar	20		45		40	
Tea	13		23		16	
Coffee	23		23		2	
Cocoa	0		0		1	
Rum	0		0		3	
Wine	0		0		10	
Tobacco . . .	0		23		4	
Tropical food, &c. .		56		114		75

[1] In every case the relative weights are given to the nearest unit.
[2] Including margarine.

TABLE V (*continued*)—Relative Weights of all Commodities in the Three Index-numbers

	Statist, 1913	Economist, 1901–5	Board of Trade, 1900
Iron	50	45	32
Steel	0	23	0
Copper . . .	24	23	10
Zinc	0	0	3
Tin	50	23	3
Lead	24	23	3
Coal	55	45	67
Minerals . . .	203	182	118
Cotton : Raw . .	42	45	75
Manufactured .	0	45	0
Wool	39	45	38
Jute	37	23	6
Flax	21	23	8
Hemp	23	23	0
Silk	13	23	18
Textiles . . .	175	227	144
Rubber . . .	0	23	3
Timber . . .	23	45	40
Bricks	0	0	6
Hides	35	0	16
Leather . . .	29	23	0
Oilseed and oil . .	70	45	17
Petroleum and paraffin .	18	23	5
Tallow	20	23	0
Indigo	10	23	0
Soda	35	23	0
Miscellaneous . .	240	227	86
Total . . .	1,000	1,000	1,000

CHAPTER II

WHOLESALE PRICES OF GROUPS OF COMMODITIES

The principal groups. Cereals; meat; cotton, yarn, and cloth. Wool, tops, and yarn. Iron, steel, coal, and other minerals. Rubber.

WHEN we leave the general index-numbers and consider the average prices of groups of commodities, and still more when we come to individual commodities, we find that their movements differ greatly one from another. Table VI and Diagram II show the monthly index-numbers in the five groups computed in the *Economist* (except that in the diagram the group of *Other Food Products, &c.* is omitted for reasons which will be apparent if the details given in the Appendix (p. 202) are examined). *Cereals* show a regular increase to the end of June 1917, when the price drops, remain nearly steady for a year and a half, and then gradually rise to the 1920 maximum. *Textiles* dropped in the first six months of the War, then rose steadily for three years; after the Armistice they dropped rapidly for six months, then rose with even greater rapidity till March 1920, when the number stood at more than four and a half times its pre-war level according to the *Economist*, and at less than three and two-thirds the same level according to the *Statist*. *Minerals* dropped a little in the autumn of 1914, doubled their price in the next eighteen months, dropped and then remained nearly steady for more than two years, and then rose rapidly in 1919 and were still rising in October 1920. The average of *Miscellaneous* commodities included by the *Economist* rose irregularly for three years to nearly two and a half times the pre-war level, remained steady for two years, then rose abruptly to March 1920 and finished by a perceptible drop. There is thus hardly anything that is common to the four movements.

Table VII and Diagram III show the quarterly movements

of the five groups separated in the *Statist* index-number. The separate statements of animal and vegetable food show a considerable divergence in the first year of the War ; their average agrees closely with the *Economist* reckoning. Textiles are markedly different in the two accounts in 1920. In minerals the *Statist* does not show the inflation in the spring of 1916. The lines representing the Miscellaneous group agree fairly well except in 1919.

As already pointed out, in the composition of the general index-numbers a great deal appears to depend on the choice of and the relative importance given to the commodities, but in the first four years general agreement between the two general index-numbers was achieved.

TABLE VI

MONTHLY MOVEMENTS OF PRICES IN FIVE GROUPS

Economist Index-numbers

Compiled from the *Economist* with the basis adjusted so that the average of the six months January to June 1914 is 100

	Cereals and Meat	Other Food Products, &c.	Textiles	Minerals	Miscellaneous
1914					
Jan. to June .	100	100	100	100	100
End of July .	102	101	98	96	98
August . .	113	105	99	98	110
September .	114	116	97	98	115
October . .	116	114	89	95	116
November .	121	116	81	98	122
December .	126	118	81	98	124
1915					
January . .	139	118	85	107	133
February .	149	117	88	116	135
March . .	149	122	95	133	142
April . .	150	126	94	130	145
May . .	158	125	92	124	145
June . .	145	122	96	129	139
July . .	147	126	96	129	138
August . .	149	125	100	126	139
September .	143	134	106	128	137
October . .	148	127	108	130	139
November .	154	127	110	138	147
December .	157	127	116	147	152
1916					
January . .	167	133	124	157	157
February .	174	149	128	165	160
March . .	168	144	126	176	162

WHOLESALE PRICES OF

TABLE VI (*continued*)—MONTHLY MOVEMENTS OF PRICES IN FIVE GROUPS

	Cereals and Meat	Other Food Products, &c.	Textiles	Minerals	Miscel- laneous
1916 (*cont.*)					
April . .	172	146	126	185	181
May . .	181	151	128	194	181
June . .	175	149	126	185	181
July . .	170	150	127	182	185
August .	177	152	140	180	193
September .	180	153	148	177	191
October . .	199	155	157	175	193
November .	208	159	173	175	196
December .	229	158	179	170	198
1917					
January . .	232	160	181	170	199
February .	232	166	189	171	206
March . .	238	174	195	172	229
April . .	241	183	197	174	230
May . .	243	184	201	173	229
June . .	253	186	229	174	228
July . .	236	173	241	173	231
August . .	237	191	239	171	234
September .	216	207	240	170	241
October . .	217	209	250	170	241
November .	218	194	260	175	240
December .	227	196	268	173	240
1918					
January . .	216	196	273	171	236
February .	219	198	276	173	235
March . .	219	199	282	172	235
April . .	220	213	280	175	239
May . .	221	222	282	175	243
June . .	225	222	288	178	246
July . .	225	222	287	183	245
August . .	228	221	305	183	248
September .	221	223	306	183	248
October . .	225	223	300	181	248
November .	228	224	294	186	247
December .	230	224	287	179	238
1919					
January . .	227	224	257	171	238
February .	228	224	254	169	234
March . .	227	224	239	174	231
April . .	231	215	240	188	230
May . .	232	222	261	192	236
June . .	237	229	277	193	244
July . .	237	230	295	213	252
August . .	244	235	298	214	246
September .	247	234	314	216	239
October . .	250	239	338	219	242
November .	252	247	351	225	249
December .	255	252	388	236	259

TABLE VI (*continued*)—MONTHLY MOVEMENTS OF PRICES IN FIVE GROUPS

1920	Cereals and Meat	Other Food Products, &c.	Textiles	Minerals	Miscellaneous
January	259	245	430	250	273
February	258	253	469	258	287
March	266	261	472	257	304
April	265	259	467	254	294
May	263	280	448	267	288
June	268	266	407	266	277
July	265	267	412	270	274
August	254	265	401	269	277
September	266	265	376	270	274
October	276	257	310	271	257
November	261	248	262	260	238
December	238	230	204	251	227

TABLE VII

QUARTERLY MOVEMENTS OF PRICES IN SIX GROUPS

Statist Index-number

Adjusted from table given in *Statistical Journal*, July 1920, p. 635, by equating the numbers for each group in the second quarter of 1914 to 100.

Year	Quarters (average)	Vegetable Food	Animal Food	Sugar, Coffee, and Tea	Minerals	Textiles	Sundry Materials
1914	2	100	100	100	100	100	100
	3	120	104	119	98	99	106
	4	135	103	123	99	93	118
1915	1	157	117	128	112	103	127
	2	160	132	140	124	107	131
	3	156	134	139	123	113	133
	4	170	127	133	134	127	145
1916	1	187	141	152	153	143	159
	2	190	161	170	159	145	164
	3	191	154	166	157	154	162
	4	244	163	178	163	177	178
1917	1	270	187	193	166	201	196
	2	282	203	207	172	222	204
	3	251	199	222	171	243	218
	4	242	197	257	176	260	234
1918	1	252	204	263	181	270	232
	2	250	207	239	185	269	252
	3	261	211	239	195	276	251
	4	265	235	244	187	264	250
1919	1	256	222	235	176	244	244
	2	254	212	244	192	254	260
	3	266	212	320	230	276	284
	4	275	232	343	255	326	294
1920	1	316	239	401	295	360	324
	2	365	256	469	301	328	308
	3	339	294	400	315	299	282
	4	311	287	244	300	229	263

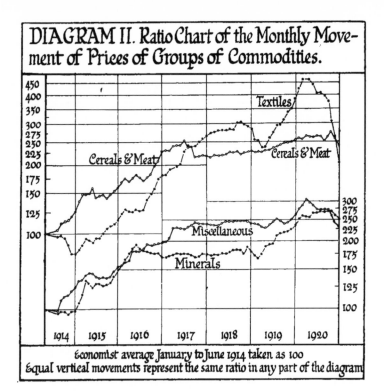

DIAGRAM II. Ratio Chart of the Monthly Movement of Prices of Groups of Commodities.

Economist average January to June 1914 taken as 100
Equal vertical movements represent the same ratio in any part of the diagram

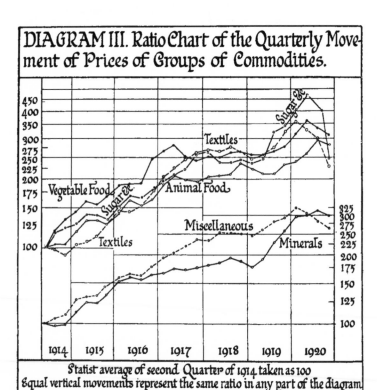

DIAGRAM III. Ratio Chart of the Quarterly Movement of Prices of Groups of Commodities.

Statist average of second Quarter of 1914 taken as 100
Equal vertical movements represent the same ratio in any part of the diagram

We can examine the detailed movements of the groups from these tables, and those of the separate commodities from the table in the Appendix, pp. 200–7.

Cereals. The upward movement of the prices of wheat, flour, barley, and oats began at the outbreak of war and continued (except for a slight drop in the summer of 1915) unchecked till control was generally established in 1917. At the highest, wheat, barley, and oats reached two and a half times the pre-war price, while flour was doubled in price. Control stabilized the prices for two years at a level perceptibly below the maximum. In the autumn of 1919 the prices of barley, oats, rice, and potatoes rose considerably, followed after some months by those of wheat and flour.

Meat. The prices of meat hardly moved till the spring of 1915, then they rose rapidly for two years with seasona fluctuations, till they reached about twice the pre-war level. In 1919 beef rose considerably, while mutton and pork were unaffected. The fluctuation at the end of 1918 shown in the *Statist* number and the upward movement from the summer of 1919 are due to the inclusion of bacon and butter in the group. The *Economist* does not include bacon, thereby omitting a commodity which has risen throughout the six years with special rapidity, and its record for butter (included in the third group) ceases in 1917.

In the group *Other Food Products, &c.,* the records are not comparable throughout either for tea, coffee, sugar, or butter. Sufficient details of the changes in these prices are given in Chapters III and V, except for coffee which is not of numerical importance. The wholesale price of tobacco rose in the summers of 1916, 1917, and 1918 to about twice its pre-war price. The retail price of ordinary good pipe tobacco rose from 5*d.* in 1914 to 1*s.* in February 1920, but the tax and cost of manufacture are of more importance than the price of the raw material.

Textiles. Cotton was one of the few commodities that fell in price at the beginning of the War, and it did not reach the pre-war level till the end of 1915. From the summer of 1916 the price advanced with great rapidity for about a year and a half, till in April 1918 American cotton was three and a third and Egyptian cotton three and a half times the pre-war level.

The details are shown in Table VII and Diagram IV. After the Armistice the price dropped, but it rose again till in January 1920 it was four times the 1914 price.

In this case we are able to compare wholesale prices in three stages of manufacture, viz. cotton, yarn, and cloth. Yarn did not fall so much as cotton in 1914, and after the recovery in 1915 followed a course not very different from that of American cotton till the autumn of 1917. From this date the price rose with great rapidity as shown on the diagram. The margin between the price of 1 lb. yarn (32's twist) and 1 lb. American cotton was $2\frac{1}{2}d.$ or $3d.$ in 1914, $7d.$ in October 1917, and $31\frac{1}{2}d.$ in October 1918; after a drop in 1919 it rose to $33d.$ in April 1919. There is nothing in the movement of wages (see Chapter XIV below) to account for this excess, and the figures point to enormous profits in the spinning trade. The price of cloth followed the same general course as that of yarn, but did not show so great an inflation in 1918. In July 1920 the changes shown over six years were the same for yarn and cloth. There was still room for considerable profits in weaving at some periods, as the following table which is purely illustrative of a possibility shows :

	Price of 8¼ lb. 32's twist		Price of cloth weighing 8¼ lb.	
	s.	*d.*	*s.*	*d.*
July 1914 . . .	6	10½	7	10
October 1918 . .	39	0	36	3
April 1919 . .	17	10	23	0
October 1919 . .	29	1	30	6
July 1920 . . .	37	6	42	6

The difference between the two increased in six years from $1s.$ to $5s.$, though the rate of increase of price was the same.

TABLE VIII
MOVEMENT OF PRICES OF COTTON, YARN, AND CLOTH

		Raw Cotton		Cotton Yarn	Cotton Cloth
		American	Egyptian		
1914	July	100	100	100	100
	October . . .	70	84	85	91
1915	January . . .	61	69	71	82
	April . . .	73	86	82	90
	July	70	82	84	87
	October . . .	91	107	101	97

TABLE VIII (*continued*)—MOVEMENT OF PRICES OF COTTON, YARN, AND CLOTH

			Raw Cotton		Cotton Yarn	Cotton Cloth
			American	Egyptian		
1916	January	. . .	103	112	120	112
	April	. . .	104	122	124	113
	July .	. . .	109	130	127	118
	October	. . .	125	165	148	133
1917	January	. . .	145	228	172	153
	April	. . .	169	300	172	153
	July .	. . .	254	333	245	206
	October	. . .	271	377	270	233
1918	January	. . .	312	366	382	320
	April	. . .	334	357	430	358
	July .	. . .	304	334	497	390
	October	. . .	335	343	567	463
1919	January	. . .	293	318	412	412
	April	. . .	215	314	260	294
	July .	. . .	261	314	395	370
	October	. . .	266	348	422	390
1920	January	. . .	408	625	555	517
	April	. . .	385	960	620	574
	July .	. . .	353	718	545	543

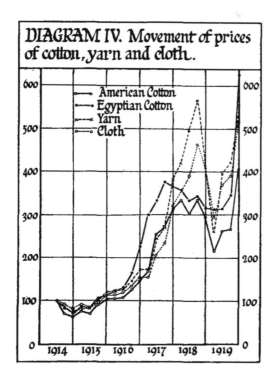

DIAGRAM IV. Movement of prices of cotton, yarn and cloth.

These numbers are based on the prices shown in Appendix I, pp. 203 seq., from the *Economist*. They are modified slightly by the use of the percentages given in the *Economist*, February 21, 1920, p. 447, which do not always correspond with the prices on the previous pages (443–6).

The headings in the *Economist* are Cotton 'middling American'; 'Egyptian, good fair brown' changed to 'fully good fair' from 1918; Yarn '32's twist'; Cloth, '37½ yards 16 by 15, 39 inch shirtings'.

Wool. The *Economist* does not give a continuous record of the prices of either English or imported wool, but Mr. A. S. Firth, in an article on 'The Increased Cost of Clothing' in the *Economic Journal*, 1918 (pp. 452–6), gives percentage figures (without stating his authority) for colonial and three kinds of English wool in selected months from July 1914 to October 1918. These are shown in Table IX in comparison with the percentages given in the *Economist* (February 21, 1920, p. 447). During the period of Government control there was evidently a difficulty in obtaining comparable records of prices. The prices of English and colonial wools had doubled by the middle of 1917.

As in the case of cotton, we can follow the prices in three stages, viz. wool, tops (i. e. combed wool), and worsted yarns (made of combed wool). Mr. Firth (*loc. cit.*) analyses the movements both for wool and for cotton. For the prices of tops and yarns we have the detailed tables published annually by the Bradford Chamber of Commerce (*Statistics relating to the Worsted and Woollen Trades of the United Kingdom*), but unfortunately the records for 1914, 1917, and 1918 do not contain these prices. Table X (p. 28) shows the prices for three grades of tops (the best (80's), that frequently quoted (60's), and the cheapest (32's)), and Table XI shows the prices of the dearest and cheapest worsted yarns; average export prices are also given, which indicate that the price per lb. in 1913 was 1*d.* lower than at our general starting-point 1914. In Table IX the figures from these sources are compared by equating the levels in January 1916; the records are not in close agreement in either case.

Mr. Firth argues that up to October 1918 the price of

tops had not risen more than was justified by the price of wool. But since wages [1] had risen less than the price of wool and other manufacturing expenses probably less than wages, the whole cost of production had risen less than the price of wool. After 1918 at any rate the price of tops rose much more rapidly than that of wool, and profits must have been enormous.

On any reckoning consistent with Table IX it is clear that the price of worsted yarns from July 1917 for two years increased out of all relation to the price of wool or of tops. Mr. Firth argues that in October 1918 the spinners were making high profits and says ' there is no doubt that spinners have availed themselves of every opportunity for demanding maximum prices '. If he had written a few months later he might have added that the combers were not less astute than the spinners. The profits made in Bradford during 1919 were notorious.[2]

TABLE IX

MOVEMENT OF PRICES OF WOOL, TOPS, AND WORSTED YARNS

		English Wool Mr. Firth. Average of three kinds	Economist	Colonial Wool Mr. Firth	Economist	Tops Mr. Firth	60's super	Worsted Yarns Mr. Firth	Economist
1914	July	100	100	100	100	100	—	100	—
	November	117	—	—	—	115	—	105	—
1915	January	117	112	113	86	113	101	109	102
	July	150	—	103	—	151	152	162	189
	November	153	—	—	—	139	150	157	185
1916	January	159	144	121	120	165	165	176	176
	July	158	—	141	—	163	194	192	191
	November	169	—	—	—	196	218	218	181
1917	January	180	176	215	213	209	—	231	—
	July	206	176	239	—	206	—	266	—
	November	206	176	—	—	206	—	304	—
1918	January	217	176	239	236	227	—	328	—
	July	217	—	239	—	242	—	373 or 341[3]	—
	October	217	—	—	—	242	—	395	—
1919	January	—	176	—	236	—	280	—	480
	April	—	176	—	236	—	310	—	430
	July	—	176	—	227	—	400	—	455
	October	—	176	—	315	—	500	—	490

[1] Unless a considerable amount of expensive overtime ought to be taken into account.

[2] e. g. *Punch* represents a Bradford employer saying ' We don't make money, we just pick it up '.

[3] Both these figures are given without explanation.

TABLE X

AVERAGE PRICES OF TOPS

From *Statistics relating to the Worsted and Woollen Trades of the United Kingdom.*
Bradford Chamber of Commerce, 1914, 1915, 1916, 1919

Pence per lb.

	80's					60's super			
	1913	1915	1916	1919		1913	1915	1916	1919
January . .	32	30	49	83		26½	27½	45	76
February . .	34	32	48	83		28½	29	43	76
March . .	34	35	45	83		28½	31½	42	76
April . .	36	35	48	92		30½	32	44	84
May . .	36	39	55	98		30½	36	50	90
June . .	36	48	56	114		30½	42	52	108
July . .	36	46	58	114		30½	41½	53	108
August . .	33	44	57	114		29	40	52	108
September .	30	41	· 58	116		26½	37	53	108
October . .	34	41	61	126		30½	37	56	118
November .	32	45	70	146		29½	41	64	135
December . .	32	47	74	166		29¼	43	68	150
Year's average .	34	40	56½	—		29¼	36½	52	—

	32's			
	1913	1915	1916	1919
January . .	17	19	26	35
February . .	18¾	20	26	35
March . .	18¾	24	24	35
April . .	18½	23	24	35
May . .	18½	24	24	34
June . .	18	25	23½	35
July . .	18	22	24	35
August . .	17½	21	24½	33
September .	18¼	20	25½	32
October . .	18	20½	26½	32
November .	18	23	29	35
December . .	18	23	30	31
Year's average .	18	22	25½	—

Average Export Prices of Tops

	d.
1913	20
1914	21
1915	26½
1916	34½
1917	44

TABLE XI

PRICES OF WORSTED YARNS IN BRADFORD

From the *Yorkshire Observer*, ' Annual Trade Report ', quoted by the Bradford Chamber of Commerce

Shillings and Pence per lb.

	2/32's Worsted								2/60's Botany White							
	1913		1915		1916		1919		1913		1915		1916		1919	
	s.	d.	s.	d.	s.	d.	s.	d.	s.	d.	s.	d.	s.	d.	s.	d.
January . .	1	8	2	2	3	3	8	6	3	3	3	4	4	10	14	0
February . .	1	9	2	4	3	4	8	3	3	4	3	10	4	10½	13	3
March . .	1	9½	2	8	3	5	7	3	3	3½	4	5	4	11	12	6
April . .	1	9½	2	9	3	5	7	0	3	5½	5	0	4	10	12	6
May . .	1	9½	2	10	3	6	7	0	3	6	5	3	5	2	14	6
June . .	1	9¼	2	11	3	6	7	3	3	6	5	10	5	6	15	3

TABLE XI (continued)—PRICES OF WORSTED YARNS IN BRADFORD

Shillings and Pence per lb.

	2/32's Worsted				2/60's Botany White			
	1913	1915	1916	1919	1913	1915	1916	1919
	s. d.	s. d.	s. d.	s. d.	s. d.	s. d.	s. d.	s. d.
July .	1 9	3 1	3 6	7 0	3 6	6 0	5 6	15 9
August .	1 8½	3 1	3 5	6 9	3 6	6 0	5 6	15 9
September	1 8¼	3 0	3 6	6 9	3 4½	5 9	5 6	16 0
October .	1 10½	2 11	3 6	7 3	3 4	5 9	5 9	17 0
November	1 11½	3 0	3 10	8 0	3 7	5 11	6 0	18 6
December	2 0	3 2	4 2	8 3	3 6½	6 3	6 9	20 0
Year's average	1 9¾	2 10	3 6½	7 5	3 5	5 3½	5 5	15 5

Average Export Price of Woollen and Worsted Yarn, per lb.

	s. d.
1913	2 0
1914	2 1
1915	3 1¾
1916	4 1½
1917	4 11

Other textiles. The price of *silk* and of *jute* show relatively moderate increases. (See Appendix I.) *Hemp* was very dear at the end of the War. *Flax* and linen became very expensive owing to the closing of the usual sources of supply, but the *Economist* figure relating to flax from Riga is probably not representative. The figures for *jute*, for which at one time there appears to have been no free market, are not comparable throughout in the *Economist's* record ; the *Statist* number shows an increase of 85 per cent. when 1919 is compared with 1914.

From the preceding pages it is clear that the *Economist* general number for textiles is not necessarily representative during the war period.

Minerals. The movements in the price of *coal* (for which see also Chapter IV) are easily followed from Appendix I. Till the middle of 1919 the wholesale price of house coal had advanced less than 50 per cent., but a considerable increase took place in the following year. The price was of course dominated by the action of Government control.

The prices of *iron* and *steel* began to come under control in June 1915. That of steel was fixed in November 1917, extra costs being met by a Government subsidy,[1] and this

[1] See M. S. Birkett in the *Journal of the Royal Statistical Society*, May 1920, pp. 365–71.

involved the fixing of the price of iron. The subsidy to steel
makers was withdrawn in January 1919 and that to pig-iron
manufacturers in April of the same year. The price of pig-
iron (Cleveland No. 3) immediately jumped from £4 15s. to
£8, as compared with £2 11s. 3d. in July 1914, while that of
steel (rails) jumped from £10 17s. 6d. to £16, as compared with
£6 in July 1914. The relative rise in five years was thus less
in the case of steel than in that of pig-iron. A further considerable rise took place in 1920 till in July steel rails reached
£23 and pig-iron £10 17s. 6d.

Mr. Birkett (*loc. cit.*) gives the following interesting table
to compare the increase in the price of pig-iron with that of
the cost of manufacture.

CHANGE IN PRICES OF PIG-IRON AND ITS CONSTITUENT COSTS

	Cleveland. (Third Quarter 1919 compared with 1913.)	Scotland. (December 1919 compared with 1914.)
	Increase per Cent.	
Hematite		
Selling price . .	180	247½
Fuel	138	200
Foreign ore . .	170	225
Wages . . .	275	262
Forge and Foundry		
Selling price .	164	219
Fuel . . .	138	170
Ironstone . .	173	—
Native ore .	—	223
Wages . .	292	262
Repairs, maintenance, &c.	333	—

(See also pp. 134 seq. below for wages.)

The percentages do not suggest that excessive profits were
being made in this industry.

The prices of *lead* and of *copper* show curious fluctuations.
The increases were relatively moderate and only for short
periods reached twice the pre-war level. *Tin* also fluctuated,
but on the whole showed a more considerable increase.

A study of the figures for the mineral group in the Appendix
shows that the level of the general index-number depends very
much on the relative importance given to coal, iron, and other

metals. The prices in July 1919, expressed as percentages of those in July 1914, are for pig-iron 312, for steel rails 267, for iron bars 264, for coal 145, for lead 121, for tin 166, and for copper 148.

In the *Miscellaneous group* the records are not continuous for timber, leather, or seal-oil. Palm-oil was kept down in price till the summer of 1919, and its movements are of course connected with the control of the materials of margarine. Special interest attaches to petroleum and rubber, which are hardly given sufficient importance in the compilation of index-numbers relating to modern times. The price of petroleum followed very much the same course as that of the index-number of prices in general. Rubber, on the other hand, is peculiar in that only once in the record in the Appendix was it as much as 20 per cent. above its pre-war price, and that after the Armistice its price fell steadily till in July 1920 it was at 30 per cent. *below* the price of six years before. In view of its greatly increased use this record is remarkable. If it had been given double its present weight, it would have brought the *Economist* index-number down 5 points, from 321 to 316, in April 1920.

CHAPTER III

RETAIL FOOD PRICES

1. The *Labour Gazette* measurement. General movement, 1914–20. Change of standard and measurement of expenditure. Table of changes in prices of various foods.

2. Prices of foods in detail. Meat, bacon, bread, potatoes, sugar, milk, butter, cheese, eggs. Effect on official index-number of prices of sugar, butter, margarine, and eggs. Tea. Other foods.

1. GENERAL CHANGES

IT is expedient to treat retail prices of food separately from those of other objects of consumption, both because expenditure on food accounts for more than half of the income of the majority of families, and because it is less difficult to arrive at definitions and methods of analysis in the case of the primary articles of food than in the cases of clothing and other necessary commodities.

While the general measurement of wholesale prices, discussed in Chapter I, is designed to show the movement of prices in the abstract, without explicit reference to the purchasing power of money in the hands of consumers, the problem that we have to solve when considering retail prices is more concrete, being to find a factor by which money wages may be converted into real wages and the movement of wages expressed in terms not of money but of the goods they purchase.

The method generally adopted in the United Kingdom and in many other countries is to estimate (generally by direct investigation) a budget of actual expenditure on food, clothing, rent, &c., of an average working-class family at some selected date, and taking this budget as basis to compute from time to time the cost of precisely the same quantities of goods of the same description and quality at current prices and compare the aggregate of these costs with the cost of the basic budget.

In the United Kingdom the basis used for food from 1914 has been the average of statements of a week's expenditure collected from 1,944 workmen's families in the year 1904. There is evidence that consumption of the principal foods per head in the United Kingdom changed little between 1904 and 1914, though retail food prices rose about 13 per cent. on the average in that period and the rise varied among the foods in question. It is assumed in the official computation, not that the same quantities of food were consumed in 1914 as in 1904, but that the same proportion of the total expenditure on food was allotted in the case of each article at the two dates. The possible error resulting from this process is small, and it has been verified that no significant alteration in the index-numbers subsequently obtained would be introduced by any reasonable modification of this method, except that it is not improbable that too little importance was allotted to margarine in the budget adopted as basis in 1914. Some of the less important items of expenditure contained in the original budget, such as biscuits, cake, sausages, lard, suet, condensed milk, vegetables other than potatoes, fruit, rice, tapioca, oatmeal, coffee, cocoa, jam, syrup, pickles, have not been included in the standard budget, either because no definite prices could be assigned or because they appeared to be unimportant. The items included account for about three-quarters of the whole expenditure on food. (See *Statistical Tables and Charts relating to British and Foreign Trade and Industry*, Cd. 2337 of 1914; *Report of Committee on Cost of Living*, Cd. 8980 of 1918; *Labour Gazette*, March 1920.)

Every month information is obtained, mainly through the managers of employment exchanges and branches, as to the predominant retail prices in shops and stores conducting a working-class trade in 650 towns and villages scattered through the United Kingdom, and the average of the prices recorded is computed for each article. The percentage increase (or decrease) over the price of each article in 1914 is calculated, and the percentages thus found are applied to the amount spent according to the basic budget, so that the increase (or decrease) in expenditure necessary to obtain the same quantities of similar goods at the later date as in 1914 is found.

In the computation the original expenditure is not represented by shillings and pence but by numbers proportional to them. The latter, together with the prices to the nearest farthing, are published, and the actual quantities and expenditure in 1914 can only be found by a troublesome approximate method.

TABLE XII

BASIS OF THE *Labour Gazette* RETAIL FOOD INDEX-NUMBER

	Quality, &c.	Price per lb.	July 1914 Quantity	July 1914 Expenditure	Relative expenditure	March 1, 1920. Price, when that in July 1914 is taken as unity	Product of numbers in the two preceding columns
		d.	*lb.*	*d.*			
Beef							
British	Average of	8·1	2·0	16·2	72	2·18	157·0
Imported	rib and thin flank	6·0	2·7	16·2	72	2·09	150·5
Mutton							
British	Average of	8·4	0·96	8·1	36	2·06	74·1
Imported	leg and breast	5·4	1·5	8·1	36	2·14	77·0
Bacon	Streaky	11·25	1·1	12·8	57	2·56	145·9
Fish	—	—	—	6·1	27	2·13	57·5
Flour	—	1·5	9·0	13·5	60	1·52	91·2
Bread	—	1·44	23·5	33·9	150	1·63	244·5
Tea	—	18·5	0·8	14·9	66	1·89	124·7
Sugar	Granulated	2·1	6·1	12·9	57	3·90	222·3
Milk	New	3·6	4·7 (quarts)	16·9	75	2·97	223·8
Butter { Fresh	Fresh	14·5	0·95	13·8	61	2·49	151·9
Salt	Salt	14·0	0·98	13·8	61	2·56	156·2
Cheese	Imported	8·8	0·8	6·8	30	2·30	69·0
Margarine	—	7·2	0·9	6·8	30	1·93	59·7
Eggs	Fresh	1·2	10 (no.)	12·6	56	3·29	184·2
Potatoes	—	0·7	17	12·1	54	2·62	141·5
Totals				225·5	1,000		2,331·0

Weighted average in March 1920 is 2·331 of that at base period. Increase is therefore 133·1 per cent.

It must not be supposed that the quantities here given arise from an actually observed budget; they are given to show what quantities approximately are implicitly assumed by the system of 'weights' or, relatively, expenditures used, which (with the price-ratios) alone enter into the computation. It is important, however, to have them, as they show, for example, that it is implied that more foreign than home-meat was consumed in 1914, and since at some dates the price-ratios for these were quite unequal, the implication affects the resulting number.

The result is that the cost of this budget on March 1, 1920, was to the cost in July 1914 in the ratio 2331 : 1000, or approximately 233 : 100. This is frequently stated in the form ' the increase was 133 per cent. ', and the price-ratios are generally stated as a percentage increase, e. g. the price of British beef increased 118 per cent., the ratio being 2·18.

In the sequel we discuss the appositeness of the computation for measuring the cost of living. Actually it is correctly described as a measurement of the average change of retail food prices, the price-changes being weighted on a definite hypothesis, and in the following paragraphs we consider its general movements for the six years beginning July 1914.

TABLE XIII

OFFICIAL INDEX-NUMBERS OF AVERAGE CHANGE OF RETAIL FOOD PRICES COMPARED WITH NUMBERS SHOWING UNIFORM INCREASE

Beginning of	1914 Actual	1914 Uniform Rise	1915 Actual	1915 Uniform Rise	1916 Actual	1916 Uniform Rise	1917 Actual	1917 Uniform Rise	1918	1919	1920	1921
January	—	—	118	118	145	145	187	179	206	230	236	278
February	—	—	122	120	147	148	189	182	208	230	235	263
March	—	—	124	122	148	151	192	186	207	220	233	249
April	—	—	124	124	149	153	194	189	206	213	235	238
May	—	—	126	126	155	156	198	192	207	207	246	232
June	—	—	132	129	159	159	202	195	208	204	255	218
July	100	—	132½	131	161	161	204	199	210	209	258	—
August	—	—	134	133	160	164	202	203	218	217	262	—
September	110	110	135	136	165	167	206	206	216	216	267	—
October	112	112	140	138	168	170	197	—	229	222	270	—
November	113	114	141	140	178	173	206	—	233	231	291	—
December	116	116	144	143	184	176	205	—	229	234	282	—

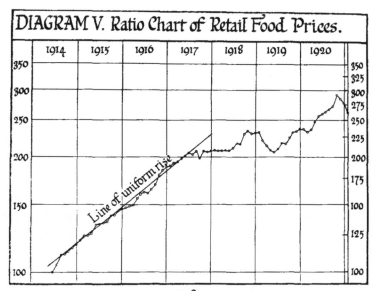

DIAGRAM V. Ratio Chart of Retail Food Prices.

From the table and diagram it is seen that average retail prices shot up 10 per cent. immediately after the commencement of the War. Then the average rose gradually with little interruption till September 1917, at which date the level was a little more than twice that of July 1914. In October 1917 there was a sudden drop owing to the effect of the bread subsidy and the introduction of a new scale of meat prices; this advantage was lost in the following month owing to the rise in other prices (as detailed in the table on p. 44), and the average remained at the level of September 1917 till June 1918. From that month there was a progressive rise till the date of the Armistice (November 1918), and the maximum level then reached was nearly maintained for three months. During the spring of 1919 the average fell and nearly reached the level of two years earlier, but another rise began in June and the level in the winter of 1919–20 was slightly above the maximum of the previous winter. The present record ends with a sharp rise to November 1920 and a subsequent fall.

The comparison between these numbers and those for wholesale price in general (p. 8) may be exhibited as follows:

TABLE XIV

MOVEMENTS OF RETAIL AND WHOLESALE FOOD PRICES

| | Retail Prices Food. June 30 or | Wholesale Prices (Statist) | |
| | | General. | Food. |
Year	July 1	End of June	Second Quarter
1914	100	100	100
1915	132	129	144
1916	161	159	173
1917	204	218	233
1918	210	233	227
1919	209	242	233
1920	258	310	328

So far as the wholesale and retail food index-numbers relate to the same commodities, evidence is afforded that in general the retailer's price rose by a smaller percentage than the wholesaler's price. This question is examined in detail in the sequel (pp. 76 seq.).

As in the account of the general movement of wholesale prices, the diagram showing these movements is drawn on a ratio scale. From it it is clear that the rise for the three years beginning September 1914 was at nearly a uniform rate, in fact at 1·7 per cent. monthly or 23 per cent. per annum ; [1] how closely this rate was maintained is shown in the table above (p. 35) where the numbers in italics show the results of uniform increase.[2] The increase in the twelve months from July 1919 (209 : 258) is also 23 per cent.

The prices included in this account are of course those paid by the consumer, and are the result not only of market and currency changes but also of control, price fixing, rationing, taxation, and subsidies. The movement shown does not reflect any general change of a definable nature as is the case with the index-numbers of wholesale prices in normal times, and it is not based on a sufficient number of independent prices (for the eight entries for meat, the two for bread and flour, and the three for milk, cheese, and butter are inter-related) to obtain the precision required in a general index-number. Further it is to be observed that the commodities themselves are not of unchanged kind and quality. The meat available has been home or imported, beef or mutton, not according to the inclination of the purchasers but according to the supplies in the control of the Ministry of Food. The quality of the bacon has changed again and again. During two years the flour and bread were of constituents and quality unknown before the War. In the period of strictest control the tea was a new blend of all available kinds, and the sugar has not always been the ' granulated ' quality to which the price nominally applies. Margarine has improved very greatly in character till the best quality purchasable in 1920 was at least as palatable and nourishing as the commoner type of pre-war butter. In general the prices are not of goods of an

[1] Twelve cumulative increments of 1·7 per cent. result in an increment of 23 per cent.

[2] Note that in the corresponding treatment of wholesale prices the monthly increment was 2 per cent., and continued to the end of 1917.

unchanged kind, but of those goods which have been available in the shops from time to time.

It might be admitted that the index-number does not satisfy the conditions necessary for abstract measurement, without condemning it as an index of some concrete quantity. It is generally assumed that this number shows the change in cost of maintaining the pre-war standard of living, but in fact this is a highly theoretical conception. During the period of acute shortage of supplies and of strict rationing, the commodities included in the budget did not exist in sufficient quantities for families in general to consume the amounts named, and in fact no family could obtain them whatever they were able to pay. This consideration was of great importance during 1917 and 1918, but may appear to be trivial in the more recent months during which control has been relaxed and in the case of many commodities abolished. The index-number is, however, greatly influenced by the price of sugar (see the table on p. 34), and in the summer of 1920 less than half the budgeted quantity could be purchased. Sugar is the extreme and obvious case, for it was still subject to legal restriction; but in fact in the summer of 1920, owing to shortage of home or of foreign supplies, it was impossible for the whole population to obtain the quantities of cheese, butter or eggs, which they consumed in 1914.

During the time of stringency the index-numbers were in fact illusory, and an alternative method was introduced by the Ministry of Food for measuring the effective change of the cost of living. The idea of measuring the cost of maintaining pre-war consumption was put aside, and in its place an attempt was made to measure the change in actual expenditure on food month by month, while the nutritive value of the food consumed was also estimated, though the two measurements were not combined. The Committee on the Cost of Living to the Working Classes, 1918 (Cd. 8980) went thoroughly into the available statistics, collecting also new budgets for the purpose, from this point of view. They found that the consumption of meat, eggs, butter, sugar, and tea had diminished considerably, while that of bacon and margarine had increased; rather more bread and flour were consumed, rather less milk (including condensed milk). As a result of the changes the nutritive value of the budget measured in 'calories' was about 3 per cent. lower on the average than in the budget taken for 1914.

The method of measuring expenditure was indirect. The budget of 1914 was taken as basis, and each item was adjusted by the change in consumption per head of the civil population as a whole (allowance made for the difference in needs of men, women, adults, and children) so as to obtain an estimate of current consumption; the quantities so adjusted were priced at current prices, and the resulting total was taken as the expenditure to be compared with pre-war expenditure on similar commodities with pre-war quantities. The investigations of the Cost of Living Committee showed that the results of this approximation were in close agreement with the averages of the budgets they collected. The statistics of consumption and the resulting estimates of expenditure were, however, related to a period two months in arrear of the date for which they were commonly given, owing to the practical necessity for averaging consumption over more than one month and other circumstances.

TABLE XV

COMPARISON OF MOVEMENTS OF PRICES AND OF EXPENDITURE

Level in July 1914 taken as 100

	Expenditure		Average retail prices
Date of prices	As stated	Corrected for time-lag	('Labour Gazette', Food Index)
1918			
February	154	144	208
March	145	141	207
April	144	152	206
May	141	167	207
June	152	181	208
July	167	184	210
August	181	189	218
September	184	—	216
October	189	—	229
November	197	—	233
December	190	—	229

TABLE XV (*continued*)—COMPARISON OF MOVEMENTS OF PRICES AND
OF EXPENDITURE

Level in July 1914 taken as 100

| Date of prices | Expenditure | | Average retail prices ('Labour Gazette' Food Index) |
	As stated	Corrected for time-lag	
1919			
January . .	—	—	230
February . .	177	—	230
March . .	179	—	220
April . . .	187	—	213
May . . .	181	—	207
June . . .	187	—	204
July . . .	197	—	209
August . .	208	—	217
September .	203	—	216
October . .	213	—	222
November . .	219	—	231
December . .	216	—	234
1920			
January . .	215	—	236
February . .	212	—	235
March . .	207	—	233

The table shows the figures in question so far as they have been published by the Cost of Living Committee or in the *Labour Gazette*.

Economy, forced or voluntary, in expenditure was at its maximum at the beginning of the record. Through the earlier part of 1919 expenditure increased, though prices fell, till the relative numbers were not far apart in October. The final difference is accounted for by the restricted use of sugar and the substitution of margarine for butter ; there were also smaller quantities of cheese and eggs available than in 1914.

Since it is probable that the pre-war budget could, with the exceptions just named, be purchased in the spring of 1920, the measurement of the purchasing power of money by the retail price index-number became less unreal than it was in 1917 and 1918, but it was still vitiated by the excessive influence of changes in the price of sugar.

It ought to be admitted that a permanent change in consumption, without any necessary reduction of standard, is almost certain to be found when a post-war period is compared with a pre-war period, and therefore that the measurement of change of prices on the assumption of an unchanged budget cannot properly be carried over the years 1914–20. But the problem of constructing an equivalent budget and comparing its cost with that of an earlier one presents many difficulties and there is no agreement as to its solution.

Both during and since the War there is another aspect of the question which ought to be considered. In the budget and in the measurement of expenditure, reference is only had to the commodities included in the table on p. 34. Some information is given later (pp. 60–1) as to the price movements of some of these, but since none was originally of much importance their inclusion in the original budget would have little effect. The point is, however, that when the usual articles of consumption are unattainable persons try to increase their purchases of others, and these if uncontrolled rise rapidly in price, and if controlled in price and not rationed are soon exhausted, unless new sources of supply become available. With a shortage of butchers' meat there is an increased demand for rabbits, poultry, &c.; with the restriction of sugar, there is a run on honey, jam, dates, and anything else that contains it. In some countries there have been purchases, legal or not, on a large scale of food that escaped control, and very high prices have been paid. In the United Kingdom such supplies have generally been soon exhausted or brought under control, so that expenditure on them cannot have been great or enduring. But there must have been a continual tendency on the part of people who had spare money to try to make good deficiencies in their food budget, and these can only be measured when a new investigation of consumption is made.

TABLE XVI

Percentage Increases in Retail Prices of Principal Foods

(Compiled from the *Labour Gazette*)

Percentage above the prices of July 1914, on the first or second day of each month

	Aug.[1]	Sept.[1]	Oct.	Nov.	Dec.
1914					
Beef					
British	7	5	6	5	6
Imported	13	15	18	18	20
Mutton					
British	6	6	7	7	7
Imported	15	16	17	17	20
Weighted average, meat	10	11	12	12	14
Bacon	17	10	11	8	7
Fish	11	18	23	19	26
Flour	20	11	11	11	15
Bread	11	9	9	10	12
Tea	0	0	0	0	12
Milk	1	2	3	5	6
Potatoes	10	−14	−17	−20	−19
Cheese	7	5	6	6	8
Weighted average of group	9	4	5	5	9
Sugar	84	72	81	72	68
Butter	15	4	4	6	8
Margarine	18	12	10	4	4
Eggs	22	13	22	47	66
Weighted average of group	32	21	25	28	33
General weighted average	16	10	12	13	16

	Jan.	Feb.	Mar.	Apr.	May	June	July	Aug.	Sept.	Oct.	Nov.	Dec.
1915												
Beef												
British	7	10	15	17	21	40	41	41	44	43	41	40
Imported	21	25	28	30	34	50	55	56	57	57	56	54
Mutton												
British	8	11	10	13	16	35	35	36	37	36	35	34
Imported	20	24	27	28	32	47	51	51	53	53	52	51
Weighted average, meat	15	19	20	22	26	44	47	47	49	48	47	46

[1] The exact dates here were August 1 and September 12.

TABLE XVI (*continued*)—PERCENTAGE INCREASES IN RETAIL PRICES OF PRINCIPAL FOODS

1915

	Jan.	Feb.	Mar.	Apr.	May	June	July	Aug.	Sept.	Oct.	Nov.	Dec.
Bacon	7	10	9	9	11	17	18	18	23	27	29	30
Fish	41	38	41	47	52	58	64	64	65	77	83	86
Flour	21	35	46	48	53	58	49	45	44	42	42	46
Bread	16	26	36	37	41	47	41	38	38	38	38	40
Tea	14	16	16	20	24	26	28	30	30	48	49	48
Milk	7	8	10	10	10	10	10	11	12	18	24	26
Potatoes	−16	−9	−5	−3	−3	−1	−2	24	−2	−6	−9	−1
Cheese	10	16	21	24	27	32	33	29	26	26	26	29
Weighted average of group	11	18	23	25	28	32	30	33	31	32	34	37
Sugar	68	68	68	68	68	70	68	68	70	93	93	93
Butter	13	16	14	15	15	16	16	19	25	34	32	33
Margarine	4	4	4	5	5	5	5	5	5	5	6	6
Eggs	63	44	30	5	3	11	24	26	41	63	79	107
Weighted average of group	35	32	28	23	22	25	27	29	36	50	52	59
General weighted average	18	22	24	24	26	32	32½	34	35	40	41	44

1916

	Jan.	Feb.	Mar.	Apr.	May	June	July	Aug.	Sept.	Oct.	Nov.	Dec.
Beef British	40	41	43	46	56	69	70	70	70	68	67	68
Imported	55	58	59	64	74	90	91	88	88	87	86	88
Mutton British	34	36	41	45	54	66	67	67	67	67	66	67
Imported	52	58	64	73	85	102	103	99	100	99	99	100
Weighted average, meat	46	49	52	57	67	81	83	80	80	80	79	80
Bacon	31	32	32	34	37	38	38	38	46	49	52	55
Fish	97	106	96	91	99	86	81	81	87	106	132	126
Flour	49	58	62	60	59	57	48	48	62	66	76	85
Bread	42	51	54	52	51	51	44	44	54	58	65	71
Tea	48	48	48	49	49	50	50	50	50	50	50	51
Milk	29	30	31	31	34	33	33	34	35	39	49	52
Potatoes	−5	−3	−1	3	47	58	109	86	52	53	104	112
Cheese	32	37	41	45	49	53	51	42	46	52	57	68
Weighted average of group	38	43	44	44	50	50	52	49	52	56	67	72
Sugar	93	103	119	128	152	155	158	160	163	166	168	170
Butter	33	32	33	34	34	33	32	34	48	54	61	67
Margarine	7	10	15	16	17	18	17	17	18	19	20	22
Eggs	105	70	49	36	20	27	45	53	82	101	138	178
Weighted average of group	58	53	53	53	55	56	60	63	77	84	96	108
General weighted average	45	47	48	49	55	59	61	60	65	68	78	84

TABLE XVI (continued)—Percentage Increases in Retail Prices of Principal Foods

1917

	Jan.	Feb.	Mar.	Apr.	May	June	July	Aug.	Sept.	Oct.	Nov.	Dec.
Beef												
British	74	82	88	93	95	104	114	115	114	97	94	89
Imported	93	103	111	117	119	129	138	139	140	132	128	125
Mutton												
British	76	82	87	92	92	114	121	119	118	92	87	83
Imported	103	113	124	131	136	153	162	163	163	153	151	147
Weighted average, meat	85	94	102	107	109	122	131	132	132	117	113	110
Bacon	56	60	73	78	79	80	76	83	96	110	127	134
Fish	131	131	122	132	138	134	127	119	136	156	163	191
Flour	88	91	95	100	105	109	109	109	109	52	52	52
Bread	73	75	80	93	97	100	100	106	100	55	54	54
Tea	51	52	59	63	69	73	74	75	79	84	103	107
Milk	57	59	60	60	61	60	60	60	61	78	88	96
Potatoes	122	131	118	117	142	144	144	52	39	40	44	39
Cheese	75	87	106	117	122	128	108	97	95	91	92	92
Weighted average of group	76	79	83	89	95	97	96	86	87	73	80	83
Sugar	170	170	171	172	172	178	188	189	190	190	190	188
Butter	72	73	79	78	71	66	65	70	90	98	115	99
Margarine	25	29	36	49	56	68	74	67	66	66	70	65
Eggs	175	136	118	72	78	85	95	127	142	160	212	239
Weighted average of group	110	102	102	94	93	94	99	108	120	127	147	144
General weighted average	87	89	92	94	98	102	104	102	106	97	106	105

1918

	Jan.	Feb.	Mar.	Apr.	May	June	July	Aug.	Sept.	Oct.	Nov.	Dec.
Beef												
British	91	91	93	91	91	91	91	91	91	115	114	114
Imported	126	126	127	141	156	156	156	156	156	190	190	190
Mutton												
British	89	87	88	84	84	84	84	82	81	104	104	104
Imported	148	149	149	154	172	172	172	172	172	211	211	211
Weighted average, meat	112	112	113	117	125	125	125	125	125	154	154	154
Bacon	139	142	139	140	139	140	138	140	141	142	142	141
Fish	196	218	220	219	220	188	190	189	189	191	167	166
Flour	52	52	52	52	52	52	52	52	52	52	52	52
Bread	54	54	54	54	54	54	54	54	55	55	55	55
Tea	98	93	90	79	73	73	73	73	73	73	73	73
Milk	99	102	102	101	65	60	77	88	95	133	141	150
Potatoes	37	36	36	37	39	52	57	114	66	63	59	50
Cheese	91	92	92	91	94	94	94	125	130	130	130	130
Weighted average of group	83	84	83	82	76	76	78	88	85	90	89	90

TABLE XVI (*continued*)—PERCENTAGE INCREASES IN RETAIL PRICES OF PRINCIPAL FOODS

1918

	Jan.	Feb.	Mar.	Apr.	May	June	July	Aug.	Sept.	Oct.	Nov.	Dec.
Sugar	189	189	187	187	237	240	240	241	241	241	241	241
Butter	104	106	107	107	107	107	100	97	97	107	110	109
Margarine	66	67	68	69	69	69	69	97	97	97	97	69
Eggs	242	245	240	211	202	221	248	295	294	329	412	348
Weighted average of group	148	149	148	142	151	155	158	170	170	182	201	184
General weighted average	106	108	107	106	107	108	110	118	116	129	133	129

1919

	Jan.	Feb.	Mar.	Apr.	May	June	July	Aug.	Sept.	Oct.	Nov.	Dec.
Beef												
British	114	114	91	91	91	91	91	91	91	91	118	118
Imported	190	190	156	156	156	121	121	105	105	105	144	144
Mutton												
British	104	104	81	81	82	82	82	82	82	82	106	106
Imported	211	211	173	173	173	134	134	114	114	114	153	114
Weighted average, meat	154	154	125	125	125	107	107	98	98	98	130	124
Bacon	141	142	141	138	139	142	143	151	153	153	154	155
Fish	166	167	159	154	137	114	133	121	118	139	140	131
Flour	52	52	52	52	52	52	52	52	52	52	52	52
Bread	55	55	55	55	55	55	55	55	59	61	62	62
Tea	73	73	73	65	65	63	65	66	67	72	78	83
Milk	154	157	158	156	85	82	111	108	122	173	198	209
Potatoes	57	60	64	66	72	84	84	225	146	127	113	117
Cheese	130	130	130	107	107	107	107	107	107	108	108	108
Weighted average of group	91	92	92	89	78	78	84	99	93	102	105	107
Sugar	241	242	242	242	242	242	242	243	242	243	243	289
Butter	110	110	110	110	110	109	110	110	112	111	111	111
Margarine	69	69	48	27	38	64	82	83	84	85	85	84
Eggs	347	343	286	207	201	195	231	261	281	312	332	339
Weighted average of group	184	184	169	150	150	151	161	168	173	179	184	195
General weighted average	130	130	120	113	107	104	109	117	116	122	131	134

TABLE XVI (continued)—PERCENTAGE INCREASES IN RETAIL PRICES OF PRINCIPAL FOODS

	Jan.	Feb.	Mar.	Apr.	May	June	July
			1920				
Beef							
British	118	118	119	119	120	120	120
Imported	144	109	109	109	109	109	109
Mutton							
British	106	106	106	107	107	108	108
Imported	114	114	114	82	83	82	82
Weighted average, meat	124	114	114	108	106	106	106
Bacon	156	156	156	157	170	168	170
Fish	128	130	113	120	97	95	109
Flour	52	52	52	53	118	118	118
Bread	62	62	63	63	116	117	118
Tea	87	87	89	90	90	88	84
Milk	212	202	197	185	158	125	124
Potatoes	126	142	162	178	196	214	297
Cheese	122	130	130	130	136	135	135
Weighted average of group	109	110	111	112	133	130	139
Sugar	290	290	290	386	387	580	581
Butter	113	126	153	153	154	147	124
Margarine	85	85	93	96	96	96	88
Eggs	341	329	229	181	174	181	208
Weighted average of group	196	200	192	202	202	241	236
General weighted average	136	135	133	135	146	155	158

2. PRICES OF SELECTED FOODS

Meat. Immediately after the declaration of war imported meat generally rose 1d. a lb. and home-grown meat ½d. A very gradual rise took place during the nine months to May 1915, the best cuts of British and imported beef rising 1d., and of mutton ½d. or ¾d., while inferior cuts rose ¼d. more ;[1] the first phase of war economy was shown in an increased demand for lower grade goods at the expense of better grade and a consequent levelling up of prices. In May 1915 there was a sudden rise of

---

[1] In the formation of the retail price index-number the price movements of ribs and thin flank are averaged for beef, and of legs and breast averaged for mutton. It had been found that this method generally gave an accurate view of the general movement for all cuts.

$\frac{3}{4}d.$ to $1\frac{1}{2}d.$ a lb., so that on June 1 British beef and mutton were 40 and 35 per cent. and imported beef and mutton 50 and 47 per cent. above the pre-war price. Practically no change took place during the second half of 1915. During the first six months of 1916 there was a rise of $2\frac{1}{4}d.$ to $3d.$ a lb., the greatest rise being that of imported mutton whose price in June 1916 was twice that in July 1914. From June to December 1916 there was no further change of importance. A rapid rise followed, till in July and August 1917 prices reached the maximum recorded in the six years July 1914 to July 1920, except in the winter 1918–19; British meat was then generally $9\frac{1}{2}d.$ above the pre-war price, while the best cuts of imported meat had risen in all $9d.$ and inferior cuts $7\frac{1}{2}d.$ The percentage increases in the three years were much higher in the case of imported than of home-grown meat. The change in the relation of the prices had a disturbing effect on the measurement of the cost of living; on the one hand, people who at the beginning of the War had been in the habit of buying the cheaper kinds of foreign meat had to pay two and a half to three times as much a lb., while others, who from economy or difficulty in supplies changed from home to foreign meat, paid only 50 to 100 per cent. more than three years earlier for meat which was little inferior to their earlier purchases.

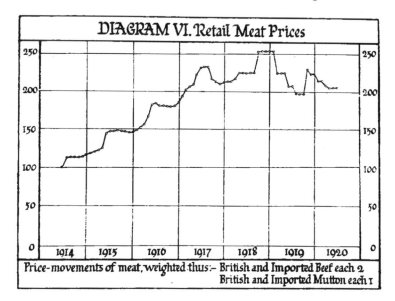

DIAGRAM VI. Retail Meat Prices

Price-movements of meat, weighted thus:– British and Imported Beef each 2
British and Imported Mutton each 1

TABLE XVII

RETAIL MEAT PRICES

Pence per lb.

	British		*Foreign*		*British*		*Foreign*	
	Beef (*Rib*)	*Mutton* (*Leg*)	*Beef* (*Rib*)	*Mutton* (*Leg*)	*Beef* (*Thin flank*)	*Mutton* (*Breast*)	*Beef* (*Thin flank*)	*Mutton* (*Breast*)
1914								
July 1	9¾	10½	7½	6¾	6½	6½	4¾	4
Aug. 8	10¼	11	8½	7¾	7	7	5½	4¾
1915								
May 1	11¼	12	9¼	8¼	8¼	8¼	6½	5½
June 1	13	13½	10½	9½	9½	9¼	7¼	6¼
1916								
Jan. 1	13¼	13¼	11	9½	9½	9¼	7¾	6½
June 1	15½	16	13½	12½	11¾	11½	9½	8¾
1917								
Jan. 1	16¾	16½	13¾	12½	12	12	9½	8¾
July 1	19¼	21	16½	15¾	15	15¾	12¼	11½
Nov. 1	17¾	18¼	16¼	15¾	13½	13	11¼	10¾
1918								
May 1 to Sept. 1	18	18¾	18	19	13	11¼	12¾	11
Oct. 1	20	20¾	20	21	15	13¼	14¾	13
1919								
Feb. 1	20	20¾	20	21	15	13¼	14¾	13
Mar. 1	18	19	18	19	13	11½	12¾	11
May 1	18	19	18	19	13	11½	12¾	11
Aug. 1	18	19	15	16	13	11½	9¾	8
Dec. 1	20¾	21	17¾	16	15	13½	11¾	8
1920								
April 1	20¾	21	15¾	15	15	13½	9¾	6
July 1	20¾	21¼	15	14¾	15	13½	9¾	6
Dec. 1	24½	27½	15¾	15½	17¾	18½	9¾	7

The prices from August 8, 1914, to September 1, 1918, are calculated to the nearest farthing from the percentages; for other dates the prices are the averages as recorded, in both cases, from the monthly accounts in the *Labour Gazette*.

In August 1917 the Ministry of Food fixed wholesale prices of meat (to take effect in September) at 8*s*. 8*d*. per stone (8 lb.) for home-killed beef, veal, mutton, and lamb, and about 1*s*.

lower for imported meat. Retailers were forbidden to sell meat over the counter at prices which, in the aggregate, exceeded the prices paid by them by more than $2\frac{1}{2}d.$ a lb. or 20 per cent., whichever was the less, and out of this margin expenses of carriage and all shop expenses had to be met. The price of home-killed beef fell $1\frac{1}{2}d.$ and of mutton $2\frac{3}{4}d.$; the better cuts of foreign meat did not fall in price. The effect on the purchaser depended on the kind of meat he was able to buy. The Ministry during the following six months extended its control till the supply of home and foreign meat was regulated in all the districts of Great Britain, and a system of rationing was developed, first by limiting the supplies to butchers, and then by personal rationing which was nearly universal from April 1918 till May 1919. Prices were strictly controlled and the amount purchasable adjusted to the available supply, while in general consumers were unable to choose between home and foreign meat or even in some cases between beef and mutton. The control was only relaxed very gradually, and maximum prices were still fixed in the summer of 1920 and the Ministry still administered the supplies of imported meat. Prices were decontrolled on April 29, 1921.

During the ten months after the fixing of prices there was very little change in the prices of home-grown meat, but those of imported meat rose in the spring of 1918 till in May they were the same as for British meat. In September 1918 all prices went up $2d.$, and in February 1919 the $2d.$ was taken off. In May 1919 imported meat was reduced $3d.$ Subsequent changes can be followed from the tables.

As has been seen, the process of control resulted in a levelling of prices, but by April 1920 the pre-war relation had been nearly restored.

	British		Imported		British		Imported	
	Beef (Rib)	Mutton (Leg)	Beef (Rib)	Mutton (Leg)	Beef (Thin flank)	Mutton (Breast)	Beef (Thin flank)	Mutton (Breast)
July 1914	93	100	71	64	62	62	45	38
Feb. 1919	96	100	96	101	72	64	71	63
April 1920	98	100	75	71	71	64	46	29

1569·34   E

In this table the price per lb. of each joint is expressed as a percentage of the price per lb. of a leg of mutton at the same date.

Bacon. The movement of retail prices of bacon is shown sufficiently by the following table :

TABLE XVIII

RETAIL PRICES OF BACON

Date	Price per lb. (*streaky*) ('*Labour Gazette*' *measurement*)
	d.
July 1914 . .	11¼
„ 1915 . .	13¼
„ 1916 . .	15½
„ 1917 . .	20
February 1918 .	27
July 1919 . .	27
August 1919 .	28½
April 1920 . .	29
July 1920 . .	30¼

The price rose 10 per cent. in the first six weeks of the War and then remained at the same level for eight months. The increase was relatively less than that of meat, bread, or of retail food prices in general till the summer of 1917, after which it rose rapidly. In November 1917 the profits of all importers, curer and wholesale and retail dealers, were fixed. In February 1918 the price was 140 per cent. above the pre-war level. In the spring of 1918 very large consignments of bacon, much of it of unattractive quality, were received ; bacon, after a quite short period of rationing, was freely saleable after July, but there was some difficulty in disposing of it at the price necessary to meet its cost. Retail prices (2*s.* 4*d.* a lb. for the best cuts) were fixed in June 1918. The price remained stationary till August 1919 when it rose as shown in the table above. It must be remembered that though the *Labour Gazette* prices are as far as possible for the same kind of bacon throughout, yet they refer to the quality commonly sold, and this has been by no means unchanged during the six years.

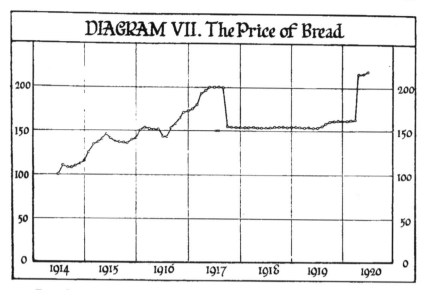

DIAGRAM VII. The Price of Bread

Bread and flour. In July 1914 the price of the 4 lb. loaf varied from 4½d. to 7d. in different towns and shops in Great Britain (*Labour Gazette*, 1914, p. 267). The average adopted in the calculations for the retail index-number was about 5·8d. The price rose rapidly in the first year of the War to 8¼d., at which it stood in July 1915 and January and August 1916, but it had been 9d. in the early part of 1916. From August 1916 it rose rapidly till from June to September 1917 it stood at 11½d. The Commission on Wheat Supplies was appointed in October 1916, and during the winter 1916–17 it took control of imported wheat and of milling, raised the percentage of flour to be extracted from grain, and caused the admixture of other cereals with wheat. Flour used in bread was of the current Government Regulation standard from December 1916 for three years ; approximate pre-war quality was restored in December 1919, but the millers were still controlled and the percentage extraction fixed. During these three years the price of the 4 lb. loaf can be stated, but it is evident that it will not be the price of a commodity of un-changed quality, though it is believed to have been of nearly the same nutritive power throughout, and except in the earlier part of 1917 people generally found it palatable. Partly owing to the nature of the flour and partly owing to pre-occupations, women in the northern counties gave up home baking to some extent and therefore in effect suffered a greater rise in price than the figures suggest. Bread was never rationed, the efforts made to obtain economy in consumption, though their effect was not great and limited to the summer of 1917, proving sufficient to avert the necessity. Beginning in September 1917 the Government granted a subsidy on bread and flour sufficient to keep the price of the 4 lb. loaf sold over the counter and at least 12 hours after baking at 9*d.*, and it remained at that height from September 17, 1917, for two years. In September 1919 a rise of $\frac{1}{2}$*d.* for the 4 lb. loaf was permitted (to allow for the increase in wages and other bakers' expenses), but it was not universally charged. In May 1920 the price was raised to 12$\frac{1}{2}$ or 12$\frac{3}{4}$*d.*, since with the rising price of wheat and flour the subsidy was becoming very heavy, and a further increase took place in August. The retail price of 1 lb. of flour (not including baking-powder) has throughout been practically the same as that of 1 lb. of bread.

Potatoes. The price of potatoes is seasonal, falling rapidly from August and rising in the spring, till as new potatoes become available it becomes difficult to define the average price. Unfortunately the basic price for the general retail food index-number is that of July 1914, and as potatoes account for more than 5 per cent. of the weights (p. 34) and have been much affected by vicissitudes of supply and bad seasons, the general effect is rather misleading. The following table shows the movements in price. June is selected as the month of highest price before new potatoes are in the market and October, November, or December as showing the lowest price for the season.

TABLE XIX

POTATOES: PRICE OF 7 LB. RETAIL

	d.		*d.*
June 1914	4$\frac{3}{4}$	November 1914	3$\frac{3}{4}$
,, 1915	4$\frac{3}{4}$	,, 1915	4$\frac{1}{2}$
,, 1916	7$\frac{1}{2}$	October 1916	7$\frac{1}{2}$
,, 1917	11$\frac{3}{4}$	,, 1917	6$\frac{3}{4}$
,, 1918	7$\frac{1}{4}$	December 1918	7$\frac{1}{4}$
,, 1919	8$\frac{3}{4}$	November 1919	10$\frac{1}{4}$
,, 1920	15$\frac{1}{4}$	October 1920	10$\frac{3}{4}$

There was a sudden rise after October 1916. In 1917 a great development of allotment cultivation took place and continued in 1918, the supply was increased considerably, and many persons were independent of the market price.

Sugar. The supplies of sugar were taken over by the Sugar Commission immediately after the outbreak of War and the retail price fixed. Individuals were rationed from December 1917, and though the form of rationing was changed in 1919 the limitation continued. The price increased more seriously than that of any other commodity and affected the price of jam and some other foods. In July 1914 the ordinary price of granulated sugar was 2*d.* a lb.; the Commission at once raised it to $3\frac{3}{4}d.$; from December 1914 to September 1915 it was $3\frac{1}{4}d.$ or $3\frac{1}{2}d.$; in November 1915 and the following two months it was 4*d.* It then rose gradually till it reached 6*d.* in September 1917; in April 1918 an additional duty of $1\frac{1}{4}d.$ a lb. was imposed and sugar was sold at 7*d.* for nineteen months. In November 1919 the price rose to 8*d.*, in April 1920 to 10*d.*, and in June 1920 to 14*d.*

Milk. In normal times the price of milk varied about $\frac{1}{2}d.$ a quart from one place to another, but in spite of the seasonal variation of the supply was usually unchanged through the year, and in fact had been delivered at 4*d.* a quart with few interruptions in many places for perhaps forty years. In months and places where milk was temporarily scarce the retailer used to ration his customers informally. This regularity of supply was disturbed during the latter years of the War owing to the scarcity of oil-seed cake and other semi-artificial foods and to the disturbance in the equilibrium of the herds, and as the diagram shows there have been very marked seasonal variations of price since the summer of 1917. From early in 1917 maximum prices were fixed for the producer, and from time to time since then maximum producers' and retailers' prices were fixed at those rates which it was believed would encourage the farmer to supply the milk and allow a reasonable profit to the distributors and retailers. Notwithstanding these arrangements there was an acute shortage of milk in the winter 1919–20. The average price in July 1914 was taken for the index-number at $3\frac{1}{2}d.$

a quart. The average rose very gradually till September 1915 (4*d*.), more rapidly till February 1916 (4½*d*.), gradually again till September 1916, and then rapidly to 5½*d*. at which price it remained till September 1917. So far there had been an upward step each autumn and no recovery in the spring; the whole increase was 60 per cent., which was less than that of any other commodity included in the general index-number except potatoes. The subsequent marked seasonal movement may be shown as follows :

Lowest summer price		d.	Highest winter price		d.
June 1917	. . .	5½	February 1918	. .	7
„ 1918	. . .	5½	March 1919	. .	8¾
„ 1919	. . .	6¼	January 1920	. .	10¾
July 1920	. . .	7¾	February 1921	. .	10½

These prices, which are the averages of returns from all over the country stated to the nearest farthing, are in some cases lower than the maximum allowed.

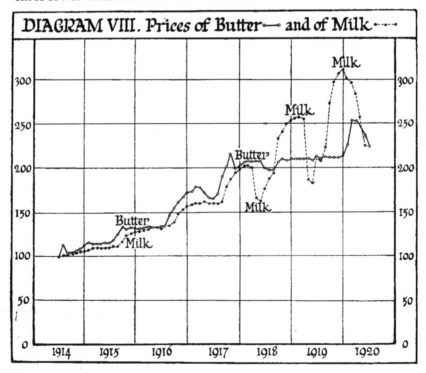

DIAGRAM VIII. Prices of Butter — and of Milk ----

Butter. The price of butter was of only academic interest to many would-be purchasers during a considerable period, since it was often either unobtainable or at a prohibitive cost. The scarcity was partly due to the great diminution of imports— in 1913, 1916, 1917, 1918, 1919 the average weekly imports were respectively 3,867, 2,080, 1,749, 1,522, and 1,540 tons, a fall from about 14 oz. per household weekly to 5½ oz., and partly to a deliberate policy of encouraging milk production at the expense of butter by the fixing of more favourable prices for the former. In the winters 1917–18 and 1918–19 the butter ration was almost negligible.

The diagram shows the movements of prices. In each year the summer prices of butter and of milk show nearly the same proportion (1 lb. of butter cost the same as 4 quarts of milk); prior to 1918 butter rose in the autumn more rapidly than milk. During 1918 and 1919 what butter there was was sold at a nearly uniform price of 2s. 6d. a lb., the pre-war price having been about 1s. 2d.; in the winter of 1919–20 it reached 3s. and was subsequently reduced to 2s. 8d. These prices are those of ' Government butter '; other could be obtained at a higher price.

Cheese. The supply of cheese was limited by the same causes which affected butter. It is not necessary to discuss the prices in detail, since it is (except in particular localities and occupations) a relatively unimportant food. The average movement of prices generally paid for imported American cheese is adequately shown in the table (pp. 42–6).

Margarine. The deficiency of the butter supply was completely compensated so far as the provision of nutrition is concerned by a great development and improvement of the manufacture of margarine, which was taken over by the Ministry of Food in 1917, great attention being paid to the supply of the necessary materials. Except for a quite short period at Christmas 1917 the supply has been equal to reasonable requirements. Margarine became the principal supply of fatty food (being hardly second to bacon in this respect) to the bulk of the population. Its price movements are of great importance, but (as with so many commodities) the quality purchased at the prices stated was not unchanged in the period. No doubt the quality as a whole improved very considerably, but the average prices given are of the kinds most usually bought and it is not possible to know in detail what these kinds were.

TABLE XX

RETAIL PRICES OF MARGARINE

	1914	1915	1916	1917	1918	1919	1920
	d.	d.	d.	d.	d.	d.	d.
January 1 . .	—	7½	7¾	9	12	12¼	13¼
April 1 . . .	—	7½	8½	10¾	12¼	9¼	14¼
July 1 . . .	7¼	7½	8½	12¾	12¼	13¼	13½
October 1 . .	8	7¾	8¾	12	14¼	13¼	13¾

During the period of complete control the prices were 1s. or 1s. 2d., but there was some variety of kinds, and the averages lead to the odd farthings in the table. Margarine was decontrolled and de-rationed in March 1919, and there was a temporary cut in price by the large distributive firms.

The price of margarine at its highest was equal to the pre-war price of butter, and those households who made a complete turnover from the latter to the former actually spent no more in 1918–20 than in 1914. This consideration tends to vitiate all ordinary comparisons of the cost of living taken in its obvious sense.

Eggs. The movement of the price of eggs, when imports are cut off, is strongly seasonal. The increase in prices, whether measured by the summer or winter levels, is sufficiently clear from the accompanying diagram. In 1913, 2,590 million eggs were imported, sufficient for five each week for every household in the kingdom; during the War this great total was reduced to quite insignificant proportions. The home supply was greatly reduced owing to the dearness of corn for fowls, while the demand for eggs for some purposes is always urgent. There is then nothing surprising in the high price reached in November 1918. Nevertheless the dearness was mitigated for the large number of households who keep a few fowls, fed to a great extent on household waste, and who preserve eggs from the

summer for winter use. The inclusion of about 12 eggs at
1s. 1d. in the basic budget has had misleading results. The fact
that the price was taken at the cheaper period of the year
exaggerates greatly the percentage increases tabulated for the

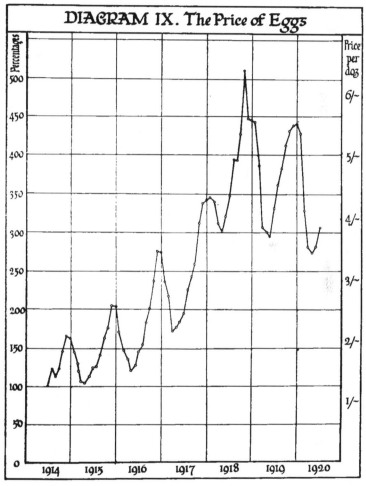

DIAGRAM IX. The Price of Eggs

winter months. If eggs had been omitted (with other of the
less important foods) in the computation of the index-number,
the general increase shown to November 1918 would have been
112 per cent. instead of 129 per cent., and in August 1919
the percentage increase would have been 109 instead of 117.

In Table XVI on pp. 42–6 the foods included in the retail
index-number are divided into three groups. The first merely
puts together the various entries for butchers' meat. In the
second are contained other foods as to which no important
difficulty in treatment is found when an index-number is
formed, except that the consumption of bacon increased in one
period at the expense of meat the price of which had risen less
rapidly. In the third group are put together those items whose
inclusion in a measurement of the cost of living presents very
difficult problems.

The following extract from the Report of the Working
Classes Cost of Living Committee, to which reference has already
been made, shows the nature of the problem :

WEEKLY EXPENDITURE OF STANDARD FAMILIES

	1914 Summer			1918 Summer		
	Quantity	Cost		Quantity	Cost	
		s.	d.		s.	d.
Sugar . . .	5·9 lb.	1	1	2·83 lb.	1	8
Butter . .	1·70 lb.	2	0½	0·79 lb.	1	11½
Margarine . .	0·42 lb.		2½	0·91 lb.		11
Eggs . . .	13	1	1	9·1	3	0½
Other food . .		20	6		39	8
Total . .		24	11		47	3

If the same quantities of the four items distinguished had
been bought in 1918 as in 1914 the second total would have
been 52s. 1½d., and the increase over 1914 would become 109 per
cent. instead of 90 per cent. Now no more sugar, butter, or
eggs were on the average available. If 5d. more had been spent
on margarine in 1918 the aggregate weight of butter and
margarine would have been the same at the two dates. But
there was no substitute for sugar to be obtained, and though the
lost nourishment of four eggs, which is trifling, could have been
replaced cheaply, a substitute would not have yielded the same
satisfaction. It is clear that the retail index-number does not
give an adequate measurement of the change in the cost of
living, and it is equally clear that it cannot be replaced by an
index of expenditure. It is not proposed here to discuss the

questions raised further, but the group index-numbers compared with the general index-number indicate how far they are important when taken in conjunction with the table of ' weights ' on p. 34.

Of the foods included in the table, pp. 42 seq., we have still to speak of *fish* and *tea*. It is evident that no definite average price can be given for fish, and fortunately it has little importance in the computation of the index-number. The average price of tea as usually bought is given as 1s. 6½d. a lb. in July 1914. The price was unchanged till December 1914, but then it rose till in October 1915 it was 2s. 3½d. or 2s. 4d., where it remained till after February 1917. During 1917 it rose till the average as recorded reached 3s. 2d. in December in spite of various efforts at control; during November and December of that year a sudden shortage of stock became apparent and the retailers rationed their customers strictly. By March 1918 the price had fallen to 2s. 11d. Early in 1918 the Ministry of Food, having failed to regulate prices of different kinds to its satisfaction, mixed together the various supplies and issued one uniform blend to be sold at 2s. 8d., and this was the price from April or May 1918 till March 1919 when control was removed. The price of tea as usually bought was 2s. 6d. or 2s. 7d. for the following six months and then rose 4d. and continued at 2s. 10d. or 2s. 11d. till July 1920.

Food not included in the index-number. The following table shows the items of food not included in the basic budget and resulting index-number, with the amounts spent on them in the average of 416 budgets of families with incomes between 30 and 35s. weekly in 1904 (Cd. 2337, p. 23).

TABLE XXI

LESS IMPORTANT FOODS. EXPENDITURE IN 1904

	s.	d.
Biscuits and cake		4½
Pork and sausages ; not stated, say . .		8
Offals, rabbits, fish		10
Lard, suet, dripping		5
Condensed milk		1
Vegetables other than potatoes . .		6¼

TABLE XXI (*continued*)—LESS IMPORTANT FOODS. EXPENDITURE IN 1904

	s.	*d.*
Fruit, fresh		3¾
Currants		1½
Raisins		¾
Rice		2
Tapioca		¾
Oatmeal		3¼
Coffee		1¼
Cocoa		2¼
Jam and marmalade		5¼
Treacle and syrup		¾
Pickles		1
Condiments		2¼
Other food, unspecified		2¾
Meals out		4
Total excluded	5	6¼
Total included	15	3
Grand total	20	9¼

Of these, jam, marmalade, treacle, and syrup have been dependent on the supply and prices of sugar; biscuits and cake on those of sugar and flour; and lard, suet, and dripping on meat and bacon; and all these together would by their inclusion in the budget tend to affect the relative importance of these principal entries and make little difference in the general index-number. The demand for all food that contained sugar or fat was no doubt accentuated in 1917 and 1918 and in the case of sugar continued in 1920.

The Ministry of Food received information for two years beginning March 1917 relating to the ordinary retail prices of lard, oatmeal, rice, &c., condensed milk, and preserved peas and beans, and were able to compare them with equivalent pre-war prices.

The relative prices of American lard were :

July 1914	*March* 1917	*September* 1917	*March* 1918	*September* 1918	*March* 1919
100	230	220	257	286	286

the rise was considerably greater than in the case of bacon.

Dripping was for a considerable period unobtainable, but was sold unextracted with the meat.

The price of *oatmeal* was regulated in September 1917; its relative prices were :

July 1914	100
April 1917	240
May 1917	270
June 1917	260
July–October 1917 . .	250 (225 in Scotland)
November–December 1917 .	241
January–February 1918 .	200
March–June 1918 . . .	213
July 1918–February 1919 .	220
March 1919	213

Oatmeal thus became dear relatively to wheat-flour.

Rice was used to an important extent in the manufacture of regulation flour, but it was also purchasable in the shops.

Its relative prices were :

July 1914	100
March–April 1917 . .	190
May 1917–February 1918 .	200
March 1918–March 1919 .	217
April 1919	200

Sago rose to three and four times its pre-war price in 1918; *tapioca* was at its dearest at the end of 1918 when it was three and a half times its pre-war price.

Condensed milk was naturally in great demand when fresh milk was scarce.

The price movements of the two may be thus compared :

	July 1914	*June 1917*	*February 1918*	*June 1918*	*March 1919*
Condensed milk . .	100	200	239	252	226
Fresh milk . .	100	160	202	260	258

Butter *beans* and haricot *beans* (white) were respectively 110 and 140 per cent. above the pre-war price from August 1917 to February 1919, after which date the prices fell.

Raisins were generally not to be obtained. Very limited quantities of *currants* were distributed from time to time.

The prices of nearly all the foods named in these paragraphs increased more rapidly from 1914 to the Armistice than did the average of the goods included in the index-number, and to the limited extent to which they were obtainable accentuated the increase in the cost of living.

CHAPTER IV

OTHER RETAIL PRICES. CHANGE IN COST OF LIVING

1. Other retail prices. Rent. Fuel and light. Coal. Clothing; investigation by the Cost of Living Committee; the index-number of the Ministry of Labour.

2. Changes in the cost of living. Combination of prices of food, clothing, &c. Index-number, 1914–20. Relation of index-numbers to cost of living. Alternative measurement.

1. OTHER RETAIL PRICES

It is very difficult to give an account of the movement of retail prices of commodities other than food. Articles of luxury cannot be adequately described or defined for statistical measurements, nor can typical objects be selected and their prices followed. It would be hopeless to try to record for statistical purposes prices of motor-cars, bicycles, expensive clothes, furniture, or apparatus for sports. Tobacco and alcoholic drinks increased in price mainly through the increase of duties; beer and whisky have altered greatly in quality. Railway travelling became dearer, first by the reduction of facilities for excursion and cheap fares, then in 1918 by raising ordinary fares 50 per cent. and contract tickets 20 per cent., while workmen's fares were unaffected; a further general rise took place in August 1920. Postage was increased from time to time, till in June 1920 the lowest letter-rate was 2d. for 3 oz., as compared with the pre-war rate of 1d. for 4 oz. inland. In the summer of 1920 it was difficult to name any article the price of which was not more than twice that in 1914.

Attention has been specially directed to the study of prices of those things which are necessary in working-class house-keeping. These are generally classified as food, clothing, fuel and light, rent and miscellaneous.

The *rent* of houses of a working-class type was kept by law at its height in 1914 throughout the War and till July 1920, but where (as is generally the case with small rentals) local rates were included in the rents, the landlord was entitled to raise the rent to recuperate himself. In 1918 the increases made for this reason were trifling (Cd. 8980, p. 24), but a greater effect was marked in the latter part of 1919, and by June 1920 the increase in rates resulted in an average increase of 15 to 20 per cent. on pre-war working-class rents (*Labour Gazette*, June 1920, p. 295). Since then a further increase has been permitted to allow for the expense of repairs.

Fuel and light. Information was obtained by the Working Class Cost of Living Committee (Cd. 8980, pp. 24–5), and percentage changes were estimated in the *Labour Gazette* monthly from November 1919.

The mean price of *coal* ascertained by an inquiry into ' Working Class Rents and Retail Prices in 1912 ' (Cd. 6955) varied from $8\frac{1}{2}d.$ to 10*d.* (Nottingham) to 1*s.* 4*d.* or 1*s.* 5*d.* (Dover) per cwt. The general average was about 1*s.* The price paid in the summer of 1918 averaged about 1*s.* 8*d.*, an increase of 65 or 70 per cent. In November 1919 it was at more than double the price in 1914 (which differed little from that in 1912), but at that date household coal was reduced 10*s.* a ton, and the effect of this was to bring coal retailed in cwt. to 65 or 70 per cent. above the 1914 price. There was a slight increase during the early months of 1920, and in May the price of household coal was raised 14*s.* 2*d.* per ton, with the result that working-class purchases were at 135 per cent. above the price in 1914.

In the summer of 1918, *gas* was about 41 per cent. dearer than in 1914, though the increase varied greatly from 24 per cent. in the east and south-east of England to 71 per cent. in Scotland (Cd. 8980, p. 25). By November 1919 the average increase was somewhat under 100 per cent. ; in February 1920 it had fallen till it was under 70 per cent. above 1914, and in March, April, May, June, July 1920 the percentages are estimated as 75, 75, 60, 65, and 85.

The prices of oil, candles, and matches (on which household expenditure is trifling) increased more rapidly than those of coal or gas.

Clothing. Since a good deal depends on the estimate of the price of clothes, when a general measurement of the purchasing power of money is attempted, and there is not agreement on the subject, it will be well to give what evidence there is in some detail.

The Cost of Living Committee (Cd. 8980, pp. 21–3) obtained from a number of retailers, 'in various towns of Great Britain, detailed statements showing the prices in 1914 and 1918 of the main articles of clothing of the qualities usually purchased by the working-classes'. The results were summarized as follows :

TABLE XXII

AVERAGE PRICES OF CLOTHING ORDINARILY PURCHASED BY THE WORKING CLASSES IN 1914 AND 1918

MEN'S

	Price per article 1914		1918		Increase per cent.	'Weight'
	s.	d.	s.	d.		
Suits . . .	28	6	60	0	110	34
Overcoats . .	27	4	46	8	71	23
Shirts (union flannel)	4	6	8	2½	82	6
Underwear (union) .	2	11	5	5	86	5
Hosiery (union) .		10	2	1	150	3
Boots (working) .	10	10	21	7	99 ⎞	
„ (lighter) .	12	10	26	10	109 ⎠	16
„ repairs . .	3	4¹	5	11¹	78	7
Hats . . .	3	0	6	2	106	3
Caps . . .	1	5	2	7	82	1
Collars . . .		5		7	40	2
						———
						100

WOMEN'S

	Price per article 1914		1918		Increase per cent.	'Weight'
	s.	d.	s.	d.		
Costumes . .	44	0	80	3	82	30
Dresses . .	8	0	15	11	89	13
Underwear . .	3	2	6	0	90	15
Corsets . .	4	0	6	11	73	2
Hats . .	10	7¹	19	2¹	81	15
Stockings . .	1	8	3	8	120	4
Aprons . .	1	4¹	2	3¹	69	3
Boots . .	11	6	22	4	94 ⎞	
Shoes . .	9	6	21	9	129 ⎠	14
Boot repairs . .	2	1¹	3	10¹	84	4
						———
						100

¹ These items were estimated from rather scanty information in family budgets received by the Committee. They are not very reliable, but they have little influence on the general result.

TABLE XXII (*continued*)—AVERAGE PRICES OF CLOTHING ORDINARILY
PURCHASED BY THE WORKING CLASSES IN 1914 AND 1918

BOYS OF SCHOOL AGE

	Price per article				Increase	
	1914		1918		per cent.	' Weight '
	s.	d.	s.	d.		
Suits	15	9	35	1	123	23
Shirts	2	6	4	0	60	8
Underwear	2	5	4	4	80	6
Stockings	1	7	3	1	95	6
Collars		5¹		7¹	40	2
Caps		11¹	1	11¹	109	2
Overcoats	15	5¹	31	5¹	134	23
Boots	6	11	12	7	82	23
Boot repairs	2	4¹	4	5¹	89	7
						——
						100

GIRLS OF SCHOOL AGE

	Price per article				Increase	
	1914		1918		per cent.	' Weight '
	s.	d.	s.	d.		
Dresses	18	2	33	7	85	27
Underwear	3	7	6	4	77	18
Stockings	1	8	3	8	120	5
Hats	2	6	4	9	90	14
Boots	7	3	14	8	102	28
Boot repairs	1	11¹	3	8¹	91	8
						——
						100

YOUNG CHILDREN

	Price per article				Increase	
	1914		1918		per cent.	' Weight '
	s.	d.	s.	d.		
Frocks	4	4	8	3	90	19
Pinafores	1	10	3	4	82	19
Underwear	1	1	2	7	138	23
Socks		9	1	10	144	4
Shoes	3	0¹	4	7¹	33	35
						——
						100

¹ These items were estimated from rather scanty information in family budgets
received by the Committee. They are not very reliable, but they have little influence
on the general result.

The relative importance or ' weights ' to be assigned to the different articles was estimated from budgets. Though they cannot be precise, it will be found by experiment, as is to be expected from the theory of weighted averages, that no substantial difference in the result is made by reasonable modification of them. The resulting percentage increases for the clothing of a man, woman, boy, girl, and child, were respectively 94, 90, 102, 91, and 89 per cent., and these combined give 93 per cent. Sufficient evidence was received that there was a tendency to purchase goods of a higher grade in 1918 than in 1914,[1] though the quality of separate grades had deteriorated, except that hosiery and repairs of boots were inferior. In the end the conclusion was that with an increased expenditure of about 96 per cent. a family would have been as well clothed in 1918 as in 1914, but that there would have been some change in the materials.

The Ministry of Labour did not publish a separate index-number for clothing till November 1919. In August 1919, the date to which the Cost of Living Committee's clothing statistics refer, the account in the *Labour Gazette*,[2] August 1918, p. 309, is as follows :

' Retail prices of the principal articles of food have [on the basis described, p. 34 above] increased by about 118 per cent., and although the average level of rents has only increased very slightly as a result of increases in local rates, the prices of other items have advanced so substantially that the general increase in the prices of all the items ordinarily entering into the working-class family budget (including food, rent, clothing, fuel, and light, &c.) between July, 1914 and August 1, 1918, is estimated at about 110 per cent., taking for this calculation the same quantities of the various items in August, 1918 as in July, 1914.'

The relative importance assigned in this calculation to the various constituents of this general index-number are stated in the *Labour Gazette* of March 1920 (p. 119), and may be put in the following form :

---

[1] The cheapest grades were often unobtainable.

[2] The *Labour Gazette* was published by the Board of Trade till June 1917, and thereafter by the Ministry of Labour without change of method.

	Relative importance in 1914	Increase of prices to August 1918
Food	60	118
Rent, including rates . .	16	—
Clothing	12	—
Fuel and light		
Coal	4·8	—
Gas	2·4	—
Oil, candles, and matches .	0·8	—
Other items . . .	4·0	—
	100·0	110

Now if we take the rise in rent and rates at 3 per cent., in fuel and light at 78 per cent., and sundries at 114 per cent., as did the Cost of Living Committee, a simple calculation shows that clothing must have risen 233 per cent. if the aggregate increased 110 per cent. If we take higher percentages, say 5 per cent., 100 per cent., 150 per cent., instead of those just named (and these are as high as any evidence allows), then clothing must have risen 200 per cent. There is little doubt that in the *Labour Gazette* an increase of at least 200 per cent.[1] must have been assigned to clothing in August 1918. But the Committee on the Cost of Living found only half this increase in the prices of ' the main articles of clothing of the qualities usually purchased by the working-classes ', and the table on pp. 64-5 shows that no adjustment of weights can raise this estimate much.

The method followed in the computation of the *Labour Gazette* estimate is thus described (*Labour Gazette*, March 1920, p. 119): ' In order to estimate the increase in the prices of clothing, information is obtained as to the movement of retail prices of men's suits and overcoats (ready and bespoke), woollen and cotton materials for women's outer garments (viz. costume cloth, tweed, serge, frieze, cashmere, print, zephyr, sateen, drill, and galatea), woollen and cotton underclothing (viz. woollen vests, men's and women's, woollen pants, men's merino and cotton socks, women's woollen and cotton stockings, flannel, flannelette, calico, longcloth, shirting), and boots. The in-

---

[1] *Labour Gazette*, April 1921, p. 179, gives June 1918 210, September 260.

formation relates to those descriptions of articles which are most generally purchased by the working classes, i. e. relatively low-priced grades.' The dealer 'is asked to quote the current price for the same article and quality' as in the previous monthly inquiry, ' or for the most nearly corresponding article or quality'. The percentage changes shown in the various returns are then averaged for each article, those for similar articles averaged together, and the group percentages thus obtained averaged to give the general figure. This process of averaging does not appear to correspond to any logical system of weighting. The result is stated for each month since November 1919, thus 'it is estimated that the level of prices of clothing, quality for quality, taking goods of the kind purchased by the working-classes ', is so much above that of July 1914.

The *Labour Gazette* inquiry draws from a larger number of districts and informants than did the Cost of Living Committee, but this consideration is not of much importance. The method of averaging may give undue importance to dress stuffs, which with the very high price of woollen manufactures had in 1918 risen acutely, and some reduction might have been obtained if more attention had been given to the relative importance of different articles of clothing. The main cause of the difference is, however, probably to be found in fixing attention on the pre-war kinds and qualities of goods, a method similar to that employed in the food index-number, where pre-war quantities of sugar, butter, and margarine are supposed to be purchased. Some of the cheaper qualities of clothing had in 1918 risen much more rapidly in price than had the better grades, and were in some cases nearly unattainable. Also the process of accumulating percentage changes from month to month may easily lead to error.

There must remain considerable doubt whether the official method of measuring clothing prices was valid in 1918 or subsequently. But we are not justified in assuming that the rather slight inquiry of the Cost of Living Committee gives us a better estimate, especially for 1919 and 1920. With the continued rise of prices the modification of quality has probably become of less importance, and without a further investigation it is not possible to determine the effect of weighting. It is much to be regretted that the *Labour Gazette* did not show till April 1921 the details on which its clothing estimate is based, for readers had no power of checking the assumed expenditure with their own experience or of testing the validity of the method of averaging.

2. CHANGES IN THE COST OF LIVING

The system of weights (p. 67) used for obtaining a general index-number of the movement of retail prices is hardly capable of improvement with the limited information we have on the subject. The relative importance of food, rent, and fuel rests on good evidence ; but no investigator has succeeded in ascertaining what proportion of working-class income is spent on clothing, and there is no doubt that this varies enormously according to the income and constitution of the household and on the various makeshifts practised by the thrifty or the poor. It is well to test from time to time what would be the effect on the index-number if the importance of clothing in 1914 were lowered from 12 to 5 or raised to 20. The 12 per cent. is generally accepted as reasonable.

To ' Other items ' is only assigned one-twenty-fifth of expenditure in 1914. This is certainly too low for an average working-class family. It has to include insurance and subscriptions of all kinds, cleaning materials, replenishment of utensils, travelling, amusements, newspapers, tobacco, and beer. It is not, however, probable that the increase in the cost of this miscellany has differed so much from the increase under the other headings, taken together, that a change in the weight assigned to it would have much effect on the general number.

In the following table the food index-number is repeated from p. 35, and set alongside the general index-number (including food). From November 1919 more detail is shown.

TABLE XXIII

CHANGES IN RETAIL PRICES (OFFICIAL COMPUTATION)

Beginning of	1914 Food	1914 General	1915 Food	1915 General	1916 Food	1916 General	1917 Food	1917 General	1918 Food	1918 General	1919 Food	1919 General
January	—	—	118	110–15	145	135	187	165	206	185–90	230	220
February	—	—	122	115	147	135	189	165–70	208	190	230	220
March	—	—	124	115–20	148	135–40	192	170	207	190	220	215
April	—	—	124	115–20	149	135–40	194	170–5	206	190–5	213	210
May	—	—	126	120	155	140–5	198	175	207	195–200	207	210
June	—	—	132	125	159	145	202	175–80	208	200	204	205
July	100	100	132½	125	161	145–50	204	180	210	200–5	209	205–10
August	116	—	134	125	160	145–50	202	180	218	210	217	215
September	110	—	135	125	165	150	206	180–5	216	210	216	215
October	112	—	140	130	168	150–5	197	175–80	229	215–20	222	220
November	113	—	141	130–5	178	160	206	185	233	220–5	231	225
December	116	—	144	135	184	165	205	185	229	220	234	225

	Food 60	Rent 16	Clothing 12	Fuel and light 8	Other items 4	Together
Relative importance		Approx.			Not stated.[1]	
Beginning of						
1919 November	231	105	300+	210		225
December	234	105	300+	185		225
1920 January	236	105	300–400	185		225
February	235	105	400	180		230
March	233	110	400	180–5		230
April	235	110	410–20	180–5		232
May	246	115	420–30	185		241
June	255	115–20	430	225		250
July	258	115–20	430	230		252
August	262	115–20	430	235		255
September	267	135	430	235		261
October	270	139	430	245–50		264
November	291	142	420	245–50		276
December	282	142	400–10	240		269
1921 January	278	142	390	240		265
February	263	142	350–60	240		251
March	249	144	340	240		241
April	238	144	320–30	245		233
May	232	144	310	250		228

NOTE.—These are not percentage increases, but relative numbers to be compared with 100 in July 1914.

[1] Other items appear to have been reckoned as increasing 100 to 150 per cent.

Up to the middle of 1917 the balance of increase in food and other prices and stationariness in rent resulted in the increase in the general index-number being about three-fourths of that of food. In the subsequent three years the greater increase assigned to clothing brought up the general number very nearly to the food number.

The result may be described as showing the increase in the cost of maintaining the pre-war standard of living, with no change in quantity and a minimum change in quality, and with no reference to the actual possibility of obtaining the goods included. The most important practical question to which an answer ought to be attempted is whether the increase of wages has kept pace with or exceeded the increase in the cost of living, or (in different words) whether the working classes have preserved or improved their standard of living. At a later stage we estimate the movement in average earnings; here we ought to measure the decrease in the purchasing power of money. Though the increase of prices has no doubt affected differently the unmarried man, the young woman, the widow, the married couple without children, and what is regarded as the normal household, viz. the married couple with three dependent children, yet we shall get as good an approximation as the data will permit if we confine attention to the last named, whose expenditure is taken as the standard for the basic budget which leads to the general retail index-number.

The question then is, ought we to accept the official index-number as an adequate measurement of the change in the cost of living, if not whether it is too high or too low, and what better measurement can be proposed?

Sugar, butter, eggs, and cheese have been unattainable in their pre-war quantities, and a practical measurement ought not to assume that they were bought. As regards cheese, we need not make any correction, for the amount included in the budget is very small, and a slight increase in bread and in meat would make good its deficiency at a price which would not affect practically the official index-number.

A reasonable assumption about butter is that the pre-war quantities (p. 34) of 1·93 lb. butter and 0·9 lb. margarine, costing together 34·4d., are replaced by the same weight equally divided, viz. 1·42 lb. butter at 2s. 8d. (Government butter, July 1920), and 1·42 lb. margarine at 1s. 1½d. (price in July 1920), which together cost 65d.

For sugar we may assume that half the former quantity is consumed, after allowing for a slight possible increase in the use of jam, and in the dearth of accurate information we cannot do better than halve also the consumption of eggs. We do not know how in fact thus deficiency is made good, but a possible method of computation is to divide the pre-war expenditure on sugar and eggs into two equal parts, to assign to one of these the actual increase in price of sugar and eggs, and to assign to the other the increase of the remainder of the budget after sugar, eggs, butter, and margarine have been cut out ; by this method we assume that an increase has been made in the consumption of all other goods of such an amount that if made in 1914 on them instead of on sugar and eggs, it would have left the total expenditure unaffected.

The changes thus supposed would then be as follows :

	July 1914 Quantity	July 1914 Cost	July 1920 Quantity	July 1920 Cost	July 1920 Quantities as in 1914 Cost
	lb.	d.	lb.	d.	d.
Butter . . .	1·93	27·6	1·42	45·4	61·8
Margarine . .	0·9	6·8	1·42	20·2	12·8
Sugar : one-half .	3·05	6·4	1·05	43·6	43·6
Eggs : one-half .	5	6·3	5	19·4	19·4
Sugar : one-half .	3·05	6·4 }12·7	—	29·2[1]	{ 43·6
Eggs : one-half .	5	6·3	—		19·4
Other food . .	—	165·7	—	381·2	381·2
		225·5		539·0	581·8

With the original quantities the increase is 158 per cent. ; with the modified quantities it is 139 per cent.

[1] $12·7 \times \dfrac{381·2}{165·7} = 29·2$

The results of a similar calculation once in six months from July 1916 are as follows :

TABLE XXIV

MEASUREMENTS OF COST OF LIVING

RETAIL FOOD PRICES

	Official Index-number	Modified Index-number	Actual Expenditure per cent. (p. 39)
July 1914 . . .	100	100	100
July 1916 . . .	161	158	—
January 1917 . .	187	178	—
July 1917 . . .	204	200	—
February 1918 . .	208	198	144
July 1918 . . .	210	198	184
January 1919 . .	230	217	177
July 1919 . . .	209	198	200 approx.
January 1920 . .	236	225	210 ,,
July 1920 . . .	258	239	—

The lower numbers shown for expenditure indicate the existence of greater modifications, and possibly some fall of standard, than are indicated by the suggested modified index-number, which is intended to correspond to no fall of standard.

It is clear that no exact calculation of a change in consumption without a reduction of standard is possible without further data, and it is always possible that the curtailment of normal supplies resulted in the purchase of more expensive substitutes instead of the economies here indicated ; but these numbers, it is believed, give a reasonable measurement of the changes that have probably taken place, and show the direction and indicate the magnitude of the kind of correction that ought to be made. The correction is not great, and the official index-numbers do not give a seriously wrong impression. On the official reckoning the value of £1 spent in food has fallen to £1 ÷ 2·58 = 7s. 9d. in the six years from July 1914 ; by the modified reckoning it has fallen to 8s. 4d.

It does not seem possible to amend the index-number for clothing on any definite principle, but we may perhaps regard the official reckoning as a maximum and assume that some modifications can be (and indeed are forced by the shortage of goods) made without any real lowering of the standard. In order to compute alternative index-numbers, which may serve as a minimum estimate of the increase of retail prices in general, we take as hypothesis that the increase in the cost of clothing is (as is suggested above for the summer of 1918) half that calculated for the official number. The numbers for rent, fuel and light, and other items need not be adjusted.

On this basis of supposing modifications in the kinds of food and clothing purchased we should have the following results :

| | General Retail Index-number | |
	Official	Modified
July 1914 . . .	100	100
July 1918 . .	200–5	180
January 1919 .	220	200
July 1919 . .	205–10	185
January 1920 . .	225	200
July 1920 . .	252	220

It is evident that a considerable amount of approximation enters into the calculation, but as in the case of the modified food index-number it shows the direction and indicates the magnitude of the change that may be introduced by a modification of purchases in accordance with supplies without necessarily any lowering of standard. On the two hypotheses the purchasing power of £1 is lowered to 8s. and to 9s. respectively.

CHAPTER V

COMPARISON OF WHOLESALE AND RETAIL FOOD PRICES

The problem. Fixed charges and percentage additions. Bread and flour. Flour and wheat. Meat. Bacon. Butter. Potatoes.

IT would be very interesting to trace the relative movements of retail and wholesale prices and to determine whether dealers and retailers had profited by the rapid changes of supply, but it is not possible in view of the great complication of the problem and the dearth of information to do more than carry out a few tentative inquiries.

The complications are mainly due to the difficulty of defining the raw material or materials of the articles finally retailed, and to the number of manufacturers, merchants, dealers, and retailers who handle the goods between the original producer and the final shopkeeper. Thus in the case of bread the producers are the farmers at home and abroad, the intermediaries are the corn and flour factors, the transport companies, the millers, and the bakers. Here we can ascertain the prices of the grain, the flour, and the loaf, but we cannot distribute the margin between the agencies concerned.

When, generally in 1917, the Ministry of Food took complete possession or effective control of the whole of the supply and distribution and regulated the prices at every stage, the allocation of the margin between the initial and final price could only be determined from the unpublished records of the Ministry. All we can do is to investigate the relation of the margin in 1914 to that immediately before and that immediately after the establishment of control. In some of the cases for which we have data the termination of control was so recent at the date of writing, and we cannot therefore determine the new equilibrium after the markets are free.

For one reason or another the only foods with regard to which an investigation is possible are flour, bread, meat, bacon, butter, and potatoes. For the other items of the retail index-number : *Sugar* was owned and distributed by the Government from August 1914 till the end of the record ; there are so many varieties of *fish* and of *tea* that we cannot connect wholesale with the corresponding retail prices. For *milk, cheese,* and *eggs* there are not sufficient records of producers or of wholesale prices throughout the period concerned. *Margarine* is composed of a variety of materials, and its contents and quality have been modified.

We ought to distinguish as clearly as possible between two methods by which middlemen's and retailers' charges are made, namely, the method of adding a definite sum (if, for example, the baker adds $2\frac{1}{2}d$. per 4 lb. loaf to the cost of the flour in it), and the method of adding a fixed percentage (as when a building contractor adds, say, 20 per cent. to his estimated outlay in drawing up his tender). By the first method retail prices rise less rapidly than wholesale, by the latter the rates of increase are identical. The question is investigated by the present writer in *The Economic Journal,* December 1913 (' The Relation between the Changes in the Wholesale and Retail Prices of Food '), and the conclusion there reached is that in the period 1896–1910 in the United Kingdom retail food prices moved as if fixed amounts, not fixed percentages, were added to wholesale prices.

In the first year or two years of the War the expenses of the dealer did not increase at all, or not nearly so fast as did the costs of materials. Internal transport rates were unchanged ; rent and rates were stationary ; fuel and light rose little, and for some time wages were steady. During this period the dealer made nearly the same profit if he added the same sum per unit handled to the wholesale price he paid. The purchasing power of his income from profit fell, but only to the same extent as that of all other individuals. In the latter years of the War, and especially in the year after the Armistice, conditions changed. Wages rose rapidly, the cost of transport, fuel, and light rose considerably, and finally rates rose ; the only outgoings that were nearly stationary were those for rent.   At the same time people generally tended to return to pre-war rates of consumption, and wages and many incomes increased till their purchasing power was not very different from that in 1914.   In 1920 the dealer would have been in the same relative position as before the War, if the margin between wholesale and retail prices had borne the same percentage to the former as in 1914, less a small deduction because of the absence of any great increase in rent.   In the long run, when all control is removed and equilibrium again obtained, equality with former conditions would be shown by the exact restoration of the pre-war percentage, if the former methods of marketing and dealing return.

In the preceding paragraph it is tacitly assumed that the amount of goods handled is unchanged.   It is evident that the dealer's gross profit falls if he handles fewer goods, while his fixed expenses are the same and he may not be able to economize in labour, so that his net profit falls more than his gross.   In 1917, when the Ministry of Food took control, supplies were very short, the butcher handled less meat, the baker was greatly restricted in the sale of confectionery, and the grocer's shop was depleted;   on the other hand, the wage bill was lowered by the drawing off of men to the Army.   The Ministry of Food appears to have followed the policy of so fixing prices that the retailer should make what was considered to be a reasonable aggregate net profit based on a diminished turnover.

The estimates in the following pages afford some means of determining whether the relation between wholesale and retail prices was such as to afford the retailer a livelihood comparable with that before the War, the considerations just discussed being borne in mind.   They do not, however, relate to the articles the high prices of which have led to the accusation of profiteering, since these are generally marked by an absence of definite information as to cost of materials.

Bread and flour.   In the article referred to above, the relation between the price of bread and of flour was given by the formula :

Price of quartern loaf =

2·27d. + 3·33d.

$$+ \frac{\text{excess of price per cwt. over } 11s. \text{ expressed in pence.}}{39·6}$$

Here 39·6 is the number of loaves estimated to be made from 1 cwt. of flour, 11s. was the mean price of flour in the years 1906–13 ; 3·33d. is the mean cost of the flour in the loaf, and 2·27d. the margin for the baker's expenses and profit. The formula fitted with remarkable closeness the prices of bread and flour recorded monthly in the *Labour Gazette* from January 1906 to June 1913.

The prices of bread stated during the War are calculated on a different system of averaging, and the basic price in July 1914 corresponds to 2·34d., instead of the 2·27d. of the formula. This adjustment is made for the following table, in which the price of flour per cwt. is taken from the records of the price of 'town households' in the *Economist*,[1] and the price of bread is deduced from the monthly statements of change in the *Labour Gazette* on the basis that the price in December 1917 was 9d. (as fixed by the Ministry of Food).

TABLE XXV

PRICE OF THE 4 LB. LOAF, ACTUAL AVERAGE AND BY FORMULA

	1914		1915		1916		1917	
	Formula	Actual	Formula	Actual	Formula	Actual	Formula	Actual
	d.	d.	d.	d.	d.	d.	d.	d.
January .	5·74	—	7·31	6·79	8·40	8·32	9·49	10·12
February .	5·74	—	8·40	7·37	8·88	8·85	9·52	10·23
March . .	5·79	—	8·64	7·96	8·88	9·20	9·58	10·53
April . .	5·68	—	8·52	8·02	8·40	8·90	9·61	11·29
May . .	5·74	—	8·88	8·25	8·15	8·85	9·79	11·53
June . .	5·85	—	8·64	8·61	8·03	8·85	9·79	11·71
July . .	5·79	5·85	7·67	8·25	8·15	8·43	—	11·71
August. .	—	6·49	7·79	8·08	8·64	8·43	9·58	11·77
September.	6·82	6·38	7·67	8·08	9·12	9·03	9·67	11·71
October .	6·70	6·38	7·55	8·08	9·24	9·26	7·70	9·00
November .	6·76	6·44	7·91	8·08	9·61	9·55	7·70	9·00
December .	7·00	6·70	8·01	8·23	9·49	9·97	7·70	9·00

[1] During 1917 the price is for 'G.R.' flour.

During the winter 1914–15 the bakers appear to have sacrificed $\frac{1}{4}d.$ to $\frac{1}{2}d.$ a loaf, which they nearly regained in the latter part of 1915 ; during the sixteen months from September 1914 the average of the formula price is 7·77d. of the actual price, 7·60d. In 1916 the price of bread did not fall in the summer with the price of flour ; in the whole year the formula average was 8·75d., and the actual average 8·97d. At the end of 1916 the baker's margin had increased by $\frac{1}{2}d.$, and was 2·82d., instead of the pre-war amount of 2·33d.

The introduction of ' G.R.' flour with its raised rate of extraction from grain and the admixture of flour other than wheat may have affected the number of loaves obtained from a sack or have increased the cost of baking. The margin rose rapidly till in August 1917 the actual price was more than 2d. above the formula ; and this was diminished when the price of bread was fixed to 1·3d., so that the margin was 56 per cent. above the pre-war amount when the price of the quartern loaf was fixed at 9d. with G.R. flour at 17·7s. per cwt. At the fixing of the prices the same *percentage* increase over July 1914 was allowed for bread and for flour, viz. 54 per cent. It is doubtful whether baker's expenses had increased by so much as 54 per cent. at that date, but no change was allowed for two years, after which the price of the loaf was raised $\frac{1}{2}d.$, and during that period wages and other expenses increased considerably while the purchasing value of money fell, so that in the whole period 1917–19 it is not certain that the baker profited.

Flour and wheat. To obtain the price of wheat, the average of 5 quarters No. 1 Manitoba (as quoted in the *Economist*) and 1 quarter of British (*Gazette* average) has been taken. Prior to the War the average price of a sack (280 lb.) of flour equalled four-fifths (more exactly 0·794) of the price of a quarter of wheat computed on a similar basis.

The relation during 1914, 1915, 1916 was as follows :

TABLE XXVI

PRICES OF WHEAT AND FLOUR

	1914			1915		1916	
	0·794 Quarter of Wheat	280 lb. Flour		0·794 Quarter of Wheat	280 lb. Flour	0·794 Quarter of Wheat	280 lb. Flour.
	s.	*s.*	*d.*	*s.*	*s.*	*s.*	*s.*
January	27·8	28	0	41·6	41	51·5	50
February	28·0	28	0	49·0	50	54·9	54
March	29·0	28	6	48·1	52	55·4	54
April	28·5	28	3	52·1	51	51·0	50
May	28·0	28	0	55·9	54	42·9	48
June	29·4	29	0	48·9	52	42·7	47
July	28·7	28	6	45·2	44	·41·3	48
August	34·2	—		46·3	45	50·6	52
September	37·9	37	0	46·0	44	54·9	56
October	34·6	36	0	45·3	43	58·4	57
November	37·9	36	6	47·4	46	62·4	60
December	37·9	36	6	47·4	47	61·7	59 (' G.R.')
Year's average	31·8	31·4		47·8	47·4	52·3	52·9

The relationship, therefore, remained unchanged during the period, and the miller's margin increased at the same *percentage* as the price of wheat, and doubled in actual amount in rather more than two years. Before the War the value of the flour obtained from a quarter of wheat was very nearly the same as the cost of the quarter, the miller's remuneration being obtained from the sale of the offal. The four-fifths of a quarter of the wheat in fact yields approximately a sack of flour. The miller then obtained throughout the value of the offal, and increased his profit in whatever proportion that increased. That this increase was considerable is indicated by the following figures from the *Mark Lane Express* :

				Bran (ordinary)	Shillings per Ton Fine Middlings	Pollard
1914	January 5.	.	.	96 to 98	138 to 140	96 to 98
	April 27	.	.	100 to 102	132 to 136	96 to 98
1916	July 3	.	.	100 to 115	200 to 205	138 to 140
	October 2 .		.	170 to 180	270 to 272	190 to 192
	December 11	.	.	280 to 282	345 to 350	305 to 307
1917	January 1.	.	.	290 to 292	345 to 350	295 to 300
	April 9	•	•	—	—	{250 to 252 {240
	October 8 .	.	.	—	—	260 to 262

At April 30, 1917, the Government prices of bran and middlings were 260s. and 300s. From the end of 1916 the higher rate of extraction of course diminished the yield of offals, and millers' profits generally were regulated from the middle of 1917. Before regulation the value of the offals appears to have been about two and a half times the pre-war value.

TABLE XXVII

WHOLESALE AND RETAIL MEAT PRICES

| | Beef | | | | Mutton | | | |
| | Home | | Imported | | Home | | Imported | |
	Wholesale	Retail	Wholesale	Retail	Wholesale	Retail	Wholesale	Retail
1914								
July	100	100	100	100	100	100	100	100
August	104	105	112	115	105	106	128	116
September	102	106	115	118	98	107	132	117
October	104	105	96	118	103	107	138	117
November	102	106	104	120	95	107	132	120
December	111	107	108	121	98	108	132	120
1915								
January	115	110	115	125	108	111	134	124
February	119	115	113	128	108	110	138	127
March	122	117	113	130	131	113	144	128
April	128	121	127	134	131	116	144	132
May	151	140	138	150	141	135	163	147
June	141	141	142	155	122	135	175	151
July	144	141	127	156	128	136	168	151
August	143	144	115	157	131	137	163	153
September	126	143	104	157	125	136	156	153
October	130	141	132	156	122	135	156	152
November	111	140	112	154	115	134	144	151
December	119	140	127	155	125	132	175	152
1916								
January	126	141	123	158	131	136	197	158
February	130	143	133	159	144	141	194	164
March	133	146	135	164	148	145	219	173
April	163	156	161	174	154	154	209	185
May	180	169	173	190	190	166	228	202
June	167	170	159	191	164	167	228	203
July	155	170	154	188	162	167	228	199
August	148	170	150	188	152	167	—	—
September	133	168	142	187	158	167	—	—
October	137	167	135	186	152	166	—	—
November	141	168	128	188	158	167	—	—
December	185	174	154	193	172	176	—	—

TABLE XXVII (continued)—WHOLESALE AND RETAIL MEAT PRICES

	Beef				Mutton			
	Home		Imported		Home		Imported	
	Whole-sale	Retail	Whole-sale	Retail	Whole-sale	Retail	Whole-sale	Retail
1917								
January .	189	182	185	203	164	182	—	—
February .	193	188	185	211	172	187	—	—
March . .	193	193	185	217	184	192	—	—
April . .	193	195	173	219	191	192	—	—
May . .	204	204	185	229	243	214	—	—
June . .	222	214	196	238	230	221	—	—
July . .	215	215	230	239	211	219	—	—
August . .	200	214	204	240	197	218	—	—
September .	185	197	181	232	172	192	—	—
October .	181	194	181	228	172	187	—	—
November .	174	189	177	225	172	183	—	—
December .	185	191	177	226	172	189	—	—
1918								
January .	185	191	177	226	182	187	—	—
February .	185	193	177	227	182	188	—	—
March to July	181	191	—	—	172	184	—	—
September to December .	211	214	—	—	197	204	—	—

Meat. In Table **XXVII** the percentage movements of wholesale and retail prices of meat are compared. For wholesale prices the weekly returns of market prices issued by the Board of Agriculture have been used. The entries abstracted are: Dead meat—London—prices per cwt.: English Beef, 1st quality; Argentine Beef, chilled hind-quarter; English Mutton, 1st quality; Australian Mutton, 1st quality. The last complete week in each month is taken, beginning with the week ended July 25, 1914, at which date the prices are equated to 100. The *Labour Gazette* prices for the first day of the following month are placed alongside these, so that the wholesale prices are throughout a few days ahead of the retail. The wholesale. prices are for the carcase (sinking the offal), while for the retail prices are (see pp. 42–4) the averaged movements of the rib and thin flank of beef, and the leg and breast of mutton; these were chosen for the food retail index-number as reflecting accurately in pre-war times the average movements of the prices of beef and mutton as retailed.

TABLE XXVIII

ABBREVIATED TABLE OF MEAT PRICES

	Beef				Mutton			
	Home		Imported		Home		Imported	
	Whole-sale	Retail	Whole-sale	Retail	Whole-sale	Retail	Whole-sale	Retail
	Averages				Averages			
July 1914 .	100	100	100	100	100	100	100	100
Jan. to June 1915	129	124	125	137	123	120	150	135
July to Dec. 1915	129	141	120	156	124	135	160 .	152
Jan. to June 1916	150	154	147	173	155	152	212 .	181
July to Dec. 1916	150	169	146	188	159	168	—	—
Jan. to Aug. 1917	201	201	193	224	199	203	—	—
Sept. 1917 to Feb. 1918 .	182	192	178	227	175	188	—	—
Mar. to July 1918	181	191	—	—	172	184	—	—
Sept. to Dec.1918	211	214	—	—	197	204	—	—

In September 1917 retail prices were fixed so as to allow the retailer $2\frac{1}{2}d.$ per lb., or 20 per cent. (whichever was less) over the cost to him, and the wholesale price was fixed for home-killed beef and mutton at $13d.$ a lb., and for imported beef at $12\frac{1}{2}d.$ hind-quarter, and $10\frac{1}{2}d.$ fore-quarter. The retail prices [1] then averaged $15\frac{1}{2}d.$ for home-killed meat, and $1d.$ or $1\frac{1}{2}d.$ less for imported beef. In 1914 the percentages show that the wholesale prices of home-killed beef and mutton on the same basis were $7d.$ and $7\cdot6d.$, and the retail prices $7\cdot9d.$ and $8\cdot1d.$ The retailers' profit was thus allowed to be $2\frac{1}{2}d.$ per lb., while at pre-war rates it was only $\frac{1}{2}d.$ to $1d.$ If there are no unknown factors this was a bargain very favourable to the retailers, unless the amount handled was very seriously diminished.

Till July 1917 the *percentage* changes in the retail prices of home-killed meat were nearly the same as those in the wholesale prices, and the margin had increased from $\frac{3}{4}d.$ in 1914 to $1\frac{3}{4}d.$; the new arrangement added $\frac{3}{4}d.$ to this. In the case of imported meat the retail price continually approximated to that of home-killed meat, as has been discussed above (p. 49), while the wholesale prices of the two rose at nearly the same rate, the rise in imported being slightly the lower. The retailer appears to have gained even more in handling imported meat than with British meat, and the high margin obtained before the fixing of prices was in this case cut down. On the whole it seems

---

[1] Prices for joints ordinarily bought for the table were higher than these, which are the averages for all outs.

possible that taking all meat together, the $2\frac{1}{2}d.$ per lb. allowed was about equal to the margin in existence immediately before the control of prices.[1]

Owing to the change in the sources of supply there is no consecutive record of the price of imported *mutton* available.

Bacon. To obtain a comparative record of wholesale prices the averages of the prices per cwt. in London of Irish (dried), Canadian sides (green), and Danish sides (green), all first quality, were abstracted from the weekly return of market prices, at the same dates as in the case of meat.

The following table compares the results with the movement of retail prices :

TABLE XXIX

PRICES OF BACON, WHOLESALE AND RETAIL

	1914		1915		1916		1917	
	Whole-sale	Retail	Whole-sale	Retail	Whole-sale	Retail	Whole-sale	Retail
January	—	—	109	110	137	132	163	160
February	—	—	106	109	131	132	—	173
March	—	—	111	109	138	134	181	178
April	—	—	113	111	143	137	182	179
May	—	—	124	117	142	138	180	180
June	—	—	123	118	141	138	176	176
July	100	100	127	118	149	138	198	183
August	114	110	135	123	162	146	210	196
September	111	111	135	127	152	149	218	210
October	94	108	135	129	153	152	219	227
November	100	107	135	130	155	155	243	239
December	104	107	134	131	155	150	241	239

In November 1917 retailers were limited to a margin of $3d.$ per lb. on the average of all bacon sold, the effect of which arrangement appears to have been to stabilize the prices at the maximum then attained ; there was no further change in retail prices for a year and a half. In December 1917 the retail price of streaky bacon was $2s.\ 3d.$ If we take the corresponding wholesale price at $2s.$, we find that in July 1914 the wholesale and retail prices were respectively $10d.$ and $11\cdot3d.$ In thirty months the retailers' margin increased from about $1\frac{1}{3}d.$ to $3d.$, and throughout the period it was one-eighth, the same proportion, of the wholesale price. In May and June 1920 after the removal of control, retail and wholesale prices still bore

[1] It is possible that the method of averaging the increases of the rib and thin flank exaggerates slightly the increase for all cuts, but any correction on this account would be very small.

nearly the same proportion (viz. +176 per cent. wholesale, +169 per cent. retail) to their prices in July 1914. It appears that the dealers in bacon did as well at the expense of the consumer as did the dealers in meat. In neither case can the expenses of the retailer (rent, wages, &c.) have risen so rapidly as the price of the goods they handled; in and after 1917, though the butcher had a small turnover in quantity, the consumption of bacon increased.

Butter. The retail prices (pp. 42 seq.) show to the end of 1917, when the price was fixed and the supply controlled very closely, the same movements as do the market prices of ' Dairy Fresh ' and ' Danish '.

Potatoes. The following table shows the relative movements of the wholesale price of potatoes (' good English ' per ton as stated in the *Economist*) and the retail price from the *Labour Gazette.* Since the price in July is easily confused with that of new potatoes, the equation is made in November 1914. At that date the wholesale price was 70s. per ton, or 2·62d. per 7 lb., and the retail price averaged 3·9d. The expenses of distribution bear a high proportion to the wholesale price, and it is not surprising that the movements are not parallel.

TABLE XXX

PRICES OF POTATOES, WHOLESALE AND RETAIL

	1914 Whole- sale	1914 Retail	1915 Whole- sale	1915 Retail	1916 Whole- sale	1916 Retail	1917 Whole- sale	1917 Retail	1918 Whole- sale	1918 Retail	1919 Whole- sale	1919 Retail
Jan.	71	—	104	105	143	119	343	277	200	171	283	196
Feb.	95	—	129	114	146	121	336	289	207	170	293	200
Mar.	104	—	136	119	143	124	314	272	193	170	293	205
Apr.	100	—	139	121	143	129	343	271	193	171	304	208
May	111	—	125	121	243	184	343	302	232	174	337	215
June	122	—	129	124	286	200	343	305	246	190	337	230
July	—	125	114	123	343	261	—	305	371	196	237	230
Aug.	104	137	132	155	143	232	214	190	200	267	271	406
Sept.	104	107	118	123	157	190	164	174	221	208	271	308
Oct.	95	104	111	118	193	191	200	175	214	204	285	284
Nov.	100	100	129	114	357	255	218	180	214	199	286	266
Dec.	114	101	143	124	343	265	200	174	264	188	314	281

PART II. WAGES

[The author is much indebted to the Intelligence and Statistics Department of the Ministry of Labour, who gave much detailed help in the interpretation and completion of their published records].

CHAPTER VI

GENERAL MOVEMENT OF WAGES

The position in 1914. War-time conditions. Earnings contrasted with wages. The official account of aggregate changes in wages. Wage movements in 1915 and 1916. Standardization of increases. The munitions bonus of October 1917. Relative increases of wages and prices at the date of the armistice. Reduction of hours in 1919. Movement of women's wages.

In the ten years prior to the War wages in general had moved upwards about 9 per cent. The index-numbers of the Board of Trade (*XVIIth Abstract of Labour Statistics*, p. 66) being, when 1904 is taken as 100.[1]

End of year	1904	1905	1906	1907	1908	1909	1910	1911	1912	1913
	100	100	102	105	105	103	104	104	106	109

In the same decade retail food prices had increased, when measured by the index numbers described on pp. 32–4, by 12 per cent. and wholesale prices by rather more, so that wages measured in purchasing power had fallen a little or at best were stationary. In the first seven months of 1914 there was a perceptible downward movement in wholesale and in retail prices, in employment, and in wages governed by sliding-scales, but on the whole there was still a tendency to an increase in wages. In some important industries there were definite trade-union programmes to press for higher wages, in order to compensate for the rise in prices of previous years and to raise the standard of living, and it was impossible to forecast what measure of success they were likely to attain. At the outbreak of the War these programmes were postponed, but they played an important part in the wage-movements after the Armistice ; at the same time outstanding disputes, including a builders' strike, were composed. Unemploy-

[1] There was a slight downward movement from 1900 to 1904, following a cumulative rise of long duration.

ment was prevalent in some industries in the autumn of 1914, but from the beginning of 1915 the general demand for labour was acute, and throughout the War and till the autumn of 1920 employment was extremely plentiful, except for the difficulty of placing the residuum of demobilized men not attached to a trade.

In normal times it is not necessary to distinguish, except for general comparisons over a decade or more, between the various ways in which wages can be measured. When we know the changes in time wages for a normal week and in piece-rates we can measure the effects on weekly and annual earnings (after allowing for variations in employment) with fair precision, and even make a good estimate of the effect on average wages all over the country of the gradual shifting of the population from one industry to another. But in the abnormal conditions produced by the War many difficulties of measurement are found. The most able-bodied men were swept into the War, and their places taken by lads, old men, and women. The supply of skilled men in engineering and munition work ran short, and apprentices were promoted, other men and women and girls trained, and the work was often re-arranged so as to permit unskilled workers to take part in jobs hitherto reserved for skilled men. At the same time the personnel of non-essential industries was diminished in number, while essential and new industries drew many recruits. Under these circumstances it would be difficult with complete knowledge, and is impossible with the meagre information available, to define or measure the movement of average wages in single industries or in the country as a whole ; this difficulty is illustrated below in the discussion of miners' earnings, where the number of coal-getters in 1918 formed a smaller proportion of all employed than in 1913.

In dealing with time wages and resulting earnings we ought to take account of not only the nominal rates for a normal week, but also the disappearance of broken time and the prevalence of overtime and night work. With piece rates the question is much more complex. It has never been safe to assume that a percentage change in piece rates results in a proportional change in earnings for the same effort, or that when piece rates are unchanged there has been no change in earnings; for piece rates are some times adjusted when machinery is improved with the definite intention of dividing the advantages of the improvement between the employer and the operative, and the gradual modification and development of machinery which is generally taking place may tend to higher earnings with the same rates, while every change in production modifies the relation of rates to earnings. These considerations have been found to be important when it has been possible to compare over a period the movement of rates with that of earnings. This want of proportional relationship was, of course, greatly accentuated by the revolutionary changes in processes that took place in and after 1915. There is no doubt that earnings increased more rapidly than rates from two distinct causes. The first was the acuteness of demand which induced extra effort for patriotic reasons, while the fear that this effort would lead to cutting of prices was temporarily removed, and this made overtime (at higher rates) normal and night work (at still higher rates) common; increased earnings from this cause corresponded to more strenuous work carried on for longer hours. The second was due to circumstances which increased earnings without calling for greater effort; machinery was improved, the orders were so large and urgent that waiting for material became rare, and the same processes had to be followed with such endless repetition that machines did not have to be re-adjusted, and also the processes became easy from continual practice. It is partly for these reasons that women and others not previously trained were able rapidly to learn to carry out processes formerly regarded as skilled. High earnings in munitions work were notorious, but two indications of the effect of the tendencies described may be adduced. Foremen and other men who normally received high time rates found that the men on piece rates who were their inferiors in skill were earning more than they. In 1915 time wages of engineering artisans were generally raised 4s. weekly, and 10 per cent. was given as an equivalent to piece workers; in 1916 a further 3s. was given to time-workers, but it was not necessary to increase piece rates. Munitions work to which these considerations

primarily apply employed directly or indirectly a very large
proportion of the non-combatant population, and other industries (except when suffering from a shortage of material) were
affected in the same direction; for with the drain of able-
bodied men to the forces more work was done and more pay
received by those left to carry on production short-handed.

The general effect of the increased demand for and diminished supply of labour was so to raise earnings as to produce
the appearance, at any rate, of great prosperity among the
working-classes. Those who continued at their former work
got more pay; many were promoted in the scale of work;
women and girls' wages approximated more nearly to men's,
and in some cases they undertook men's work at men's rate of
pay. Nearly every able-bodied or partially able-bodied person
was able to get work and to get it continuously. At the same
time multitudes of families received government allowances
on account of their absent men folk. Even if rates of wages
increased less rapidly than prices, the household earnings often
increased more rapidly.

In the first year of the War a record (hitherto unpublished)
was taken of the total of the wages paid out of money drawn by
cheque from certain banks, which affords some index of the movement of total earnings. This account yields the following results:

TABLE XXXI

TOTAL WAGE-CHEQUES DRAWN ON BANKS IN VARIOUS PARTS OF
ENGLAND AND WALES

Week

1914	£000s
July 27–August 1	9,358
August 24–August 29 . . .	7,516
September 28–October 3 . . .	8,140
October 26–October 31 . . .	8,469
November 23–November 28 . .	8,347
December 14–December 19 . .	8,484
1915	
January 25–January 30 . . .	8,931
February 22–February 27 . .	9,054
March 22–March 27 . . .	9,072

Since the whole weekly wage bill in the United Kingdom
may be computed at about £16,000,000 in 1913, it is clear
that these cheques account for a very great part of the

industrial workers in England and Wales. The record ends before the rise of prices or wages had attained any serious importance. The rapid recovery from the disorganization of the autumn of 1914 is marked, and it is seen that in spite of the withdrawal of men to the forces, already on a large scale in 1915, the wage bill in March 1915 was less than 3 per cent. below that of the previous August.

These inflated earnings tended to cease after the Armistice. Overtime and night work became uncommon, relaxed factory legislation was reinforced, trade-union restrictions relating to the employment of unskilled labour were restored, women retired to a great extent from their novel occupations, patriotic fervour was abated, and except that the demand for labour continued without interruption till the miner's strike of October 1920 pre-war conditions were to a great extent reached. We cannot, as has been explained, measure earnings during the War, and must restrict ourselves generally in the sequel to an account of the changes of rates ; but when we compare 1920 with 1914 the comparison of rates will afford a good approximation to the comparison of earnings, though not so good as would a comparison of 1914 with 1908.

In the following chapters the detailed movements of wages in several industries are discussed and women's wages are separately considered. In this chapter we consider the general movements chronologically and analyse certain tendencies towards definite changes in the relationship between wages of different occupations and different districts. In Chapter VII an attempt is made to compare the increase in wages with the increase in the cost of living.

Every January there is published in the *Labour Gazette* a summary account of the wage-changes of the previous year. These are based on the changes reported to the Ministry of Labour (formerly to the Labour Department of the Board of Trade), of which the principal alterations are recorded each month. The summary is often quoted as if the total increase tabulated included the whole of the changes in all manual occupations, which is not the case, and it is important to realize the exact meaning and limitations of the statistics.

In the first place many important industries are excluded altogether from the computation, for the purely technical reason that the numbers affected by changes are not reported to the Department in the same way as for the industries included. For this reason the table contains no figures for agriculture, railways, seamen, police, government employees, domestic servants, or employees in wholesale or retail commerce.[1] This list, which is not complete, probably cuts out 7 million of the 16 million men, women, boys, and girls commonly counted as wage-earners, and the changes apply to only £450 to £500 million out of the annual wage-bill computed as about £770 million in the United Kingdom in 1913.

In the second place certain classes of changes are definitely excluded. Among these are ' Changes in the average earnings in a trade which are due, not to an alteration in the scales of pay for particular classes of work, but to alterations in the proportions which the higher and lower paid classes of work people bear to each other ' ; ' Changes in the rates of pay for individuals due to promotions, or progressive increments of wages ' ; ' Purely seasonal changes ' ; ' Changes in the terms of employment which merely provide for compensation for extra work ' (*Report on Changes in Rates of Wages and Hours of Labour in the United Kingdom in 1909*, Cd. 5324, p. 9). The changes are thus narrowly confined to those for the same work, and no modification of organization has any effect on them. Also changes in piece rates are taken as always resulting in proportional changes in earnings for the same effort, whereas, as has already been pointed out, the proportion is not exact but alters in a cumulative way. The changes are throughout in rates for the normal week and do not reflect in any way the special opportunities for increasing earnings in the war-period. They are weekly, not hourly rates, and are quite independent of the general reduction of hours in 1919.

It is not credible that all changes affecting the 9 million persons in the industries included are reported and recorded. The weekly wages of these persons in the aggregate were about £10,000,000 in 1914 ; the total of the computed changes in

[1] Since the war some of these have been included.

weekly wages from July 1914 to the end of 1919 is about £6,750,000, indicating an increase of 67 per cent. It will be seen in the sequel that wages for the normal week had in the industries for which there are adequate records at least doubled in the period. Again in 1919 changes are recorded for only 5,647,000 persons, while it is hardly possibly that there was a single wage-earner whose wages did not rise in that year. A similar discrepancy between the changes computed on the method of this table and those computed by index-numbers has been observable throughout the years for which these statistics have been published.[1]

The movements by the two methods are similar, but not proportional, especially when the change is rapid. The differences in normal times are probably due to the fact that the frequent changes in wages in coal mining and the iron and steel industries are readily and completely recorded and exercise a great influence on the figures, and also the less frequent changes in other well-combined industries are known ; but the changes in scattered trades and in those occupations where unionism is weak or standard rates are not recognized are sometimes missed. The Department receives ' returns from Employers and Employer's Associations, Trade Unions, its own

	Changes as recorded	Index-numbers on basis of £9,000,000 weekly in 1900	Index-number. General course of wages, Abstract of Labour Statistics
[1]			
	£000		
1897	—	95·8	90·0
1898	+81	96·7	92·6
1899	+90	97·7	95·1
1900	+209	100·0	100·0
1901	−77	99·1	98·6
1902	−73	98·3	97·0
1903	−38	97·9	96·2
1904	−39	97·5	95·6
1905	−2	97·5	95·9
1906	+58	98·1	97·6
1907	+201	100·3	101·8
1908	−59	99·7	101·0
1909	−69	98·9	99·4
1910	+14	99·1	99·7
1911	+34	99·4	99·8
1912	+139	101·1	102·5
1913	+175	102·9	105·3

Correspondents, and other sources. The daily and trade papers were searched for references to any changes in wages or hours ' (*loc. cit.*, p. 10) ; hence changes which take place individually on a small scale may 'escape attention. When a change is reported a letter (pp. 131–2) is sent to employers and workers' representatives asking for details and especially for the ' number of workpeople directly affected by the change ' and asking whether this number ' relates to all the firms involved '. Consequently if other firms subsequently adopt the change, or, as must be quite common, the movement spreads to allied industries or to neighbouring places, these additional numbers do not come into the computation (the effect on wages is obtained by multiplying the change to an individual by the number affected), and there appears thus to be a tendency to under-estimate the numbers. This would explain the discrepancies shown in the note on p. 93, where the movement shown by these changes is generally less than that shown by the index-numbers.

These difficulties were greatly increased during the war, when changes of personnel as well as of wages were frequent, so that the numbers immediately as well as those subsequently affected cannot have been known, and there is also the difficulty of computing the effect on wages of the very complicated wage arrangements described in the sequel.

Further the figures for each change apply (if computed by rule) to the persons then in the industry, and when in 1919 the numbers in the industries changed the changes in the previous years were partly wiped out ; but a man who left an ordinary occupation to make munitions, though credited with the increases he received during the war, is not debited with the subsequent loss. Consequently the war-time figures are of an approximate and undefinable nature, and they cannot be used for computing the effect in five years on the natural wage-bill nor for any similar calculations. They have their use, however, in indicating the periods of rapid change, and to a more limited extent for comparing the movements in the main industrial groups.

For the years 1914–19 the statements are as follows :

TABLE XXXII

AGGREGATE CHANGES IN RATES OF WAGES IN CERTAIN GROUPS OF INDUSTRIES, UNITED KINGDOM, 1914-19

From the January numbers of the Labour Gazette, 1915-20

Groups of Trades	Number of Workpeople whose rates of Wages were reported as changed						Total net increase in the weekly Wages of those affected					
	1914	1915	1916	1917	1918	1919	1914	1915	1916	1917	1918	1919
	000s.	000s.	000s.	000s.	000s.	000s.	£000	£000	£000	£000	£000	£000
Building	134	116	222	250	389	290	13	16	36	100	254	197
Coal mining	364	887	865	1,000	921	1,110	−26	278	227	473	421	597
Other mining and quarrying	33	37	37	51	58	59	−1	10	11	24	24	31
Pig-iron, and iron and steel manufacture	67	126	131	160	184	184	−5	37	42	95	95	118
Engineering, shipbuilding, and other metal trades	213	882	715	1,489	1,747	1,715	15	158	115	946	765	500
Textile	23	621	857	866	826	521	1	55	80	272	475	153
Clothing	6	104	120	260	355	390	1	15	15	59	115	104
Road transport and docks	26	178	180	200	292	267	5	41	43	82	196	59
Paper, printing, &c.	20	55	90	92	102	157	2	6	11	31	68	61
Glass, brick, pottery, and chemical	26	119	104	201	281	208	2	14	14	71	127	59
Other trades	29	213	142	310	647	561	4	31	25	101	339	182
Local authority services	19	132	130	150	196	185	2	17	18	54	109	50
Total	960	3,470	3,593	5,029	5,998	5,647	13	678	637	2,307	2,988	2,111

Up to August 1914 preliminary returns show a net decrease of £12,800. The increase during the last five months of 1914 was therefore about £25,000.

The broad lessons of the table are evident. The movements in 1914 were trifling. Those in 1915 and 1916 were nearly equal and considerable, amounting to about 4s. and 3s. 6d. respectively per head of those whose wages were changed. In 1917 and 1918 the increases were spread wider and were on a handsomer scale, averaging 9s. and 10s. respectively. In 1919 they were a little less important and averaged 9s., but in that year the mass of manual workers obtained their money for shorter hours. A cursory comparison with the course of retail prices shows that these wage movements followed to some extent that course, and it is clear that to determine whether prices or wages moved first and which in the end moved most will need close analysis.

In the first six months or year of the War wages in many industries were not changed, and in others the increase seldom exceeded 10 per cent. By the middle of 1915, however, a general movement became evident. The patriotic efforts of men to work their best, irrespective of wage questions and without much notice of the rise of prices which was perceptible soon after the outbreak of war, showed signs of diminution. The demand for labour was acute and there was no difficulty in obtaining moderate increases. Wages governed by sliding scales moved upwards. Piece rates in coal mines were raised about 15 per cent. by June 1915. Woollen operatives received a bonus in April, and engineers generally obtained 4s. in the first half of 1915. There was practically no change however in the wages of builders, printers, or dock labourers till after the end of 1915. During 1916 wage movements were general, and several different methods were introduced for adjusting wages. In some cases a definite increase in time rates or percentage or piece rates was arranged on pre-war lines. In others a war-bonus or war-wage was granted, on the assumption that the rise of prices was temporary and the former level would be regained at the end of the War which was always popularly expected in the near future. Under war conditions the idea that wages ought to increase systematically with the cost of living gained adherents, but the questions whether this increase ought to be a general flat rate, on the ground that all workmen needed the same minimum amount of food, or a rate proportional to earnings so that the skilled man got a greater increase than the unskilled, or even a greater amount to the lowest paid so that their low standard of living should at least be maintained while better paid men could afford to lower their standard, was not decided and in fact has not yet been decided. No definite criterion has yet replaced the pre-war method of determination of wages by the market value of labour. In March 1915 in the South Wales iron and steel works a bonus was given of 1s. to those earning less than 15s., 2s. to those earning from 15s. to 20s., 3s. to those earning 20s. to 30s., but only 2s. to those earning from 30s. to 40s. Similarly in the Huddersfield woollen industry a bonus in April 1915 was 6d. to those earning less than 10s., 1s. to women earning more than 10s. and to men earning less than 20s., 2s. 6d. to men earning from 20s. to 30s., but only 2s. to those earning from 30s. to 40s. Thus the adult unskilled man obtained a greater absolute increase than the skilled. In Huddersfield the next increase was 6d. all round (Jan. 1916), in the next two changes men earning more than 20s. all received 2s., while others received 1s. 6d., while in January 1917 the best paid obtained the higher bonus with the result that all men originally earning over 20s. received the same aggregate increase during the first 2½ years of the War, viz. 10s.

On the other hand, artisans and labourers in the engineering trade generally received the same flat increase, reaching 7s. by January 1917.

Another method was introduced on railways, where the first bonus (Feb. 1915) was 3s. to men with less and 2s. to men with more than 30s.; but in October this was replaced by 5s. all round.

In the building trades the general method was to increase the wages of artisans and of labourers by the same number of pence per hour, but in Manchester and in Southampton the labourers gained a ½d. at the first increase and lost it subsequently.

On the other hand, in several industries wages moved by

the same percentage for all occupations. In the cotton industry, for example, the pre-war method of percentages was never altered.

During 1917 greater uniformity was introduced in wage bargains, in which various departments of the Government took an increasingly dominant part. The method generally preferred was to give a flat weekly war-wage to adult male time-workers and piece-workers alike, added either to the pre-war wage or to the wage at the beginning of 1917. On railways this was the method from October 1915, and by the end of 1917 the war-wage was 21s. In coal mines percentage increases, which had averaged about 33 per cent. on the earnings of July 1914, were abandoned, and from then till March 1920 flat time-rates per day or per shift were given in all districts; in March 1920, on the other hand, the increase was 20 per cent. in all districts reckoned on the rates prior to the first flat increase. In iron and steel trades regulated by sliding scales, however, there was no general change in method.

In 1917 and 1918 there was a pressure in the direction of widening the area of bargaining; standard rates were introduced in districts and occupations where hitherto they had not obtained, and towns were grouped together for the purposes of securing uniform wage treatment.

The woollen and worsted industries again showed peculiarities, for here the flat rates were abandoned in June 1917, and percentage increases were substituted (higher for time-workers than for piece-workers), subject to a maximum money increase, after March 1918.

At the end of three years of war, in the summer of 1917, rates of wages in general had definitely advanced less than the cost of living, whatever the method by which this is measured, but since earnings had increased more rapidly than rates and employment was very plentiful, it is probable that the standard of life had not fallen, though inconvenience was felt because of the shortage of supply of butter, sugar, beer, and other commodities. A good deal of discontent, however, was manifested, and partly in order to lessen this the bread subsidy was instituted in October 1917. A special cause for discontent was the inequality of the earnings of time- and piece-workers in munition industries, for the latter were making good money, while skilled men on time rates had only received increases amounting to 34 per cent. of the pre-war standard for normal hours. From October 12, 1917, a bonus of $12\frac{1}{2}$ per cent. on weekly earnings (which owing to overtime were generally greater than the standard time rates) was given to all skilled time-workers employed on munitions work in the engineering and iron-foundry industries, whose standard wages equalled or exceeded the district time-rate for turners and fitters. The occupations affected included blacksmiths, borers, core-makers, electrical fitters, fitters, gauge-makers, gear-cutters, grinders, hardeners and temperers, gig-makers, millers, millwrights, moulders, pattern-makers, planers, scientific instrument makers, shapers, slotters, toolmakers, toolsmiths, and turners. The earnings for normal hours became 50 per cent. above the pre-war standard time rates, and with a moderate amount of overtime the increase in earnings was as great as that in the cost of living. Labourers, whose wages had already advanced 54 per cent., since they had received the same flat rates of increases as artisans, obtained the same percentage advance by a subsequent award. This increase had very far-reaching effects ; intended no doubt to equalize increases in earnings, it in fact destroyed what balance still remained between payments for different kinds of work. In January 1918 piece-workers on munition work in the engineering iron-foundry and shipbuilding industries were awarded an increase of $7\frac{1}{2}$ per cent. on earnings. Workers in other munition industries claimed similar advances, as did workers on non-munition work in engineering, &c. In other industries generally there was a movement for a rise which often took the form of an immediate increase of $12\frac{1}{2}$ per cent. to be merged in subsequent rises where wages were already governed by a systematic arrangement.

Though this increase to munition workers was thought by many people to be unnecessary, since their earnings were believed to be high, and inexpedient since there was not enough food in the country to allow consumption to be increased, yet there can be little doubt that the acute rise in prices during 1917 and 1918 would in any case have led to an increase of wages, and it was the method and date of the award rather than the award itself that was open to criticism. In fact by the date of the Armistice wages generally had risen considerably more than 12½ per cent. since October 1917.

At the date of the Armistice the cost of living reached a temporary maximum at 125 per cent. above the pre-war level by the *Labour Gazette* measurement, or about 100 per cent. by the modified measurement explained on pp. 72–5. It may be affirmed with some confidence that in November 1918 the time rates of unskilled men had on the whole increased at a rate between these two measurements, while those of skilled men had in general not reached the lower rate of increase. Earnings, especially of piece-workers, were probably enhanced by as large a percentage as was the cost of living on the more liberal measurement.

Wages continued to advance in 1919, but not at once in all industries; prices fell in the first half of the year and the expectation was rather that part of the war wage would be cancelled than that there should be further increases. Miners' wages at the beginning of the year were raised in accordance with the recommendation of the Coal Industry Commission, and it appears to have been intended to fix them at such a rate that the pre-war standard of living would be raised.

The principal change in 1919 was in hours rather than in wages. An Industrial Conference of Employers and workmen was arranged in February, and the first recommendation of its Provisional Joint Committee was ' The establishment of a statutory forty-eight hour week, subject to provisions for varying this (with adequate safeguards) in proper cases, and for giving statutory force, when required, to agreements between employers and employed, arranging different time bases. The discouragement of systematic overtime, and the regulation of necessary overtime ' (*Labour Gazette*, April 1919, p. 124). The Coal Industry Commission also recommended the reduction from eight hours to seven hours in the statutory regulation for coal miners' work under ground from July 16, 1919, and in Mr. Justice Sankey's report (adopted by the Government) a further reduction to six hours, subject to the economic position of the industry from July 13, 1921.

Hours of time-workers in a great number of industries were reduced without any change of weekly wages. Where hourly rates were customary (see pp. 112 seq., 166 seq., 215) they were increased so as to give the same (or in many cases rather higher) weekly wages. Piece rates were generally, but not universally, raised so as to allow the same weekly earnings to be reached with normal work.

The *Labour Gazette* (Jan. 1920, p. 4) records reductions affecting 6,400,000 persons during 1919 (including railway workers, but excluding police and agricultural labourers), and no doubt the record is incomplete. The average of the reductions recorded is $6\frac{1}{2}$ hours weekly, that is, one-eighth or one-ninth of the former average normal week. If we are considering the wages received for the same number of hours (instead of for the week as is customary) an equivalent fraction must be added to the wage changes considered in this chapter. It is too early to say to what extent, if any, output has increased per hour, or broken time diminished ; indeed, it will never be possible to make any exact estimate on this question. Since the records of reduction of hours are important and interesting, and information about pre-war hours is not always easy to obtain, a table from the *Labour Gazette* showing the principal changes up to November 1920 is given in Appendix III (p. 215).

In the *Labour Gazette* of May 1919, p. 170, and again in April 1920, p. 170, accounts are given of the changes of wages since the beginning of the War. The sections below (pp. 111 to 183) show the detailed movements in the more important industries, but the *Labour Gazette* summary affords a convenient method of dealing with the industries not separately treated. The following paragraphs are reproduced from the *Labour Gazette* of April 1920.

 · *Other Metal Trades* :—The general increases granted in the engineering and shipbuilding trades have been extended to a large number of workpeople in other metal trades, including the manufacture of iron castings, railway carriage and wagon building, sheet metal working, gas meter making, heating and domestic engineering, bolt, nut, screw, and rivet making, and tube manufacture. In some other branches, however, different amounts have been given. . . . As regards those sections of the metal trades in which minimum rates of wages are fixed under the Trade Boards Acts, the minimum rate for women in the chainmaking trade had been raised from 2¾d. per hour at August 1914 to 7½d. per hour by the end of February 1920, in cases where the employer provides the workshop, tools, and fuel, and to 10d. per hour when the worker provides any or all of these. In the hollow-ware trade a minimum rate of 3d. per hour fixed for women in January 1916 had been raised to 30s. 9d. per week of forty-seven hours ; and in the tin-box trade a minimum rate of 3¼d. per hour for women, fixed in November 1915, had been raised to 7½d. per hour.

' *Other Textile Trades* :—In the bleaching, dyeing, printing, and finishing sections, wages are varied in accordance with the fluctuations in cost of living. In Lancashire, Cheshire, Derbyshire, and Scotland, the increases over pre-war rates at the end of February were 37s. 10d. per week for men and 22s. 6d. per week for women, with certain additions to basis rates. In Yorkshire the increase for time-workers was 125 per cent. on basis rates, which have also been increased by 8 per cent.; for piece-workers it was 100 per cent. on basis rates, increased by 5 per cent. In these trades also the weekly hours of labour have been reduced to 48 without any reduction in weekly wages. Amongst other bodies of textile operatives, workpeople in the linen industry in Ireland had received advances equivalent to 25s. for a full week in the case of men, and of 18s. a week in the case of women, but much short-time is being worked in this industry. Workpeople engaged in the manufacture of carpets had received 110 per cent. on pre-war time-rates and 105 per cent. on pre-war piece-rates, excluding 15 per cent. granted in compensation for a reduction in hours ; hosiery workers in Leicestershire, Nottinghamshire, and Derbyshire, had received a war bonus of 6½d. in the shilling (54 per cent.) on their earnings, and, in addition, 10s. per week to men and 6s. per week to women ; and at Dundee men in the jute trade had a minimum advance of 29s. a week and women one of 21s. a week, plus a full-time bonus of 2s. a week in each case.

' *In the wholesale boot and shoe manufacturing industry* the minimum rate for clickers, lasters, and finishers at July 1914 was 29s. per week in some of the principal centres, and 30s. per week in others, whereas at the end of February last it was 56s. per week. This represents an increase of about 87 to 93 per cent. For piece-workers new price lists have been adopted, resulting in additional increases. It has recently been arranged that the minimum rate of 56*s*. shall be raised to 68*s*. per week in April, with certain increases on piece-rates.

' *Other Trades* :—In the following table particulars are given of the increases in rates of wages in certain other industries between July 1914 and the end of February 1920. In some of these cases, e. g. the furniture, baking and electricity industries, further increases have since been granted, or are being arranged, to take effect from later dates.

Industry or Occupation	*Usual Amount of Increase between July 1914 and the end of February 1920*
Bookbinders . . .	41*s*. 6*d*. to 47*s*. 6*d*. a week.
Furnishing :	
Cabinet Makers . .	46*s*. to 50*s*. a week.
Upholsterers . . .	44*s*. to 53*s*. a week.
French Polishers . .	47*s*. to 55*s*. a week.
Baking :	
Table Hands . . .	32*s*. to 41*s*. a week.
Pottery Manufacture (North Staffordshire)	80 per cent. together with increases in basis rates for some classes.
Chemical Manufacture .	33*s*. 6*d*. a week and a bonus of 12½ per cent. on total earnings. The rates for week-end shifts have also been raised.
Electricity Undertakings .	33*s*. 6*d*. a week and a bonus of 12½ per cent. on total earnings. In addition, the basis rates have been increased in some districts.
Gas Undertakings . .	31*s*. 6*d*. to 33*s*. 6*d*. a week (for 6-day workers) according to the size of the undertaking and a bonus of 12½ per cent. on total earnings. Shift-workers, for whom the general adoption of 8-hour shifts involved no reduction in hours, received an additional increase of 6*d*. a shift.
Police Constables (Great Britain)	Minimum of 72*s*. a week adopted for men with one year's probationary service, resulting in increases of 42*s*. to 51*s*. in the minimum rate (apart from probationers).'

The article in May 1919 concludes as follows : ' To locate the precise position within this (wide) range of increases, of the average increase in rates of wages for all classes of workpeople, careful examination would be necessary, both of the relative numbers of workpeople employed in 1914 in the different industries, districts, and occupations in which varying amounts of increase have been given, and of the changes which have occurred since 1914 in the proportions of men, women, boys and girls employed in each case. The information available on these points is insufficient to provide a trustworthy basis for precise calculations ; but taking all industries together, it is evident that rates of wages, for manual workers generally, have been more than doubled, on the whole, during the war ; and, while the material available is not sufficiently complete to enable an exact calculation of the general average increase on pre-war rates to be made, there is little doubt that it lies between 100 and 120 per cent., apart from enhancements of hourly and piece rates in certain industries, the effect of which, on weekly wages, has been neutralized by reductions in the weekly hours of labour.' In the article in April 1920 we find that the average percentage increase for all industries and occupations is estimated up to *February* 1920 as 120 to 130 per cent. on pre-war rates. If the record had been continued to August 1920 a further substantial increase would certainly have been found. In the *Labour Gazette* of February 1921 it is estimated in the same way that the average increase in rates till the end of 1920 was 170 to 180 per cent., but it is suggested that if all increases could have been included the average might be a little lower.

In Chapter XV below, the changes in women's wages are discussed. The employment of women in munitions work and in occupations hitherto followed only by men brought up their average earnings to a relatively high level by the end of the War ; but after the return to ordinary employment and the reduction of hours in 1919 their average wages for a normal week were little more than double the pre-war rates, while by the summer of 1920 they had risen to be about $2\frac{1}{2}$ times those rates, which is as near as we can measure the same relative increase as for men.

CHAPTER VII

WAGES AND THE COST OF LIVING, 1914-20

General summary of the increases of wages and prices. The levelling up of wages. Minimum and cost of living wages.

WE are now in a position to bring together estimates of the movements of wages and of the increase of the cost of living, using for the latter the results obtained in Chapter IV above, where two measurements are given, viz. : the *Labour Gazette* index which allows for no alteration in the kind or quality of goods purchased, and an alternative measurement in which some modification is assumed without sensible deterioration of standard.

TABLE XXXIII

ESTIMATES OF MOVEMENTS OF TIME-RATES (FOR NORMAL WEEK) AND OF PIECE-RATES IN CERTAIN INDUSTRIES COMPARED WITH THE CHANGE IN THE COST OF LIVING

July	Brick-layers	Brick-layers' labourers	Composi-tors	Railway-men	Dock labourers	Cotton operatives	Woollen and Worsted operatives
1914 .	100	100	100	100	100	100	100
1915 .	102	103	100	110	111	103	115
1916 .	108	115	105	120	130	107	126
1917 .	122	134	120	155	150	119	144
1918 .	157	185	156	195	193	157	164
1919 .	185	224	196	225	209	202	196
1920 .	235	300	246	280	266	259	239

July	Engineering artisans	Engineering labourers	Shipbuilding Platers' time-rates	Coal mining	Agriculture England and Wales
1914 .	100	100	100	100	100
1915 .	110	—	—	113	112
1916 .	111	—	—	129	—
1917 .	134	154	130	136	—
1918 .	173	213	169	187	189 (Aug.)
1919 .	199	255	193	224	226
1920 .	231	309	223	260	{254 (May) {277 (Aug.)

TABLE XXXIII (*continued*)—Estimates of Movements of Time-rates (for normal week) and of Piece-rates in certain Industries compared with the Change in the Cost of Living

July	Wages General rough average of Percentages above	Cost of Living Labour Gazette Index	Modified Index
1914 . .	100	100	100
1915 . .	105 to 110	125	(120)
1916 . .	115 to 120	145	(135)
1917 . .	135 to 140	180	(160)
1918 . .	175 to 180	205	180
1919 . .	210 to 215	210	185
1920 . .	260	252	220

The increases in piece-rates to compensate for reduction of hours are not included in these estimates.

For details of wage-changes see the following chapters, of cost of living see Chapter IV above.

The changes up to July in each of the years 1915 to 1920 are estimated [1] for a number of important industries in the following table, and a rough average of these estimates is also given to enable a general comparison to be made with the movement in the cost of living. So far as a general statement can be made, we may say that *rates* of wages for the same work increased less rapidly than the cost of living in the first three years of the War, in the fourth year wages gained and their increase over four years was nearly that of the modified index. In 1918–19 wages gained rapidly and reached the official cost of living measurement, and they kept pace with it in the year 1919–20. This equality is the result of a balance between a lesser increase in the case of artisans and a greater in the case of labourers.

It is evident from this table and from the detailed accounts in subsequent chapters that the ratio of the rates for unskilled workers to the rates for skilled workers has increased. The nature of this increase is best illustrated from the building trade (p. 114). The bricklayer who had 10*d.* an hour in 1914 had 22*d.* at the beginning of 1920 ; his labourer had 6½*d.* and 18½*d.* at these dates. For both the increase is 1*s.* an hour,

[1] The details will be found in subsequent chapters.

but the ratio of the labourer's to the bricklayer's wage has increased from $\frac{13}{20}$ to $\frac{37}{44}$, i. e. from 0·65 to 0·84. But otherwise we might say that if the bricklayer's 22d. was only worth 10d. at 1914 prices and he had had no real increase, the labourer's wage would be worth $\frac{10}{22}$ of 18$\frac{1}{2}d$. $= 8\cdot4d$. and he had a rise of nearly 30 per cent. At the same time there has been a tendency to level up the wages of small or outlying districts to those of larger towns in several industries, so that not only equal flat rates of increase have been obtained, but also the basis to which these increments are added has been raised where the initial rates were lowest. The general result must have been to lessen the real inequality (i. e. expressed in purchasing power, not in cash) between districts and in occupations, but in the case of districts not to any great extent. The movement as regards districts is no doubt connected with a policy of preventing competition by low-rated workers, but it may also have relation to a definite levelling up of prices in small and semi-rural towns as the result of control and deficiency of supplies. The local differences in wage rates were no doubt caused partly by the supply of low-paid labour from rural districts, partly by the relative cheapness of such foods as were produced locally, and especially by lowness of rents as compared with the largest towns, so that the difference was greater in money than in real wages. At the same time the higher real wages in the towns attracted the best workmen and the real efficiency rates may have been nearly equal. A general artificial levelling up of wages has no doubt serious economic results, which have not yet become manifest, and it is very doubtful whether the equality will be maintained ; so far as the differences were due to natural advantages in cost of living it is very undesirable that they should be abolished, since most people desire that the concentration of population in large towns should be diminished, and if there is no advantage to employers in lower wages in smaller places a great part of the inducement to decentralize factories will disappear.

As regards the elimination of inequality between rates for different occupations, it is doubtful how far this has been the result of deliberate policy and how far it has been accidental from the introduction of flat rates of increase from other causes. The principal ideal of working-class policy in the matter of the amount of wages has been the establishment of a minimum wage which should allow to all workers a standard of living definitely above that of the unskilled labourer before the War. This ideal was in part accepted by the Industrial Conference of employers and workmen of March 1919. Their second recommendation was ' The establishment of minimum time rates of wages, to be universally applicable. . . . Extension of Trade Boards in the less organized trades. . . . ' (*Labour Gazette*, April 1919, p. 124). The statutory minimum wage, first established in coal mining and then in certain ' sweated industries ', has in fact been extended to agriculture, and to several small industries where the wages were low ; but the machinery for its general application has not as yet been developed. In the evidence to the Court of Inquiry that dealt with Dock Labourers in February 1920 the workers' representatives were prepared to sacrifice both local and occupational differences of pay in order to obtain a universal satisfactory minimum, and it appeared that many of these differences were the results of custom rather than of economic forces. On the other hand, it is highly probable that artisans will not long be content with a system that gives them in return for their skill and training so little more than it gives labourers, and even if they do not move themselves in the matter they will become relatively scarce (since young men will not be at the trouble and expense of training for so little reward), and their wages will rise owing to the failure of supply. There can be no doubt that the present rate will not long be in equilibrium.

Apart from the question of the minimum wage, there are the difficulties arising from the movement of prices. As we have seen, in the earlier years of the War the tendency was to give flat rates of increase to all workers of such an amount as to meet the increased cost of bare necessities ; if the cost of a minimum budget of bread, meat, &c., had increased from 15s. to 25s., there was the necessity that every workman with a family to support, who had had the lowest wage consistent with efficiency before the War, should receive an additional 10s.; the better paid workman could economize and actually carry on his work with a smaller increment, but since even an equal increment put him in a relatively worse position than before it was rare that less than this was given (except where wages were unusually high), and the general compromise was that all should have the same bare cost of living increment. Such a method is clearly not applicable for meeting changes in prices when standards have been agreed on which take account of differences of skill; to preserve the relations the same percentage increase, equal to whatever is shown by a recognized index-number of the cost of living, must be given to every one. At present such a relation has not been obtained in those arrangements for adjusting wages which are based on a ' cost of living' index-number. The sliding scale for railway men (p. 164) allows 1s. for every 5 points change in the index-number, with certain minima. Thus a typical rate is that of porters, grade 1, viz.: When the cost of living is 125 per cent. above the pre-war standard the rate is 60s.; it is to fall 1s. for each 5 in the index-number, but not more than 14s., so that the minimum corresponds to a cost of living 55 per cent. above the standard. If the pre-war wage in this grade was 26s. 8d. then at 60s. the increased cost of living of 125 per cent. is exactly met; but at 100 per cent. in the index the wage would be 55s. which gives an increase in real wages, and at 150 per cent. the wage is 65s. and the increase over the pre-war 26s. 8d. is only 143¾ per cent. and real wages fall. The equation 5 points = 1s. would only give an exact proportion throughout when the original wage was 20s., so that in fact the variation is based on a bare living standard for all ranks and not on the whole wage.[1]

The sliding scale in the woollen and worsted industries presents some of the same features. The ' cost of living wage ', added to the basic rate of earnings, was not proportional to the

---

[1] For details of the application of the sliding-scale method to railway clerks and to police see the *Labour Gazette*, March 1920 and October 1920.

whole of this rate, but to the pre-war rate which had since been raised 10 per cent. ; the percentage is, therefore, only calculated on $\frac{10}{11}$ths of the accepted standards, or put otherwise only $\frac{10}{11}$ths of the change of cost of living is allowed, up or down.[1]   There is also a limitation that the increase shall not be greater in any case than 3s. for 10 points, that is, for men whose rates before the War were over 30s., only 30s. is taken into account.

These sliding-scale arrangements tend to assume the existence of some normal price level considerably above that before the War, but below those of 1920.   If such a normal could be found about which prices oscillated, but from which they did not depart far, a strong argument could be adduced for giving wages smaller oscillations ; but, as it is, it is clear that the whole arrangement is provisional, and that its varieties of application are experimental, while the index-numbers on which it is based are generally recognized as being unsatisfactory.

The question whether the general establishment of minimum wages with variations proportional to those in the cost of living is possible or even desirable is outside the scope of this book.

---

[1] From August 1920 the percentage was applied to the whole revised basic rates.

CHAPTER VIII

BUILDING

Increases in eight large cities in hourly and weekly rates. Comparison of the movements of artisans' and labourers' wages with that of the cost of living. Detailed table of changes. Local variation of hourly rates in 1915 and 1920 compared.

THE study of wages in the building trades is specially illuminating and important both because a number of interesting tendencies can be observed and because available information is complete and detailed.

Only small changes are recorded during the first two years of the War in spite of the considerable increase in prices, but unusually regular employment no doubt tended to compensate the falling value of money. During the latter half of 1916 and throughout 1917 there were throughout the country a number of successive increases generally of 1*d.* an hour each, and at the beginning of 1918 wages were in different towns from 2*d.* to 5*d.* above the pre-war level, but quite generally the rise was less than that in the cost of living however reckoned. In January 1918 a bonus of 12½ per cent. on earnings was awarded to builders engaged directly or indirectly in munitions work, and this was generally extended to all builders in the spring of 1918. Further considerable increases were obtained in the latter part of 1918, and wages rose by considerable and not infrequent steps throughout 1919, and a general increase again took place in the summer of 1920. Since the Armistice there has been a definite movement towards the reduction of summer hours to a uniform forty-four throughout the country and in nearly every case hourly rates were raised at the time of the reduction so that the week's earnings should be at least as high as before.

Since wage rates in 1914 varied greatly from town to town and the dates and amount of change were arranged locally it is impossible to give full detail and impracticable to calculate the movement of average wages minutely. The movement can, however, be followed in outline from the details given below (pp. 116 seq.) for eight selected towns (London, Southampton, Bristol, Birmingham, Leeds, Manchester, Glasgow, and Belfast); the wages of the various artisans (bricklayers, carpenters, &c.) are not always equal and there is no rule which shows their relation to one another, for this relation varies from place to place, but the differences are always small and the increases have normally (though not universally) been made to all artisans at the same time ; in the tables given the bricklayers' wages have been taken as typical of all. Labourers' wages have often moved at different dates from those of artisans, and consequently the course of bricklayers' labourers' wages is also shown in detail in the tables.

In general the increase in labourers' rates has been the same number of pence per hour as the increase in artisans'; in some cases (e. g. Southampton, June 1916, and London, November 1919 and May 1920) the increase has been the greater for labourers. Prior to the War (and indeed during the whole of the nineteenth century) the labourers' wage in London was almost exactly two-thirds of the bricklayers'; the process of equal increments has, of course, diminished the relative inequality, till in London in June 1920 the labourers' rate was as much as $\frac{25}{28}$ths of the bricklayers'. The percentage increase for the labourer has from the same cause been considerably higher than that for the artisan. The painter, whose rate is intermediate between those of the bricklayer and labourer, has in a similar way gained relatively to the artisan. These tendencies are shown in the following table, in which the rates at eight towns are shown for July of each year.

Since the number of hours worked per week in the summer has been reduced (as shown below, p. 114 and pp. 116 seq.) the increase in the hourly rate and the expense of building have risen more rapidly than this table suggests.

Summaries given in the *Labour Gazette* for all large towns give a more complete view of the movement at two selected dates.

TABLE XXXIV

SUMMARY OF BRICKLAYERS' WEEKLY SUMMER RATES IN EIGHT CITIES

	London	Southampton	Bristol	Birmingham	Leeds	Manchester	Glasgow	Belfast	Average of Eight	
									Rate	Percentage
	s. d.	s. d.	s. d.	s. d.	s. d.	s. d.	s. d.	s. d.	s. d.	
July 1914	47 11	42 0	41 8	42 1	41 3	43 4	43 9	40 6	42 10	100
,, 1915	47 11	42 0	43 9	45 4	41 3	43 4	45 10	40 6	43 9	102
,, 1916	52 1	45 3	45 10	47 5	44 4	45 5	47 11	41 3	46 2	108
,, 1917	56 3	49 8	50 0	55 8	50 6	53 7	54 2	47 10	52 2	122
,, 1918	71 6	57 5	66 1	74 3	67 3	70 1	71 6	61 3	67 5	157
,, 1919	87 6	70 8	73 4	82 6	77 6	77 6	83 5	81 3	79 2	185
Mar. 1920	91 1	82 3	88 4	89 1	89 1	89 1	88 0	81 3	87 3	204
July 1920	102 8	88 0	97 2	102 8	102 8	102 8	102 8	106 4	100 7	235

SUMMARY OF BRICKLAYERS' LABOURERS' WEEKLY SUMMER RATES

	London	Southampton	Bristol	Birmingham	Leeds	Manchester¹	Glasgow	Belfast	Average of Seven	
									Rate	Percentage
	s. d.	s. d.	s. d.	s. d.	s. d.	s. d.	s. d.	s. d.	s. d.	
July 1914	33 4	28 9	29 2	29 9	28 10	26 10	27 1	—	29 1	100
,, 1915	33 4	28 9	31 3	33 0	28 10	26 10	29 2	—	30 2	103
,, 1916	37 6	34 3	33 4	35 1	33 0	30 11	31 3	—	33 7	115
,, 1917	41 8	38 8	37 6	43 4	39 2	37 1	35 5	—	39 0	134
,, 1918	55 1	46 4	52 10	60 4	53 4	53 7	53 10	—	53 7	185
,, 1919	70 10	57 5	64 2	70 1	65 10	62 0	66 0	—	65 2	224
Mar. 1920	77 6	68 6	73 4	77 6	77 6	73 7	70 7	—	74 1	254
July 1920	91 8	77 0	86 2	91 8	91 8	88 0	85 3	—	87 4	300

¹ See note, p. 119.

TABLE XXXV

AVERAGE (UNWEIGHTED) OF BUILDERS' WAGES IN TOWNS WITH POPULATIONS OVER 100,000

(Compiled from the *Labour Gazette*, May 1919, April 1920, and February 1921)

| | Hourly rates | | | | Weekly rates | | | Percentages Aug. 1914 = 100 | | | | |
| | | | | | | | | Hourly rates | | | Weekly rates | |
	Aug. 4, 1914 d.	Apr. 30, 1919 d.	Feb. 29, 1920 d.	Dec. 31, 1920 d.	Aug. 4, 1914 s. d.	Feb. 29, 1920 s. d.	Dec. 31, 1920 s. d.	Apr. 1919	Feb. 1920	Dec. 1920	Feb. 1920	Dec. 1920
Bricklayers	9·9	18·6	22·0	27·5	40 7	83 7	100 10	188	223	278	206	248
Masons	9·8	18·7	22·1	27·5	39 8	83 9	100 10	191	226	281	211	254
Carpenters and joiners	9·7	18·5	22·0	27·4	39 11	83 5	100 6	191	226	282	209	252
Plumbers	9·6	19·6	22·3	27·8	39 9	83 9	101 11	204	232	289	211	256
Plasterers	9·7	18·5	22·0	27·5	40 2	83 9	100 10	191	226	282	209	251
Painters	8·8	17·9	21·5	27·1	36 3	81 5	99 3	203	244	308	224	274
Labourers	6·5	14·9	18·5	23·8	26 11	70 3	87 3	229	284	365	261	324

Bricklayers' average summer and winter hours 1914, 49·2 ; 1920, February 45·6, December 44.

It is seen that the eight towns selected in the former table shows practically the same changes for bricklayers and labourers up to December 1920, and since further the movements are the same for all artisans, it may be taken that the eight towns form a sufficient sample for other dates.

The average increase for artisans and labourers was 1s. 5d. an hour up to December 1920, and after allowance is made for the reduction of hours the increase in weekly rates was approximately 43s. to February and 60s. 3d. to December 1920.[1]

Since the Armistice there has been a movement towards grouping towns together for wage bargaining; thus the towns of Lancashire are arranged in three grades, within each of which building artisans' rates are equal, while the rates differ by 1½d. or 2½d. an hour from one grade to the next. This grading has no doubt had a perceptible effect in levelling up wages, and so far as it relates to towns with a population under 100,000 this effect is not reflected in the figures in the table above. This aspect is considered further on pp. 121 seq. below.

By July 1918 the increase in labourers' wages was as great as that of the modified measure of the cost of living, discussed above, and it was considerably greater than the official measure by July 1920. The bricklayers' weekly rate, however, did not catch up even the modified measure in the cost of living till 1919, and the increase was definitely less than that in the official measure in July 1920.

TABLE XXXVI

BUILDERS' WAGES AND COST OF LIVING

	Average of eight towns Bricklayers' summer wages	Average of seven towns Labourers' summer wages	Official index-number of cost of living	Modified index-number
July 1914	100	100	100	100
„ 1915	102	103	125	(120)
„ 1916	108	115	145–150	(135)
„ 1917	122	134	180	(160)
„ 1918	157	185	200–205	180
„ 1919	185	224	205–210	185
„ 1920	238	300	252	220

[1] Hours were at the end of 1920 44 hours weekly with no change between summer and winter.

It must be remembered, however, that there has been very regular employment, at any rate for artisans, from the time that the War began its drain on the population, whereas before the War considerable lost time was normal.

TABLE XXXVII

DETAILS OF CHANGES OF BUILDERS' WAGES IN SELECTED TOWNS

LONDON

	Bricklayer and Carpenter			*Bricklayer's labourer*		
	Hourly rate	*Weekly hours (summer)*	*Weekly rate*	*Hourly rate*	*Weekly hours (summer)*	*Weekly rate*
	d.		*s. d.*	*d.*		*s. d.*
July 1914	11½	50	47 11	8	50	33 4
July 1916	12½	50	52 1	9	50	37 6
June 1917	13½	50	56 3	10	50	41 8
Jan. 1918	15¼	50	63 6½	11¾	50	48 11½
May 1918	15¼+12½%	50	71 6	11¾+12½%	50	55 1
Oct. 1918	17+12½%	50	79 8	13½+12½%	50	63 3
Feb. 1919	21	50	87 6	17	50	70 10
Nov. 1919	23½	50	97 11	20	50	83 4
May 1920	28	44	102 8	25	44	91 8

The increases of 1¾*d.* hourly granted generally in January 1918 and October 1918 were given to those engaged on munitions work about three months earlier in each case.

The 12½ per cent. bonus granted generally in May 1918 had already been allowed to those engaged in work for the Ministry of Munitions and other departments in January 1918.

SOUTHAMPTON

	Bricklayer and Carpenter			*Bricklayer's labourer*		
	Hourly rate	*Weekly hours (summer)*	*Weekly rate*	*Hourly rate*	*Weekly hours (summer)*	*Weekly rate*
	d.		*s. d.*	*d.*		*s. d.*
July 1914	9½	53	41 11½	6½	53	28 8½
June 1916	10¼	53	45 3	7¾	53	34 3
May 1917	11¼	53	49 8	8¾	53	38 8
Jan. 1918	12¼	53	54 1	9¾	53	43 1
May 1918	13	53	57 5	10½	53	46 4½
May 1919	16	53	70 8	13	53	57 5
Sept. 1919	18	47	70 6	14½	47	56 9½
Apr. 1920	21	47	82 3	17½	47	68 6½
May 1920	24	44	88 0	21	44	77 0

The general bonus of 12½ per cent. granted to those engaged on munitions work in January 1918 was not extended to other operatives in Southampton. It ceased after the increase in rates in May 1919.

TABLE XXXVII (*continued*)—Details of Changes of Builders' Wages in Selected Towns

Bristol

	Bricklayer and Carpenter				*Bricklayer's labourer*			
	Hourly rate	*Weekly hours (summer)*	*Weekly rate*		*Hourly rate*	*Weekly hours (summer)*	*Weekly rate*	
	d.		*s.*	*d.*	*d.*		*s.*	*d.*
Aug. 1914	10	50	41	8	7	50	29	2
Jan. 1915	10½	50	43	9	8	50	31	3
July 1916	11	50	45	10	8	50	33	4
Nov. 1916	11	50	45	10	8½	50	35	5
July 1917	12	50	50	0	9	50	37	6
Nov. 1917	13	50	54	2	10	50	41	8
Dec. 1917	14¼	50	59	4½	11¼	50	46	10½
Mar. 1918	14¼+12½%	50	66	10	11¼+12½%	50	52	9
July 1918	15+12½%	47	66	1	12+12½%	47	52	10½
Dec. 1918	18	47	70	6	15	47	58	9
May 1919	20	44	73	4	17½	44	64	2
Dec. 1919	21	44	77	0	18½	44	67	10
Feb. 1920	22	44	80	8	19½	44	71	6
Mar. 1920	23	44	84	4	20	44	73	4
May 1920	24	44	88	0	21	44	77	0
July 1920	26½	44	97	2	23½	44	86	2
Sept. 1920	28	44	102	8	25	44	91	8

The increase of 12½ per cent. was awarded to all in March 1918, two months after its grant to those on Government work.

Birmingham

	Bricklayer and Carpenter				*Bricklayer's labourer*			
	Hourly rate	*Weekly hours (summer)*	*Weekly rate*		*Hourly rate*	*Weekly hours (summer)*	*Weekly rate*	
	d.		*s.*	*d.*	*d.*		*s.*	*d.*
July 1914	10	50½	42	1	7	50½	29	5½
Oct. 1914	10½	49½	43	4	7½	49½	30	11
Apr. 1915	11	49½	45	4½	8	49½	33	0
Oct. 1915	11½	49½	47	5	8½	49½	35	1
Dec. 1916	12½	49½	51	7	9½	49½	39	3
July 1917	13½	49½	55	8	10½	49½	43	4
Dec. 1917	14¾	49½	60	10	11¾	49½	48	6
Apr. 1918	14¾+12½%	49½	68	5	11¾+12½%	49½	54	7

TABLE XXXVII (*continued*)—DETAILS OF CHANGES OF BUILDERS' WAGES IN SELECTED TOWNS

BIRMINGHAM (*continued*)

	Bricklayer and Carpenter				*Bricklayer's labourer*			
	Hourly rate	*Weekly hours (summer)*	*Weekly rate*		*Hourly rate*	*Weekly hours (summer)*	*Weekly rate*	
	d.		*s.*	*d.*	*d.*		*s.*	*d.*
June 1918	16+12½%	49½	74	3	13+12½%	49½	60	4
Oct. 1918	17¼+12½%	49½	80	0½	14¼+12½%	49½	66	2
Feb. 1919	20	49½	82	6	17	49½	70	1½
Aug. 1919	21	49½	86	7½	18	49½	74	3
Nov. 1919	22	49½	90	9	19	49½	78	4½
Jan. 1920	23	49½	94	10½	20	49½	82	6
May 1920	24	44	88	0	21	44	77	0
June 1920	28	44	102	8	25	44	91	8

The increase in December 1916 was first given to those on war work, but soon extended to all.

The increase in April 1918 had been granted to those on government work in January 1918.

LEEDS

	Bricklayer	*Carpenter*		*Bricklayer*		*Bricklayer's labourer*			
	Hourly rate	*Hourly rate*	*Weekly hours (summer)*	*Weekly rate*		*Hourly rate*	*Weekly hours (summer)*	*Weekly rate*	
	d.	*d.*		*s.*	*d.*	*d.*		*s.*	*d.*
July 1914	10	9½	49½	41	3	7	49½	28	10½
Jan. 1916	10¾	10¼	49½	44	4	7½	49½	30	11
Apr. 1916	10¾	10¼	49½	44	4	8	49½	33	0
July 1916	10¾	10½	49½	44	4	8	49½	33	0
Feb. 1917	11¾	11½	49½	48	5	9	49½	37	1
July 1917	12¼	12	49½	50	6	9½	49½	39	2
Oct. 1917	13¼	13	49½	54	8	10½	49½	43	4
Jan. 1918	14¼	14	49½	58	9	11½	49½	47	5
Apr. 1918	14½+12½%	14+12½%	49½	67	3	11½+12½%	49½	53	4
Sept. 1918	15¼+12½%	15+12½%	49½	70	9	12½+12½%	49½	58	0
Jan. 1919	16¼+12½%	16+12½%	49½	75	5	13¾+12½%	49½	63	10
May 1919	20	20	46½	77	6	17	46½	65	10
Dec. 1919	22	22	46½	85	3	19	46½	73	7
Jan. 1920	23	23	46½	89	1	20	46½	77	6
May 1920	24	24	44	88	0	21	44	77	0
June 1920	28	28	44	102	8	25	44	91	8

The increase granted in January 1918 to those engaged on munitions work was extended to all in April 1918.

TABLE XXXVII (*continued*)—DETAILS OF CHANGES OF BUILDERS' WAGES IN SELECTED TOWNS

MANCHESTER

	Bricklayer and Carpenter				*Bricklayer's labourer*[1]			
	Hourly rate	*Weekly hours (summer)*	*Weekly rate*		*Hourly rate*	*Weekly hours (summer)*	*Weekly rate*	
	d.		*s.*	*d.*	*d.*		*s.*	*d.*
July 1914	10½	49½	43	4	6½	49½	26	10
Nov. 1915	11	49½	45	5	7½	49½	30	11
Dec. 1916	12	49½	49	6	7½	49½	30	11
Jan. 1917	12	49½	49	6	8	49½	33	0
May 1917	13	49½	53	7	9	49½	37	1
Nov. 1917	14	49½	57	9	10	49½	41	3
Feb. 1918	15	49½	61	10	11	49½	45	5
May 1918	17	49½	70	1	13	49½	53	7
Nov. 1918	18	49½	74	3	14	49½	57	9
Mar. 1919	20	46½	77	6	16	46½	62	0
Nov. 1919	22	46½	85	3	18	46½	69	9
Jan. 1920	23	46½	89	1	19	46½	73	7
May 1920	24	44	88	0	20	44	73	4
June 1920	28	44	102	8	24	44	88	0

The increase in January 1918 to those engaged in munitions work was merged in the increase of 2*d.* shown above in May 1918.

GLASGOW

	Bricklayer				*Bricklayer's labourer*[1]			
	Hourly rate	*Weekly hours (summer)*	*Weekly rate*		*Hourly rate*	*Weekly hours (summer)*	*Weekly rate*	
	d.		*s.*	*d.*	*d.*		*s.*	*d.*
July 1914	10½	50	43	9	6½	50	27	1
Nov. 1914	11	50	45	10	7	50	29	2
Nov. 1915	11	50	45	10	7½	50	31	3
May 1916	11½	50	47	11	7½	50	31	3
Aug. 1916	11½	50	47	11	8½	50	35	5
Apr. 1917	13	50	54	2	8½	50	35	5
Aug. 1917	13	50	54	2	10+1*s.* weekly	50	42	8
Dec. 1917	14	50	58	4	10+1*s.* weekly	50	42	8
Jan. 1918	14+12½%	50	65	7½	10+1*s.* weekly	50	42	8
Apr. 1918	15¼+12½%	50	71	6	11¼+1*s.* weekly +12½%	50	53	10
Aug. 1918	16½+12½%	50	77	4	12½+12½%	50	58	7
Dec. 1918	17¾+12½%	50	83	2	13¾+12½%	50	64	5
Mar. 1919	22¾	44	83	5	18	44	66	0
Dec. 1919	24	44	88	0	19¼	44	70	7
July 1920	28	44	102	8	23¼	44	85	3

[1] The rates are for an ordinary builder's labourer; hod-carriers received ½*d.* an hour more.

The movement of carpenters' wages, which were $10\frac{1}{2}d.$ hourly in July 1914 and $28d.$ in July 1920, differed a little from that in bricklayers'.

The increase of $1d.$ to bricklayers in December 1917 was confined to those on munitions work, but appears to have been extended subsequently to all.

The increase of $12\frac{1}{2}$ per cent. on earnings was paid on all work from January 1918.

The $1s.$ bonus granted to bricklayers' labourers in 1917 was merged in other increases in August 1918.

In *Belfast* the pre-war rate for bricklayers and carpenters was $9d.$ an hour, the summer hours being 54 weekly. During 1915 a war bonus of $3s.$ weekly was granted. In May 1916 in lieu of the bonus the hourly rate was raised to $10d.$, summer hours at the same time being reduced to $49\frac{1}{2}$. In November 1916 a further bonus of $3s.$ was granted and in May 1917 the hourly rate was raised to $11\frac{5}{7}d.$, the bonus being merged and the summer hours reduced to 49.

The hourly rate was raised to $12\frac{3}{4}d.$ in November 1917 and to $15d.$ in May 1918. The munitions workers $12\frac{1}{2}$ per cent. increase appears never to have been extended to other workers.

In October 1918 the hourly rate is stated at the unusual amount of $16\frac{22}{27}d.$[1] and the bonus appears to have been dropped. In May 1919 the rate was $20\frac{3}{4}d.$ without any bonus, and summer hours were reduced to 47. In May 1920 the rate was raised to $29d.$ and the hours reduced to 44.

The weekly rates were therefore $40s.$ $6d.$ in 1914, $43s.$ $6d.$ at the end of 1915, $41s.$ $3d.$ from May 1916, $44s.$ $3d.$ from November 1916, $47s.$ $10d.$ from May 1917, $52s.$ $1d.$ from November 1917, $61s.$ $3d.$ from May 1918, $68s.$ $8d.$ from October 1918, $81s.$ $3d.$ from May 1919, and $106s.$ $4d.$ in May 1920.

There is not sufficient information to give an account of labourers' wages.

The summary from the *Labour Gazette* quoted on p. 114 showed that from July 1914 to February 29, 1920, rates had increased

---

[1] This rate may be due to the employees of Messrs. Harland & Wolff working 54 hours, when the weekly rate would have been the more usual amount of $75s.$ $8d.$

in large towns generally by 12*d*. and 12¼*d*. We are able to make a detailed comparison for 360 districts in March 1915 and January 1920, and since changes before March 1915 and in the first two months of 1920 were not very important, the results of the two tabulations are nearly comparable.

In March 1915 the recognized wages for carpenters (who are selected for investigation because, unlike most other occupations, rates for them are stated for nearly all districts) varied from 6*d*. to 11½*d*. an hour. On the whole the highest rates were found in the large towns, but the division is geographical also. Thus in London only was the rate 11½*d*. and in Liverpool and Birkenhead only it was 11*d*. At 10½*d*. there were twenty-four districts, including Manchester and some neighbouring places (but not Stockport), Newcastle and neighbourhood, Glasgow, Birmingham, Bristol, and outlying districts of London. From 9½*d*. to 10¼*d*. come the principal towns in Lancashire, Durham, Northumberland, and South Scotland not already named, Sheffield, Hull, Leeds, Barnsley, Huddersfield, Leicester, Nottingham, Coventry, Wolverhampton, Portsmouth, and Southampton, and the larger Welsh towns, 100 districts in all. From 8¾*d*. or 9¼*d*. we find the smaller places in Lancashire and the North, Bradford and other important towns in the West Riding, and the towns of moderate size in the Midlands and South and Belfast ; 134 districts in all. Rates below 8½*d*. are stated for 99 districts, generally small manufacturing or market towns, but including Crewe and Swindon.

By January 1920 Liverpool and Birkenhead rates had increased to 24*d*., London and its outlying districts (including a greater area than in 1915) was at 23½*d*., and the most populous districts and large towns in Scotland were rated at 22¾*d*., 23*d*., or 23½*d*. In the principal towns in Lancashire and Yorkshire and Wales and eleven large towns in the Midlands the rates were uniformly 22*d*. or 21*d*., while in Northumberland and Durham they were 21½*d*. More than half the rates quoted were 21*d*. or more. Below 21*d*. the remaining places tail off in an irregular way till in three towns in the Isle of Wight the rate stated is only 12*d*.

BUILDING

The distribution of the districts rates, including those in ten towns in Ireland, is shown at the two dates in the accompanying diagram and following table.

TABLE XXXVIII

HOURLY RATES OF CARPENTERS IN 360 DISTRICTS IN THE UNITED KINGDOM

March 1915			January 1920		
Rate	No. of districts		Rate	No. of districts	
d.			d.		
6	4 ⎫		12		3
6½	6 ⎬ 11		14	1 ⎫	2
6¾	1 ⎭		14½	1 ⎭	
7	19 ⎫		15	7 ⎫	9
7¼	3 ⎬		15½	2 ⎭	
7½	20 ⎬ 46				
7¾	4 ⎭		16	11 ⎫	
			16¼	1 ⎬ 15	
8	37 ⎫		16½	3 ⎭	
8¼	5 ⎪				
8½	59 ⎬ 107		17	14 ⎫	16
8¾	6 ⎭		17½	2 ⎭	
9	62 ⎫		18	47 ⎫	
9¼	7 ⎬		18½	3 ⎬ 51	
9½	53 ⎬ 126		18¾	1 ⎭	
9¾	4 ⎭				
			19	40 ⎫	
10	41 ⎫		19½	3 ⎬ 45	
10¼	2 ⎬ 67		19¾	2 ⎭	
10½	24 ⎭				
			20	28 ⎫	30
11	2 ⎫		20¾	2 ⎭	
11½	1 ⎬ 3				
			21	71 ⎫	
	———		21¼	1 ⎬ 96	
	360		21½	24 ⎭	
			22	52 ⎫	
			22¼	2 ⎬ 65	
			22¾	11 ⎭	
			23	10 ⎫	
			23¼	1 ⎬ 26	
			23½	15 ⎭	
			24		2
				———	
				360	

Average of rates 8·83d.   Average of rates 20·05d.

Average increase 11·22d.

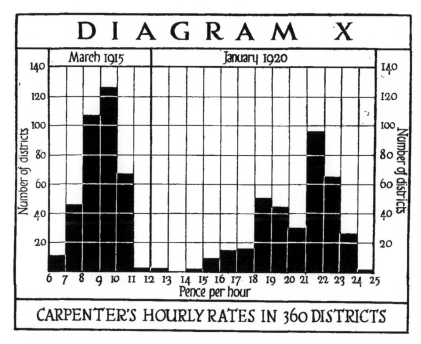

DIAGRAM X

CARPENTER'S HOURLY RATES IN 360 DISTRICTS

Except locally the rates were not more uniform or concentrated in 1920 than in 1919, nor has there been any general system in the amount of increase.

TABLE XXXIX

AVERAGE INCREASE IN CARPENTERS' RATES GRADED AS IN 1915

Rates d.	No. of districts	Average increase
6	4	11·5
6½ or 6¾	7	10·5
7 or 7¼	22	9·7
7½ or 7¾	24	10·6
8 or 8¼	42	10·9
8½ or 8¾	65	10·6
9 or 9¼	69	11·4
9½ or 9¾	57	11·9
10 or 10¼	43	12·1
10½	24	11·6
11	2	13·0
11½	1	12·0
		11·2
Total and average	360	

There is no general levelling up as is found in engineers'
wages (pp. 129–30), nor are the amounts of increase obtained
in the separate districts uniform.

Amounts of increase	No. of districts
d.	
4	1 (Cowes)
5	2 (Ryde, Newport, Isle of Wight)
6	2 (Ashford, Folkestone)
7	9
8	16
9	33
10	47
11	98
12	97
13	49
14	6
	360

CHAPTER IX

ENGINEERING, SHIPBUILDING, IRON AND STEEL MANUFACTURE

Engineering and Shipbuilding. Distinction between earnings and nominal rates. District increases in 1914–16. General increases, 1917–20. Munition workers' bonus, 1917–18. General change in time rates, 1914–20. Analysis by districts ; levelling up of wages. Time rates in shipbuilding, 1915 and 1920.

Pig-iron and Iron and Steel Manufacture. Sliding scales and the extent of their influence. Changes for blast-furnace men. Changes in the iron and steel manufacture and bonuses. The effect of fixing the price of steel. Tables of all changes. *Note* on the introduction of an eight hours' shift.

Engineering and Shipbuilding. In the case of these industries it is necessary to make a sharp distinction between nominal rates of wages or nominal changes in piece rates and actual earnings. From the beginning of the War the demand made on the products of engineering was acute, and ordinary manufacture was diverted to munition work of all kinds. As the War continued the normal resources of the industry proved quite inadequate, new factories were built and operated by or directly for the Government, and old factories were controlled. Trade Union regulations were suspended, unskilled men and women were introduced not only to do work of a novel character but also for operations hitherto carried out by skilled men, and regulations were made to ensure certain rates of pay. In many cases it became easy to make high earnings on piece work both because the work was well systematized and repetitive on a large scale and because the same rate being ensured whatever the output, there was no fear of any cutting of prices. At the same time night work and overtime at enhanced rates were common. The earnings of piece workers consequently increased greatly, independently of any increase in rates, time workers received more in return for more work, and a very large number of persons passed from unskilled to skilled rates of pay. These processes were specially marked in 1917 and 1918 ; but since the Armistice production has returned to the old conditions of earnings, subject perhaps to the advantage of improved machinery and organization.

There is no means of estimating the increase of earnings during the war period, and the changes recorded in the sequel show only some of the factors involved, namely, those factors which operated in the same way before and after the War.

The industries of engineering and shipbuilding cannot be altogether separated from each other, since both employ engineers and engine makers; but in normal times engineering wages are based on time rates to a much greater extent than those in shipbuilding, where especially in many operations peculiar to the industry piece rates predominate. The changes recorded in time rates are therefore of more importance in connexion with engineering.

During 1915 (generally in March or May) additions were made in all or most of the important districts of 3s. or 4s. a week in time rates (labourers generally receiving the same increase as artisans) and of 7½ or 10 per cent. in piece rates. During 1916 a further increase of 3s. was commonly given on time rates, while piece rates (on which earnings were increasing for the reasons indicated above) were left unchanged. (See Table XL.) In April 1917, for all classes of work in the engineering and foundry trades throughout Great Britain, the increases given since the outbreak of war to men were levelled up to a minimum of 7s., and this 7s. or more became part of their permanent time rates. Increases in piece rates appear to have amounted generally to 10 per cent. by the same time or to have been brought up to this level.

In April 1917, in addition to the levelling up of increments, the first of the war wages was granted throughout the United Kingdom in these trades; this was 5s. per full ordinary week to all males over 18 years, and 2s. 6d. to all youths and boys under 18, including apprentices. It should be noticed that these flat-time increments were given to piece workers as well as to time workers. A second increment of 3s. was awarded in August 1917. In October 1917 an addition of 12½ per cent. on the weekly earnings was granted to all skilled munition time workers in these industries and was extended to unskilled munition workers by a subsequent award.   In January 1918 a similar bonus of 7½ per cent. on earnings was granted to munition piece workers.   Since a very large proportion of the industries was devoted to the production of munitions, this increase was widespread ; the distinction between earnings of men doing the same class of work on munitions and other essential work naturally caused discontent, and the increments were gradually extended to all workers in the industries concerned.

TABLE XL

CHANGES IN ENGINEERS' TIME RATES IN IMPORTANT DISTRICTS, JULY 1914 TO APRIL 1917

Turners' rates, taken as typical

	July 1914	Increases in 1914–15	Increases in 1916–17
ENGINEERING DISTRICTS	s. d.		
London . . .	40 0	Nov. 3s.[1], Apr. 4s.[1, 2]	Nov. 3s.[2]
Manchester . . .	39 0	March 3s.[1, 2]	Apr. 1s.[1,2], Nov. 3s.
Blackburn . . .	38 0	Nov. 1s.[2], May 3s.[1]	Nov. 3s.[2, 3]
Bolton	38 0	Jan. 1s.[1, 2], May 3s.[1, 2]	Nov. 3s.[2, 3]
Sheffield . . .	41 0	Oct. 1s., Mar. 4s [1, 2]	Aug. 3s.[2]
Leeds	37 0	Mar. 3s.[1, 2]	May 1s.[1, 2], Nov. 3s.[2]
Bradford . . .	37 0	Apr. 3s.	May 1s. [1, 2], Oct. 3s. [2]
Derby	36 0	Mar. 3s.[1]	Aug. 3s.[2, 3]
Birmingham. . .	38 0	Dec. 2s.[1], Aug. 3s.[1, 2]	Aug. 3s.
Bristol. . . .	39 0	Mar. 3s.	July 3s.
SHIPBUILDING DISTRICTS			
Liverpool and Birken-			
head . . .	39 0	Jan. 3s.[1], May 4s.[1]	Oct. 3s.[2], Jan. 4s.
The Tyne and the Wear	37 0	Mar. 4s.[1, 2]	Aug. 3s.[2], Feb. 2s.[2]
Hull	38 0	Mar. 3s. [1, 2]	Aug. 3s.
Barrow . . .	40 0	Mar. 3s.[2]	May 1s.[1], Dec. 3s.
Southampton . .	40 6	Mar. 4s.[1, 2]	Sept. 3s.[2]
Cardiff . . .	40 0	Apr. 2s., Sept. 2s.	July 3s.
The Clyde . . .	38 3	Mar. 4s.[1]	Aug. 3s. 4d.[2]
Belfast . . .	42 0	Mar. 3s.[1, 2], Oct. 2s.[1]	Oct. 3s.

Where separate rates are stated for engineering, machine and marine works, that for engineering is quoted, except in the case of Southampton where the marine rate is taken.

[1] In these cases it is known that an increase in piece rates took place, usually 2½ per cent. for each 1s. on time rates.

[2] In these cases the same increase was given to labourers, except that in Bradford, October 1916, the increase was 2s., and in March 1915 4s. in Barrow and 3s. in Sheffield.   There were probably some other labourers' increases not recorded here.

[3] In Derby, August 1916, and in Blackburn and Bolton, November 1916, the increase in piece rates was 2½ per cent.

In December 1917 a further advance of 5*s.* a week was granted to men over 18, and wages generally stood for time workers at *pre-war rates* + 20*s. for normal week* + *overtime earnings* + 12½ *per cent. on weekly earnings* and for piece workers at *pre-war rates* + 10 *per cent. on rates* + 20*s. a week* + 7½ *per cent. on earnings.*

Further advances were August 1918 3*s.* 6*d.*, December 1918 5*s.*, December 1919 5*s.*, March 1920 and May 1920 each 3*s.* to time workers and 7½ per cent. on the existing piece rates.

In January 1919 weekly hours of work were reduced from 53 or 54 to a uniform 47—time rates remaining unchanged and an increase being made in piece rates to enable the same earnings to be reached in the shorter hours.

The changes in time rates are summarized in the *Labour Gazette* of May 1919 (p. 173), April 1920 (p. 170), and February 1921 (p. 63) for a number of the principal engineering and shipbuilding centres ; and the tables may be amalgamated as follows :

TABLE XLI

ENGINEERS' AND SHIPBUILDERS' AVERAGE WEEKLY TIME RATES INCLUDING THE BONUS OF 12½ PER CENT.

Occupation	Unweighted average of certain centres			Increase from Aug. 1914 to Feb. 1920		Increase to Dec. 31, 1920
	Aug. 4, 1914	Apr. 30, 1919	Feb. 29, 1920	Amount	Per cent.	Per cent.
	s. *d.*	*s.* *d.*	*s.* *d.*	*s.* *d.*		
Engineering						
Fitters and turners .	38 11	76 10	82 5	43 6	112	129
Iron moulders	41 8	79 10	85 6	43 10	105	121
Pattern-makers	42 1	—	86 8	44 7	106	122
Labourers .	22 10	58 3	63 11	41 1	180	209
Shipbuilding						
Platers . .	40 4	77 8	83 4	43 0	107	123
Rivetters .	37 9	74 9	80 5	42 8	113	131
Shipwrights .	41 4	78 11	84 6	43 2	105	121
Labourers .	22 10	58 0	63 7	40 9	178	204

Excluding the bonus, the increase may be computed to be 34*s.* 4*d.* for fitters, turners, and iron moulders ; 33*s.* 9*d.* for platers, rivetters, and shipwrights ; 34*s.* 11*d.* for pattern-makers ; 34*s.* for engineering labourers ; 33*s.* 8*d.* for shipbuilding labourers. The increases due to the 7*s.* prior to April 1917 and the advances up to February 1920 were 33*s.* 6*d.*, so that artisans in the engineering trade had gained an average of 10*d*. in addition.

The effect of the flat increases to all was, of course, to raise labourers' wages relatively to artisans. In engineering, in August 1914, the labourer's wage was 59 per cent. of the fitter's; in April 1919, 76 per cent.; in February 1920, 78½ per cent.; and in June 1920, nearly 80 per cent. These changes should be compared with the corresponding changes in the wages of building artisans and labourers.

The table above, relating only to the principal centres, does not show the whole movement, for there has been a considerable levelling up of the rates of those smaller districts in which wages in 1914 were well below the 36*s*. to 38*s*. common in the important centres. In the following table (XLII), comparative figures are given for iron moulders (in some districts called ' iron founders ') in 120 districts, and for turners in 189 districts, in July 1914 and January 1920. In the case of the turners, the average of these rates in 1914 (giving equal importance to each district) was 36*s*.; in January 1920 it was 45*s*. 2*d*., showing an increase of 9*s*. 2*d*. as compared with 7*s*. 10*d*. found above in the principal districts and 7*s*., the minimum arranged in 1917.[1] When the districts are classified according to the rates in 1914 and the average rates in each class computed for January 1920, it is found (as in the last column of the table) that the increases fall with a certain regularity as one reads down the column. The same phenomena are even more marked in the case of ironfounders.

This analysis is important as showing the general tendency to level up wages not only between occupations but also between districts; but the increase of 9*s*. 2*d*. must not be taken as the average increase in time rates of all turners and fitters, for it is simply the unweighted average of the districts and it is precisely the districts where most were employed that have received the least increase; the average increase for all employed is much nearer to the 7*s*. 10*d*. found from the *Labour Gazette* table than to this 9*s*. 2*d*.

[1] The 7*s*. arranged in 1917 was definitely added to wages; increases in 1918–19 were regarded as war wages; the 6*s*. in 1920 was added to wages.

TABLE XLII

IRONFOUNDERS

Time rates excluding 12½ per cent. bonus and war wage (26s. 6d.)

General movement				Mean increase on 1914 rate			
July 1914		Jan. 1920					
Rate	No. of towns	Rate	No. of towns	1914 rate		Increase	
s. d.		s.		s. d.		s. d.	
31 0	3	38	2	31 0		13 0	
32 0	6	39	1	32 0		12 5	
33 0	2	40	0	33 0		11 9	
34 0	4	41	2	34 0		8 3	
35 0	3	42	2	35 0		9 6	
36 0	10	43	3	36 0		9 5	
37 0	4	44	6	37 0		9 3	
38 0	16	45	11	38 0		8 8	
39 0	12	46	14	39 0		8 6	
40 0	27	47	24	40 0		7 11	
41 0	9	48	12	41 0		8 10	
42 0	19	49	15	42 0		8 3	
43 0	4	50	22	43 0		7 4	
43 6	1	51	4	43 6		9 0	
		52	2				
	120		120				
Average	38s. 8d.		47s. 4d.			8s. 8d.	

ENGINEERING TURNERS

Time rates excluding 12½ per cent. bonus and war wage (26s. 6d.)

General movement				Mean increase on 1914 rate			
July 1914		Jan. 1920					
Rate	No. of towns	Rate	No. of towns	1914 rate		Increase	
s.		s.		s.		s. d.	
27	1	37	2	27		16 0	
28	6	38	2	28		15 3	
30	8	41	3	30		12 0	
31	3	42	18	31		16 4	
32	15	43	28	32		11 8	
33	8	44	20	33		11 5	
34	18	45	24	34		9 6	
35	17	46	50	35		10 6	
36	20	47	12	36		8 1	
37	24	48	5	37		8 1	
38	26	49	6	38		8 0	
39	18	50	10	39		7 5	
40	20	51	5	40		8 1	
41	1	52	3	41		11 6	
42	1	54	1	42		7 0	
43	1			43		7 6	
45	2			45		5 4	
	189		189				
Average	36s.		45s. 2d.			9s. 2d.	

The iron moulders, though they had received the same advances as engineers, struck for a further increase in September 1919 ; after four months they accepted the 5s. increase given in December 1919 to the whole of the engineering and ship-building trades.

The general results of the changes may be estimated as follows :

TABLE XLIII

SUMMARY OF CHANGES IN ENGINEERS' AND SHIPBUILDERS' TIME WAGES.
CHANGE IN TIME RATES—APPROXIMATE AVERAGE

July	Fitters and turners	Labourers	Platers
1914	100	100	100
1915	110	—	—
1916	111	—	—
1917	134	154	130
1918	173	213	169
1919	199	255	193
1920	231	309	223

The time rates of platers, rivetters, &c., are shown for the principal districts in March 1915 and January 1920 in the table on p. 132. To those in 1920 should be added the war wage of 26s. 6d. and the $12\frac{1}{2}$ per cent. on earnings, and by July 1920 another 6s., carrying also $12\frac{1}{2}$ per cent., should be added.

We cannot compute the percentage changes in piece earn-ings, for we do not know the average earnings in 1914 nor whether facilities for earning have changed. The general additions since 1914 have been 25 per cent. on rates ; 26s. 6d. flat weekly war wage ; and, on the total so computed, $7\frac{1}{2}$ per cent. together with a compensation for shorter weekly hours. Thus, 40s. and 50s. in 1914 would have become 82s. 3d. and 95s. 8d. respectively. Further advances have been given in some cases.

Wages regulated by Sliding Scales. Pig-iron Manufacture. The wages of men employed in the manufacture of pig-iron (blast-furnace men) and of iron and steel generally are (with the exception in most cases of bricklayers, blacksmiths, main-tenance-men, and labourers) regulated by sliding-scale arrange-

K 2

TABLE XLIV

TIME RATES OF BOILER-MAKERS AND SHIPBUILDERS ON NEW WORK[1] IN CERTAIN DISTRICTS EXCLUSIVE OF WAR WAGE (26s. 6d.) AND 12½ PER CENT. BONUS IN 1920

	Angle-iron smiths and heavy platers		Light platers		Riveters and caulkers		Holders up	
	Mar. 1915 (s. d.)	Jan. 1920 (s. d.)	Mar. 1915 (s. d.)	Jan. 1920 (s. d.)	Mar. 1915 (s. d.)	Jan. 1920 (s. d.)	Mar. 1915 (s. d.)	Jan. 1920 (s. d.)
London								
Boilershops	47 0	54 0	47 0	54 0	40 6	47 6	35 0	42 6
Tees								
Boilershops	42 6	51 6	40 6	49 6	40 0	49 0	33 0	42 0
Tyne								
Shipyards	39 0	46 0	—	46 0	37 0	44 0	31 6	38 6
Hull								
Boilershops	43 0[2]	51 0[2]	42 0	50 0	37 0	45 6	31 6	39 6
Shipyards	43 6[2]	50 6[2]	42 6	49 6	37 6	44 6	32 6	39 6
Barrow-in-Furness								
Boilershops	43 6[3]	49 3	—	49 3	38 3	46 3	32 0	40 0
Shipyards	41 10[3]	46 8	39 9	46 8	37 6	44 6	32 0	40 0
Birkenhead								
Boilershops	42 6[4]	49 6	—	—	36 6	45 6	30 6	39 6
Shipyards	45 0[4]	50 0	—	—	37 0	54 0	31 6	38 6
Liverpool								
Boilershops	44 0[4]	49 6	42 0	49 6	38 0	45 6	32 0	39 6
Shipyards	42 0	50 0	42 0	50 0	38 0	54 0	32 0	38 6
Clyde								
Boilershops (north side)	48 9	55 0[5]	47 4½	50 6	46 1½	48 4	35 3	40 6
Shipyards	—	—	38 3 to 42 9	46 1	38 3	46 1	30 4½	40 6
Belfast								
Boilershops	47 6	54 10¾	47 6	54 10¾	42 0	50 0	34 0	38 6
Shipyards	42 6	50 6	42 6	50 6	40 0	48 3	34 0	—

[1] Repair work is paid at a higher rate.   [2] Heavy platers 1s. less.   [3] Heavy platers 2s. 1d. less in 1915. The rates here stated are for 47 hours.
[4] Heavy platers 2s. less in 1915.   [5] The Clyde rates in 1920 are per hour.

ments by which rates are increased or diminished by so many pence per ton of output or a certain percentage on a standard rate—when the ascertained average price of the finished product in the past two, three, or four months has risen or fallen by certain amounts.[1]

An idea of the number of men affected by these arrangements may be obtained from the following table, which is based on the *Labour Gazette* account of wage changes during the first twelve months of the War.

Ironstone mining	
Lincs., Leicestershire, Northants	3,700
Iron-ore mining	
Cumberland	5,000
Blast-furnace men	
Cleveland and Durham	5,500
South Wales and Monmouth	1,250
West Cumberland	1,400
South Staffordshire	1,000
North Staffordshire	600
West Scotland	2,500
Iron and steel manufacture.	
Northumberland, Durham, and Cleveland	
Puddlers and millmen	3,400
Consett, Jarrow, and Newburn [2]	
Steel millmen	1,200
Barrow-in-Furness	
Rail millmen, &c.	750
Midlands and South Lancs., and South Yorks.	
Puddlers and millmen	20,000
Certain firms in England and Wales	
Steel melters, pitmen, &c.	2,400
South Wales and Monmouth	
Iron and steel workers and mechanics	5,000
West Scotland	
Steel millmen, engine men, &c.	4,600
Iron puddlers and millmen	3,000

The list (which includes 62,000 workers) is not complete, but includes all the principal cases except certain firms of steel-sheet-makers in England and Wales, whose movements follow

---

[1] Sliding scales were formerly also prevalent in coal mining, but had been given up in most districts prior to the War.

[2] These places are in the neighbourhood of Newcastle-on-Tyne.

those of the Midlands Iron and Steel Board. In the sequel no account is given of the four groups where the numbers affected are printed in italics; for the remaining twelve groups, all changes from July 1914 till after the end of the War are shown in the tables which follow.

In the pig-iron trade the very large majority of the employees are in receipt of time rates of wages per shift worked, but in addition a considerable number get a bonus on the output of the furnace. In 1920 it is stated that in the case of over 80 per cent. of the men the amount of the time wage is regulated by sliding scales based on the price of iron; and this percentage tends to increase owing to the extension of the scale to classes hitherto outside its scope. The chief exceptions to its application in 1920 were platelayers, sailor men, engineers, bricklayers, and their labourers, and other men engaged on repairs or maintenance of plant.

The general movements of the sliding scales for blast-furnace men are shown in the following table :

TABLE XLV

PIG-IRON MANUFACTURE—BLAST-FURNACE MEN. SLIDING-SCALE RATES EXPRESSED AS PERCENTAGES OF LEVELS IN JULY 1914

	Cleveland and Durham	West Cumberland	South Staffs.	South Wales	West Scotland
July 1914	100	100	100	100	100
„ 1915	108	135	107	102	110
„ 1916	131	155	159	133	139
„ 1917	144	155	180	148	151
„ 1918	157	163	195	159	151
„ 1919	192	220	220	173	159
Oct. 1919	208	245	256	185	159

The divergence in the rates of increase is very striking, and it is not explained by the various bonuses and war wages awarded at various dates, of which an account is given in the following paragraphs.

Pig-iron Manufacture. War Bonuses and War Wages. In Cleveland and Durham about 5d. a shift was granted on

TABLE XLVI

PIG-IRON MANUFACTURE. BLAST-FURNACE MEN
HEIGHT OF SLIDING SCALES IN RELATION TO STANDARD 100

Date of standard	Cleveland and Durham 1879	West Cumberland 1889	South Wales 1895	South Stafford 1908	West Scotland[1] 1889
1914 July	+23¾	+25	+27¾	+2½	+22½
Aug.	,,	,,	,,	0	,,
Oct.	24	29¾	27	,,	,,
Dec.	,,	,,	,,	5	,,
1915 Jan.	23¼	30¾	20½	,,	,,
Feb.	,,	,,	,,	7½	25
Apr.	25¾	53½	22¾	,,	,,
May	,,	,,	,,	,,	35
June	,,	,,	,,	10	,,
July	33¼	68¾	30	,,	,,
Aug.	,,	,,	,,	17½	40
Oct.	40	,,	40½	27½	,,
Dec.	,,	,,	,,	37½	,,
1916 Jan.	44	84¼	45	,,	,,
Feb.	,,	,,	,,	45	55
Mar.	,,	,,	,,	,,	,,
Apr.	51	93¾	,,	55	,,
May	,,	,,	,,	,,	70
June	,,	,,	60	62½	,,
July	61¾	,,	70¼	,,	,,
Aug.	,,	,,	,,	70	,,
Oct.	69¾	,,	77¼	72½	85
Dec.	,,	,,	,,	77½	,,
1917 Jan.	71¼	,,	86	,,	,,
Feb.	,,	,,	,,	80	,,
Apr.	72	,,	87½	82½	,,
June	,,	,,	,,	85	,,
July	78	,,	89½	,,	,,
Oct.	79½	,,	,,	,,	,,
1918 Jan.	96½	104¼	91	,,	,,
Feb.	,,	,,	,,	100	,,
Apr.	95¼	,,	99½	,,	,,
July	94¾	,,	103	,,	,,
Oct.	108½	,,	103½	102½	,,
Dec.	,,	,,	,,	107½	,,
1919 Jan.	108	,,	104½	,,	,,
Apr.	115	113¾	106	117½	,,
June	,,	,,	,,	125	,,
July	137¼	174½	121½	,,	95
Aug.	,,	,,	,,	152½	,,
Oct.	158	206	136½	162½	,,
Nov.	,,	New basis	,,	,,	110
Dec.	,,	,,	,,	170	,,

[1] These percentages apply to Lanarkshire ; for Ayrshire add 5.

February 28, 1915 ; this was raised to about 1s. on the average in April 1917. A war wage of 1s. 6d. per shift was granted in August 1918. Both continued to October 1919.

In West Cumberland the first war bonus was 4d. per shift in December 1916 and was increased to about 11d. in July 1917, and to 1s. 5d. in December 1917 in lieu of the general increase to munition workers. A war wage of 1s. per shift was added in August 1918 and dropped in July 1919.

In South Wales a bonus of 2s. or 3s. weekly was granted in March 1915 and was increased to about 5s. in March 1916. From October 1917 and January 1918 the time- and piece-workers received the munition workers' bonus of 12½ per cent. or 7½ per cent. on earnings ; these were gradually merged in increases of rates.

In South Staffordshire a weekly bonus of 3s. was given in March 1915, reduced to 1s. 6d. in February, and cancelled in April 1916. A bonus of 1s. per shift in November 1917 (time-workers) and in January 1918 (piece-workers) was given in lieu of the general munition workers' bonus, and a further 1s. was added in August 1918 ; both were merged in sliding-scale increases by the end of June 1919.

In West Scotland a bonus of 6d. per day was granted in March 1915 and also 10d. per shift in August 1917. Additions of 2s. as in South Staffordshire were given in 1917–18, and a further 5d. in December 1918. The total increases were 3s. 9d. a shift.

Iron and Steel Manufacture. In the iron and steel manufacture the workpeople can be divided into four main groups, viz. (1) straight time-workers, (2) time and bonus men, (3) time and tonnage men, (4) straight tonnage men.

Men in group (4) have received the 7½ per cent. bonus granted in January 1918 to piece-workers, and they are understood to number about 30 per cent. of the total employed though the proportion varies considerably in different districts. Men in groups (1), (2), and (3) were regarded as time-workers and received the 12½ per cent. bonus granted in the autumn of 1917 to time-workers. In the majority of cases the tonnage bonus of a part-datal and part-tonnage man represents a small proportion of his total earnings. It is estimated that outside the Sheffield area (which is very largely non-scale) approximately 80 per cent. of the men in the iron and steel trades have their wages regulated by sliding scales. The chief occupations in the non-scale group are engineers and other mechanics and their labourers, enginemen, cranemen, and other steam service men, and a considerable number of unskilled labourers largely employed in melting shops.

TABLE XLVII

IRON AND STEEL MANUFACTURE

Sliding-scale rates expressed as percentages of their levels in July 1914 [1]

	Northumberland, Durham, and Cleveland	Consett (Durham)	Midlands	Certain firms of steel workers	South Wales	West Scotland	
	Iron millmen	Steel millmen	Iron millmen	Basic process	Iron and Steel workers	Iron millmen	Steel workers
July 1914	100	100	100	100	100	100	100
„ 1915	107½	107	107	100	102	107½	139
„ 1916	150	128	158	122	133	162½	156
„ 1917	167½	141	180	141	148	180	161
„ 1918	182½	157	195	155	159	192½	166
„ 1919	247½	174	220	163	173	247½	215
„ 1920	287½	250	307	224	206	295	288
Aug. 1920	287½	250	341	246	206	327½	297

In addition to these charges there were bonuses in all districts (see pp. 142–5). Most of them were merged in subsequent increases in the scale rates, but there remained in 1920 10d. a shift in South Wales. The steel workers in West Scotland received the same weekly increases as engineers during part of 1917 and 1918 while the sliding scale changed little. Even when all bonuses are included the changes vary considerably from district to district and it is not practicable to compute the average movement.

[1] Puddlers generally received an increase of 3d. per ton produced for each 2½ per cent. on the sliding scale.

Mr. M. S. Birkett ('The Iron and Steel Trades during the War', *Statistical Journal*, 1920, pp. 368, 374–5) calls attention to the circumstances affecting these wages. In November 1917 it was agreed that the prices of commercial steel (on which wage rates depend) should remain for the future unaltered, the Government paying a subsidy on production. This control continued till the beginning of 1919. Wages did not, however, remain stationary for long, partly because after a time in some districts (e. g. West Scotland) the subsidies were included in the basic rates, and partly because the award to munition workers in October 1917 and January 1918 (see p. 136) led to a claim on the part of the skilled workers which was settled as follows : ' Workers who had received no more than 20s. advance obtained the advance of 12½ per cent. on their earnings, but in the case of workers who had received War advances in excess of 20s., the excess was merged in the 12½ per cent.' This advance, which took place early in 1918, was rapidly merged in increases under the sliding scale, so that its effect is only to antedate the changes shown in the tables (pp. 140–3) in 1918 or 1919.

It is evident that these data are not sufficient to allow a computation of the change of earnings. Mr. Birkett states that the average weekly earnings of 100,000 employees in the iron and steel trades were 85s. 5d. in December 1919. At the date of the wage census (1906) a similar computation would have given about 36s. 6d. ; by 1914 prices of iron and steel had risen about 10 per cent. and average earnings were probably about 40s. ; this suggests that the increase from 1914 to the end of 1919 was only 115 per cent., which is less than that indicated by the lists.

Early in 1919 hours in pig-iron and iron and steel manufacture were reduced to a uniform 8 per shift. Formerly the shifts had been 12 or 8 hours. Weekly time wages remained unchanged (see note on pp. 145–7). The price per ton on which puddlers' piece earnings depend was raised to 13s. 6d. in the Midlands, North-eastern Counties, and West Scotland from (usually) 9s., and the existing percentages above standard of millmen's wages were applied to this new rate. As a result the

wages earned *per ton* by puddlers in the Midlands rose from
9s. 9d. in July 1914 to 21s. 11d. in June 1919 and to 47s. 3d. in
August 1920 (but see p. 147). The price of pig-iron according
to the *Economist* was 51s. 3d., 160s., and 217s. 6d. respectively
at these dates.

Before the War and up to September 1917 the movement
of earnings of Cleveland ironstone miners followed those of the
Cleveland blast-furnace men's sliding scale; from September
1917 to at least the summer of 1920 they were subject instead
to the same changes as those of coal miners; these changes
were applied to ironstone mines operated by Companies which
also operated coal mines.

CLEVELAND. IRONSTONE MINING

Relation to Standard 1879 = 100

1914 July	$+29\frac{1}{2}$	1916 Jan.	$+50$	1918 June	$+105 + 3s.$ day or shift.
Oct.	$+29\frac{3}{4}$	April	$+60$	1919 Jan.	$+105 + 5s.$,, ,,
1915 Jan.	$+29$	July	$+71\frac{3}{4}$	1920 Mar.	$+105\%$ on standard.
Apr.	$+31\frac{1}{2}$	Oct.	$+82$		$+5s.$ day or shift
May	$+46\frac{1}{2}$				$+20\%$ on gross earnings,
		1917 Jan.	$+84\frac{1}{2}$		exclusive of 5s.
		Apr.	$+95\frac{1}{4}$		
		July	$+105$		
		Sept.	$+1s.$ 6d. day or shift		

July 1919, piece rates raised 8 per cent. to compensate for reduction of shift
to seven hours.

TABLE XLVIII

IRON AND STEEL MANUFACTURE

		Midlands		Northumberland, Durham, and Cleveland		West Scotland	
		Iron puddlers	Iron millmen	Puddlers	Millmen [2]	Iron puddlers	Iron millmen
		Per ton [1]	Standard of 1908	Per ton	Standard	Per ton [3]	Standard
		s. d		s. d.		s. d.	
1914	July	9 9	+2½	8 9	−2½	9 0	0
	Aug.	9 6	0	,,	,,	,,	,,
	Nov.	,,	,,	9 0	0	9 3	+2½
	Dec.	10 0	5	,,	,,	,,	,,
1915	Feb.	10 3	7½	,,	,,	9 6	5
	May	,,	,,	9 6	5	9 9	7½
	June	10 6	10	,,	,,	,,	,,
	Aug.	11 3	17½	10 0	10	10 3	12½
	Sept.	,,	,,	11 0	20	11 0	20
	Oct.	12 3	27½	,,	,,	,,	,,
	Nov.	,,	,,	,,	,,	11 9	27½
	Dec.	13 3	37½	,,	,,	,,	,,
1916	Jan.	,,	,,	11 9	27½	12 9	37½
	Feb.	14 0	45	,,	,,	,,	,,
	Mar.	,,	,,	12 9	37½	13 9	47½
	Apr.	15 0	55	,,	,,	,,	,,
	May	,,	,,	13 6	45	14 6	55
	June	15 9	62½	,,	,,	,,	,,
	July	,,	,,	13 9	47½	15 3	62½
	Aug.	16 6	70	,,	,,	,,	,,
	Oct.	16 9	72½	14 3	52½	15 9	67½
	Nov.	,,	,,	14 9	57½	16 0	70
	Dec.	17 3	77½	,,	,,	,,	,,
1917	Jan.	,,	,,	15 3	62½	16 6	75
	Feb.	17 6	80	,,	,,	,,	,,
	Apr.	17 9	82½	15 6	65	16 9	77½
	June	18 0	85	,,	,,	,,	,,
	July	,,	,,	,,	,,	17 0	80
	Oct.	,,	,,	15 9	67½	,,	,,
	Dec.	,,	,,	,,	,,	18 0	90

[1] Inclusive of bonus of 6d. per ton till February 1919.

[2] In some firms the rates for millmen were 2½ per cent. above those shown here till March 1919, when some levelling up took place.

[3] Plus 1d. per heat till March 1919.

TABLE XLVIII

IRON AND STEEL MANUFACTURE

		South Wales and Monmouth Iron and steel workers and mechanics Standard of 1895	Consett, Jarrow, and Newburn (Durham) Steel millmen Standard[1]	West Scotland Steel millmen, enginemen, &c. In relation to level of 1905	Certain firms in England and Scotland Steel melters, pitmen, &c. Standard of 1905
1914	July	+27¾	+15	+2½	+13¾[2]
	Aug.	,,	,,	0	11¼
	Oct.	27	12½	10	,,
	Nov.	,,	,,	,,	8¾
1915	Jan.	20½	,,	,,	,,
	Feb.	,,	,,	12½	10
	Mar.	,,	,,	22½	,,
	Apr.	22¾	15	30	,,
	May	,,	,,	35	13¾
	July	30	22½	42½	,,
	Aug.	,,	,,	,,	17½
	Oct.	40½	27½	45	,,
	Nov.	,,	,,	,,	23¾
	Dec.	,,	,,	47½	,,
1916	Jan.	45	32½	50	,,
	Feb.	,,	,,	65	31¼
	Mar.	,,	,,	70	,,
	Apr.	,,	37½	72½	,,
	May	,,	,,	80	38¾
	June	60	,,	60	,,
	July	70¼	47½	,,	,,
	Aug.	,,	,,	,,	47½
	Oct.	77¼	55	,,	,,
	Nov.	,,	,,	,,	52½
	Dec.	,,	,,	,,	,,
1917	Jan.	86	60	,,	,,
	Feb.	,,	,,	,,	57½
	Apr.	87½	62½	,,	,,
	May	,,	,,	,,	60
	June	,,	,,	65	,,
	July	89½	,,	,,	,,
	Aug.	,,	,,	,,	58¾
	Dec.	,,	,,	,,	63¾

[1] i.e. the Consett standard. The percentage changes were the same in 1914–20 in the three districts.

[2] The standard here used is for men on the basic process. That for the acid process shows the same changes starting 25 per cent. lower and finishing at +155 per cent.

TABLE XLVIII (*continued*)—IRON AND STEEL MANUFACTURE

		Midlands		Northumberland, Durham, and Cleveland		West Scotland	
		Iron puddlers	Iron millmen	Puddlers	Millmen[2]	Iron puddlers	Iron millmen
		Per ton[1]	Standard of 1908	Per ton	Standard	Per ton[3]	Standard
		s. d.		s. d.		s. d.	
1918	Jan	18 0	85	16 9	77½	18 3	92½
	Feb.	19 6	100	,,	,,	,,	,,
	May	,,	,,	17 0	80	,,	,,
	Sept.	,,	,,	17 6	85	18 9	97½
	Oct.	19 9	102½	,,	,,	,,	,,
	Dec.	20 3	107½	18 3	92½	19 3	102½
1919	Jan.	,,	,,	18 6	95	19 6	105
	Feb.	New basis 13/6+107½%	,,	New basis ,,	,,	New basis ,,	,,
	Mar.	,,	,,	13/6+110%	—	13/6+115%	115
	Apr.	,,	117½	,,		,,	
	June	125		125		125	
	July	,,		142½		147½	
	Aug.	152½		,,		,,	
	Sept.	,,		147½		,,	
	Oct.	162½		,,		,,	
	Dec.	170		155		155	
1920	Feb.	175		157½		157½	
	Mar.	,,		167½		175	
	Apr.	190		,,		,,	
	May	,,		187½		195	
	June	215		,,		,,	
	Aug.	250		217½		227½	
	Sept.	,,		,,		242½	

Notes on the Iron and Steel Sliding Scales

Midlands. Part of the advances October to December 1915 replaced a bonus of 1*s.* to 4*s.* granted in March 1915, and part of the advance of February 1918 replaced the munition workers' bonus in December 1917 and January 1918 ; these bonuses are not shown in the table.

Northumberland, Durham, and Cleveland. The rises in

[1] Inclusive of bonus of 6*d*, per ton till February 1919.

[2] In some firms the rates for millmen were 2½ per cent. above those shown here till March 1919, when some levelling up took place.

[3] Plus 1*d*. per heat till March 1919.

TABLE XLVIII (*continued*)—IRON AND STEEL MANUFACTURE

	South Wales and Monmouth Iron and steel workers and mechanics Standard of 1895	Consett, Jarrow, and Newburn (Durham) Steel millmen Standard[1]	West Scotland Steel millmen, enginemen, &c. In relation to level of 1905	Certain firms in England and Scotland Steel melters, pitmen, &c. Standard of 1905
1918 Jan.	91	67½	70	63¾
Feb.	,,	,,	,,	67½
Apr.	99½	75	,,	,,
May	,,	,,	,,	76¼
July	103	80	,,	,,
Aug.	,,	,,	,,	77½
Oct.	103½	,,	,,	,,
Nov.	,,	,,	,,	76¼
Dec.	,,	,,	75	,,
1919 Jan.	104½	82½	,,	,,
Feb.	,,	,,	,,	82½
Mar.	,,	,,	85	,,
Apr.	106	87½	,,	,,
May	,,	,,	,,	83¾
July	121½	100	120	,,
Aug.	,,	,,	,,	103¾
Sept.	,,	,,	127½	,,
Oct.	136½	125	132½	,,
Nov.	,,	,,	,,	127½
1920 Jan.	136	140	142½	,,
Feb.	,,	,,	,,	133¾
Apr.	145¼	157½	155	,,
May	,,	,,	165	155
June	,,	,,	185	,,
July	178	187½	195	,,
Aug.	,,	—	205	180

January and May 1918 replaced the munition workers' bonus of October 1917 and January 1918. These workers also received war bonuses as granted to steel melters, &c. (p. 144).

West Scotland. Iron puddlers and millmen. The rise in December 1917 was to compensate for the loss in earnings due to the Government's subsidy on pig-iron, in consequence of which its actual selling value was greater than the value on which the sliding scale was based. This increase was finally merged in the

[1] i. e. the Consett standard. The percentage changes were the same in 1914–20 in the three districts.

sliding scale in September 1919. It and an equivalent 1s.
per shift to the puddlers are included in the table.

South Wales and Monmouth. In March 1915 a war bonus
was given thus : 1s. weekly to those earning under 15s., 2s.
from 15s. to 20s., 3s. from 20s. to 30s., and 2s. from 30s. to 40s.
In March 1916 this was increased as a time-keeping bonus to
5s. for those earning under 50s., while earnings between 50s.
and 55s. were made up to 55s. This continued till at least
July 1920 except that it was altered to 10d. a day in February
1919. The 55s. limit was based throughout on the standard
rate + 45 per cent., the level in March 1916.

The general munitions workers' bonus of 12½ per cent. on
earnings to time-workers and 7½ per cent. to piece-workers in
the autumn of 1917 and January 1918 was extended to these
workers but is not included in the table. It was gradually
merged in the sliding-scale changes.

Consett, Jarrow, and Newburn. A bonus of 12½ per cent. on
earnings was given to time-workers in October 1917 and of 7½
per cent. to piece-workers in January 1918 which are not
shown in the table ; they were gradually merged in the sliding-
scale increases.

West Scotland. Steel millmen, gas-producer men, charge
wheelers, enginemen, cranemen, and firemen have their wages
regulated by the sliding scale. Engineers', electricians', and
labourers' wages usually follow the general engineering awards.
During part of 1917 and the whole of 1918, when the price of
steel was controlled, the sliding scale remained nearly unchanged,
the men whose wages depended on it receiving the same flat
increases, and also the bonus of 7½ per cent. on piece earnings
(Jan. 1918) or of 12½ per cent. on time earnings (Oct. 1917),
as engineers (see p. 126).

Steel melters, pitmen, &c. In March 1915 all men were
granted a bonus of 4s. weekly if earning 20s. to 30s. a week,
3s. from 30s. to 40s., and 2s. from 40s. to 50s.; this was merged
into scale increases. Half-scale men received a further 3s. in
July 1916, also merged ; they also received 6s. in April 1917,
3s. in August 1917, 5s. in December 1917, 3s. 6d. in August

1918, and 5s. in December 1918, 22s. 6d. in all which was not merged.

In all cases the 12½ per cent. and 7½ per cent. munition workers' increase of October 1917 and January 1918 were subsequently merged in the scale increases.

NOTE [1]

Adoption of the Eight-hour Shift in the Pig-iron Trade and its effect on Wages

In some of the principal districts, including Cleveland, Cumberland, North Lancashire, and Lincolnshire, eight-hour shifts were worked at blast furnaces before the War. In some districts, however, including South Staffs., Northants, South Wales, and the West of Scotland, the twelve-hour shift system was in operation. In the early part of 1919 the length of the shift was reduced to eight hours in all the districts where twelve hours had previously been worked. In South Staffs. and Northants the change from twelve to eight hours was made without any alteration in weekly earnings. In South Wales the change was accompanied by the adoption of a scale of 'contributions' similar to that adopted in the mills governed by the Midland Iron and Steel Conciliation Board (see p. 134). In the West of Scotland no reduction in earnings took place, but the men undertook additional duties in order to reduce the number of extra men required to work the third shift.

Adoption of the Eight-hour Shift in the Manufactured Iron and Steel Trade and its effect on Weekly Wages

In the early part of 1919 it was agreed between employers and workpeople in the manufactured iron and steel trade to adopt the eight-hour shift system instead of the twelve-hour shift previously worked (i. e. to work three shifts of eight hours each instead of two shifts of twelve hours each). In order to recoup the employers for the extra cost involved in providing

[1] For this note I am indebted to the courtesy of the Intelligence and Statistics Department of the Ministry of Labour.

additional labour for the third shift, it was agreed generally that a scale of contributions towards this cost should be adopted whereby the lower-paid men contributed nothing (and so received the same earnings for eight hours' work as for the twelve formerly worked) and the higher-paid men contributed varying amounts according to earnings up to a maximum of $33\frac{1}{3}$ per cent. of their earnings. In the iron and steel mills in the North of England, in melting shops in England and Scotland, and in *steel* mills in the West of Scotland, the following method of adjusting rates and scales of contributions towards the extra cost was adopted.

The average base earnings for the normal working week were ascertained over an average of the two periods of six months each ended June 30, 1913, and June 30, 1918. A graduated percentage reduction was arranged starting with no reduction on average base earnings of 50s. per week and ranging up to a reduction of $33\frac{1}{3}$ per cent. on average base earnings of £6 a week.

Thus, men with weekly base earnings of 50s. or under contributed nothing and their earnings remained the same for the eight hours as for the twelve hours. Men with weekly base earnings of over 50s. and under 51s. had their base earnings reduced by 0·475 per cent.; weekly base earnings over 51s. and under 52s. were reduced by a further 0·475 per cent. (i. e. by 0·950 per cent.) and so on, till men with base earnings of 119s. and under 120s. per week contributed 33·25 per cent. of their base earnings, and all men with weekly base earnings over 120s. contributed the full $33\frac{1}{3}$ per cent. In the Midlands and in South Wales a similar scale of contributions towards the extra cost involved in providing for the third shift was adopted. Men with weekly earnings under £4 17s. 6d. contributed nothing, those with earnings of £4 19s. 6d. had a reduction in earnings of 0·5 per cent., and a further reduction of 0·5 per cent. was made for each additional 2s. earned, up to £11 9s. 6d. per week when 33 per cent. reduction was enforced and the full $33\frac{1}{3}$ per cent. was deducted when the earnings reached £11 11s. 6d. per week. In the West of Scotland iron mills no scale of contributions was adopted, but the change over from twelve to eight hours was accompanied by a revision of base rates which were, and are still, only *provisionally* fixed.

These scales of contributions were also adopted in puddling forges in the North of England and the Midlands, but the change was accompanied by an alteration in the method of payment.   Under the twelve-hour shift system puddlers had a base rate of 9s. per ton, with an average rise or fall of 3d. per ton for every 5s. rise or fall in the ascertained selling price of iron above a standard price.   On the adoption of the eight-hour shift a new base rate of 13s. 6d. per ton was established (upon which the current scale percentage was paid) with a rise or fall of 2½ per cent. on this base for each 5s. rise or fall in the ascertained selling price of iron.   The new base rate of 13s. 6d. cancelled all previous allowances (viz. Monday working money, prize money, level hand money, firing, and fettling) and also merged any balance of the 12½ per cent. bonus on earnings as far as underhand puddlers were concerned.

From these notes it will be seen that for men engaged in the manufacture of iron and steel the change from twelve to eight hours per shift resulted, generally, in the highest-paid men suffering a reduction in earnings up to 33⅓ per cent.   In the case of medium-paid men a reduction in earnings, according to the scale, was made, but this was accompanied by all-round promotions in order to provide the necessary skilled labour for the third shift.   The reduction in earnings was, therefore, largely counterbalanced by the increase in wages consequent upon promotions.   In the case of the lower-paid men little or no reduction was made, and in many cases earnings were actually increased owing to the promotions necessary to provide semi-skilled labour for the third shift.

CHAPTER X

COAL MINES

Percentage movements till 1917. Subsequent increases and general averages.

THE movements of miners' wage prior to the War and till September 1917 took place by percentage changes on standard rates, the standards having been fixed in 1888 in Scotland and in the Forest of Dean, in 1879 in Northumberland and Durham,[1] and in 1911 in Yorkshire, Lancashire, and the Midlands. The changes in relation to these rates from July 1914 to February 1917 are shown in Table LI, and the resulting relations to the rates existing in July 1914 in Table LII. From July 1914 to May 1915 the changes were insignificant ; in May 1915 increases took place of different amounts in the different districts, which resulted in an average rise of about 12 per cent. During the next twelve months sporadic rises brought the general level in the summer of 1915 to about 27 per cent. above the pre-War level, and further increases brought the Northumberland rate to 47 per cent., and those in other principal districts to 32 to 36 per cent. up.

In September 1917 the movement by percentages was abandoned, a general increase of 1s. 6d. per diem was given to all men, and in June 1918 this was increased to 3s. As a result of the Coal Industry Commission of March 1919 a further increase of 2s. was awarded to take effect from January 1919. In March 1920 the miners claimed an increase of 3s. a shift, and an increase of 20 per cent. on the wages paid prior to September 1917 (with a minimum of 2s. a shift) was awarded.

In July 1919 the duration of a shift was reduced from eight hours to seven hours, and piece rates were raised so as to yield the same earnings as before the change. In January 1919 the hours of surface workers were reduced to 49 (having varied before from 51 to 58 or more), and in July 1919 they were

---

[1] In Durham for many years and in Northumberland since early in 1914 the percentage movements were determined by sliding-scales based on the selling-price of coal. The sliding-scale in South Wales was given up many years ago.

further reduced to 46½. The week's time wages were not altered in consequence of any alteration in hours.

It is very difficult to compute the effect on earnings of these changes. Two sets of tables were put in evidence to the Coal Industry Commission by the Controller of Coal Mines and by the Mining Association of Great Britain, which agree closely with each other. They show that the average pre-War earnings per shift of all employed were 6s. 6d., and in November 1918, 12s. 5d. or 12s. 6d. In 1918, however, the number of coal-getters had been reduced owing to enlistment to 33 per cent. of all workers underground from 41 per cent. before the War; if this reduction had not taken place, the general average would have been 12s. 8d. instead of 12s. 6d. Coal-getters' earnings had increased from 8s. 5d. to 16s. 4d. per shift. The tables show in detail the changes in different districts and for various classes of workers, and considerable variations appear, not readily explicable by the recorded changes in rates; but since earnings depend on output, and the changes in rates only make standards from which local rates and rates for various kinds of work are computed, it is not to be expected that exact agreement will be found between movements in rates and earnings.

TABLE XLIX

AVERAGE EARNINGS PER SHIFT OF ALL EMPLOYED IN COAL MINES

	Average in 1914	Per cent. increase in rates	Resulting Average Aug. 1917	Add bonus 3/– adults 1/6 boys 1917–18	Calculated Average Nov. 1918	Recorded Average Nov. 1918
	s. d.		s. d.	s. d.	s. d.	s. d.
Northumberland	6 2	47	9 1	3 2	12 3	12 4
Durham . .	6 3	32	8 3	3 2	11 5	11 8
Federated districts . .	6 6	32½	8 7	3 2	11 9	12 1
South Wales and Monmouth .	6 9	35	9 1	3 2	12 3	13 8
Forest of Dean .	5 4	33⅓	7 3	3 2	10 5	10 6
Scotland . .	6 9	36	9 2	3 2	12 4	13 2
All . . .	6 6	34	8 9	3 2	11 11	12 5
						(12 8)[1]

The bonus in 1917–18 was per diem, not per shift. At 5½ shifts weekly, 18s. gives 3s. 3d. a shift, not 3s.

[1] This sum is that which would have been reached if the number of coal-getters had borne the same proportion to all underground as before the war.

In the foregoing table the percentage changes are applied to the average earnings (shown in Table LIV) in each district, the increase in day earnings in September 1917 and June 1918 are added, and the totals are compared with the average earnings (shown in the same table) in November 1918. It is found that earnings had increased by 6*d.* per shift on the average more than the known changes show, this excess varying from 1*d.* in Northumberland to 1*s.* 5*d.* in South Wales.

The increase of 2*s.* per shift awarded in January 1919 brought the earnings to 14*s.* 8*d.*, and the 20 per cent. or 2*s.* increase in March 1920 may be estimated at bringing the average to 16*s.* 11*d.* per shift. Sir R. Horne, in the House of Commons, October 19, 1920, said that ' over the coalfields of this country that increase had worked out at a little over 12*s.* a week ', *The Times* report. He also said that in the second quarter of 1920 the general average earnings were at the rate of £226 per annum. At 16*s.* 11*d.* a shift this is equivalent to fifty weeks at $5\frac{1}{3}$ shifts weekly, which corresponds with the estimates here given.

The resulting changes in the average may be exhibited as follows :

TABLE L

APPROXIMATE ESTIMATE OF MOVEMENT OF AVERAGE EARNINGS IN COAL MINES IN GREAT BRITAIN [1]

July 1914	.	.	.	100
July 1915	.	.	.	115
July 1916	.	:	.	129
July 1917	.	.	.	136
July 1918	.	.	.	187 from rates, 195 from earnings [2]
July 1919	.	.	.	224
July 1920	.	.	.	260

[1] Sir Hugh Bell (*Contemporary Review*, December 1920). The average annual earnings of men employed by Messrs. Bell Bros. in collieries, ironstone mines, and limestone quarries (North Yorkshire and Durham) were, in 1914, £83 ; in 1915, £93 ; in 1916, £111 ; in 1917, £131 ; in 1918, £157 ; in 1919, £184 ; and in 1920 (estimated from figures up to September), £220 ; figures showing practically the same movement as those in the table.

[2] These figures are those which would have been reached if the number of coal-getters had borne the same proportion to all underground as before the War.

The changes thus reckoned should be compared with those in the cost of living exhibited on pp. 75 and 106. It is then seen that earnings had lagged in 1917, had passed the modified scale in 1918, and passed (but only by a few points) the official scale in 1920. At $5\frac{1}{2}$ shifts weekly, the week's earnings of all men averaged 36s. 3d., and of coal-getters, 46s. in 1914, and about 93s. and 115s. in 1918, if the above computation is correct. The higher earnings sometimes quoted are exceptional. A coal-getter appears to have averaged about 3s. an hour in July 1920.

The complications of these changes, and the question whether by the award of the Coal Industry Commission the miners were to receive wages which kept their standard of living at the level obtained in March 1919 or at the somewhat lower level of July 1914, explain in part the controversies which led to the miners' strike of October 1920. The basis of the miners' claim, however, was that they were entitled to a share of the high profits made on exported coal ; in the settlement it was arranged that changes in the immediate future should depend on output. The difficulties in February 1921 in arriving at a permanent basis arise from quite different circumstances ; during the War the method of giving national flat increases destroyed the relation between wages in the different districts, and the resulting losses in the worst-paying mines (e. g. in Somerset and in the Forest of Dean) were made good from a general pool of profits. The question was, what would happen to this pool and this arrangement when Government control was removed.

TABLE LI

INCREASE OF RATES IN THE PRINCIPAL COAL DISTRICTS

Percentage increases above Standards

Date of standard 100	Northumberland, 1879	Durham, 1879	Federated Districts,[1] 1911	South Wales and Monmouth, 1879	Forest of Dean, 1888	Scotland, 1888
1914						
July	50	57½	10	60	35	75
November	—	53¾	,,	··	,,	,·
December	—	,,	,,	,,	40	,,
1915						
January	47	,,	,,	,,	45	,,
April	48	·,	,,	,,	60 (Feb.)	,,
May	63	68¾	27·05	77½	,,	93¾
June	·,	,,	,,	,,	,,	106¼
August	65 [2]	,,	,,	96¼ [3]	·,	112½
October	83	,,	,,	,,	,,	,,
November	,,	75	,,	,,	,,	118¾
December	,,	,,	32·05	88¾	,,	,,
1916						
January	78	,,	,,	,,	,,	,,
February	,,	78¾	·,	,,	,,	,,
March	,,	,,	37·05	,,	,,	,,
April	90	,,	,,	,,	,,	125
May	,,	88¾	,,	,,	,,	,,
June	,,	.	40·38	111¼	,,	137½
July	112	,,	,,	,,	70	,,
August	,,	102½	,,	,,	,,	150
September	131	,,	,,	,,	80	,,
November	,,	107½	,,	,,	,,	,,
December	,,	,,	,,	133¾	,,	,,
1917						
January	120	,,	,,	,,	,,	··
February	,,	,,	45·5	,,	,,	,,

[1] The Federated Districts include Yorkshire, Lancashire, Cheshire, North Wales, and the Midland Counties except South Staffordshire, in which in these years the changes were the same. Cumberland also follows closely the same sequence.

[2] July.

[3] In July 1915 a new standard was adopted 50 per cent. above that of 1879, and subsequent changes are stated in the records in relation to this 1915 standard. In the table the numbers have been adjusted to the old standard. 5 per cent. on the new standard is equivalent to 7½ per cent. on the old.

TABLE LII

HEWERS' RATES EXPRESSED AS PERCENTAGES OF LEVELS IN JULY 1914

	Northumberland	Durham	Federated Districts	S. Wales and Monmouth	Forest of Dean	Scotland	Weighted Average
1914							
July . .	100	100	100	100	100	100	100
November .	,,	98	,,	,,	,,	,,	100
December .	,,	,,	,,	,,	104	,,	100
1915							
January .	98	,,	,,	,,	107	,,	100
February .	,,	,,	,,	,,	118½	,,	100
April . .	99	,,	,,	,,	,,	,,	100
May . .	109	107	115½	111	,,	111	112
June . .	,,	,,	,,	,,	,,	118	113
July . .	110	,,	,,	,,	,,	,,	113
August .	,,	,,	,,	122⅔	,,	121	116
October .	122	,,	,,	,,	,,	,,	117
November .	,,	111	,,	,,	,,	125	118
December .	,,	,,	120	118	,,	,,	119
1916							
January .	119	,,	,,	,,	,,	,,	119
February .	,,	114	,,	,,	,,	,,	119
March .	,,	,,	124½	,,	,,	,,	121
April . .	127	,,	,,	,,	,,	128	122
May . .	,,	120	,,	,,	,,	,,	123
June . .	,,	,,	127½	132	,,	136	128
July . .	141	,,	,,	,,	126	,,	129
August .	,,	129	,,	,,	,,	143	130
September	154	,,	,,	,,	133¼	,,	131
November .	,,	132	,,	,,	,,	,,	132
December .	,,	,,	,,	146	,,	,,	135
1917							
January .	147	,,	,,	,,	,,	,,	134
February .	,,	,,	132½	,,	,,	,,	136

In obtaining the averages in the last column the weights taken are proportional to the output of coal in the various districts in 1914, viz. Northumberland 5, Durham 17, Federated Districts (including Cumberland and South Staffordshire) 43, South Wales and Monmouth 21, Forest of Dean 1, Scotland 13.

TABLE LIII

STATEMENT FURNISHED BY THE CONTROLLER OF COAL MINES. EARNINGS IN 1913 AND 1918

Average Earnings per Shift in four weeks of November 1913, by Occupations and Districts

Occupation	Northumberland	Durham	Yorkshire	Lancs. and Cheshire	Midland Counties¹	S. Wales and Mon.	Scotland	Other Districts²	All Districts
	s. d.	s. d.	s. d.	s. d.	s. d.	s. d.	s. d.	s. d.	s. d.
UNDERGROUND WORKERS:									
Getters (Piece-work)	8 4	7 11	8 6	8 6	8 6	8 8	8 1	7 1	8 5
Putters, Hauliers, Trimmers, &c. „	6 4	7 0	5 11	6 4	5 2	6 9	7 0	4 3	6 6
Stonemen, Brushers, Rippers, &c. „	8 7	8 3	7 9	6 8	7 2	8 3	9 1	7 8	8 1
Getters, Putters, Stonemen, &c. (not distinguished) „	—	—	8 11	7 9	8 3	—	8 0	8 2	8 2
Deputies, Firemen, Examiners, &c. (Day-wage)	7 5	7 5	7 11	7 5	7 10	8 6	7 3	6 11	7 8
Mechanical Haulage :									
Men „	4 4	4 9	5 4	5 7	4 11	6 1	5 10	5 5	5 6
Boys „	2 9	2 10	3 4	2 11	3 2	3 11	3 4	3 2	3 1
Other Underground Workers	5 1	4 7	5 6	5 11	5 4	5 8	6 2	4 9	5 6
ALL UNDERGROUND WORKERS	6 8	6 7	7 2	6 6	7 0	7 4	7 8	6 6	7 1
SURFACE WORKERS :									
Enginemen	6 8	6 9	6 5	6 5	5 10	6 6	6 7	6 0	6 5
Pitheadmen	5 9	5 7	5 1	4 7	4 10	5 5	4 7	4 10	5 0
Persons on and about Screens :									
Men	4 6	4 8	4 7	4 2	4 3	5 5	4 0	4 2	4 6
Boys and Girls	2 1	2 3	2 2	2 2	2 5	2 6	2 1	2 0	2 2
Stokers and Boilermen	4 11	5 11	5 2	4 11	5 1	5 7	4 9	4 8	5 2
Mechanics, Joiners, Blacksmiths, &c.	5 10	5 9	4 7	5 2	4 11	5 10	5 2	4 11	5 4
Other Surface Workers	4 5	4 9	4 8	4 3	4 4	5 5	4 3	4 2	4 7
ALL SURFACE WORKERS	4 9	4 11	4 5	4 8	4 5	5 6	4 4	4 2	4 8
ALL WORKPEOPLE	6 3	6 3	6 6	6 0	6 5	7 3	6 11	5 11	6 7

¹ Including Derbyshire, Nottinghamshire, Leicestershire, Staffordshire, Shropshire, and Warwickshire.

² Including Cumberland, North Wales, Forest of Dean, Bristol, and Somerset.

TABLE LIV

Numbers returned, Shifts worked, and Average Earnings per head in four weeks in November 1918. (All Districts)

Occupation	Average Daily No. on Pay Rolls	Average No. of Shifts worked per head (4 weeks)[1]	Average Earnings per Head Whole Period (4 weeks)[1] £ s. d.	Per Shift s. d.
UNDERGROUND WORKERS :				
Getters (Piece-work)	139,120	19·1	15 11 2	16 4
Putters, Hauliers, Trimmers, &c. "	24,491	19·1	12 3 2	12 4
Stonemen, Brushers, Rippers, &c. "	29,113	20·4	15 13 9	15 4
Getters, Putters, Stonemen, &c. (not distinguished) "	26,409	19·1	14 15 6	15 5
Deputies, Firemen, Examiners, &c. (Day-wage)	14,682	24·6	17 14 4	14 5
Mechanical Haulage:				
Men	24,738	21·0	11 2 11	10 2
Boys "	17,483	20·8	6 14 3	6 6
Men and Boys (not distinguished) "	1,170	18·7	7 16 8	8 4
Other Underground Workers "	91,407	21·0	11 7 0	10 10
ALL UNDERGROUND WORKERS	368,613	20·2	13 11 9	13 6
SURFACE WORKERS :				
Enginemen	6,815	27·8	16 15 9	12 3
Pitheadmen	6,243	23·1	11 9 8	9 11
Persons on or about Screens :				
Men	15,099	20·9	10 5 4	9 10
Boys and Girls	15,479	20·6	5 6 8	5 2
Stokers and Boilermen	6,515	27·0	14 4 6	10 6
Mechanics, Joiners, Blacksmiths, &c.	16,515	24·2	12 15 0	10 7
Other Surface Workers	29,913	22·9	10 13 9	9 4
ALL SURFACE WORKERS	96,579	23·1	10 16 8	9 5
ALL WORKPEOPLE	465,192	20·8	13 0 4	12 6

[1] The number of shifts worked in November, and the total earnings, were affected by holidays taken in consequence of the Armistice.

TABLE LV

Percentage Increases in Average Earnings per Shift between November 1913 and November 1918

Occupation	Northumberland	Durham	Yorkshire	Lancs. and Cheshire	Midland Counties[1]	S. Wales and Mon.	Scotland	Other Districts[2]	All Districts
UNDERGROUND WORKERS:									
Getters (Piece-work)	101·0	98·9	97·1	85·4	85·4	102·9	92·9	97·7	94·0
Putters, Hauliers, Trimmers, &c. ,,	124·7	92·5	76·3	63·6	72·3	98·8	89·2	113·7	89·5
Stonemen, Brushers, Rippers, &c. ,,	107·8	88·7	94·7	86·7	97·8	85·0	84·8	81·9	88·8
Getters, Putters, Stonemen, &c. (not distinguished) ,,	—	—	88·5	85·1	87·0	—	101·1	108·6	88·7
Deputies, Firemen, Examiners, &c. ,, (Day-wage)	87·8	74·4	93·7	93·3	91·5	98·0	86·0	91·7	89·0
Mechanical Haulage:									
Men ,,	115·4	101·8	93·7	68·7	95·2	90·0	98·6	103·0	85·9
Boys ,,	127·3	117·6	107·5	105·7	115·4	91·1	95·1	134·2	110·8
Other Underground Workers ,,	101·6	96·4	89·2	84·7	90·6	105·8	105·5	117·5	96·9
ALL UNDERGROUND WORKERS[3]	98·8	92·3	89·5	91·5	83·7	100·0	90·2	98·7	90·5[3]
SURFACE WORKERS:									
Enginemen	95·0	73·8	103·9	79·2	89·2	93·5	84·6	84·9	87·0
Pitheadmen	85·3	79·4	119·7	103·6	91·8	115·4	94·4	105·0	98·3
Persons on and about Screens:									
Men	125·9	101·8	127·3	126·0	111·8	114·8	118·8	123·5	118·7
Boys and Girls	130·0	111·1	119·2	150·0	93·3	116·7	176·0	191·7	138·5
Stokers and Boilermen	111·7	81·7	114·3	101·7	96·8	111·9	107·0	107·1	103·2
Mechanics, Joiners, Blacksmiths, &c.	94·4	82·4	140·0	103·2	100·0	94·4	87·5	111·9	98·4
Other Surface Workers	115·1	93·0	116·1	98·0	94·1	109·2	105·9	120·0	101·9
ALL SURFACE WORKERS[3]	107·0	89·8	118·7	104·0	94·3	106·1	103·8	118·0	101·8[3]
ALL WORKPEOPLE	98·7	90·5	93·6	92·0	85·9	100·0	91·6	101·4	89·7[3]

[1] Including Derbyshire, Nottinghamshire, Leicestershire, Staffordshire, Shropshire, and Warwickshire.

[2] Cumberland, North Wales, Forest of Dean, Bristol, and Somerset.

[3] The percentage increases shown for all workpeople are, of course, affected by the changes which occurred between 1913 and 1918, in the relative proportions of different classes of workpeople employed.

Cmd. 361, p. 108

TABLE LVI

STATEMENT SUBMITTED ON BEHALF OF THE MINING ASSOCIATION OF GREAT BRITAIN. EARNINGS IN 1914 AND 1918

Average Earnings per Shift in 4 weeks in July 1914 and November 1918 at Collieries in the United Kingdom employing more than 50 Workmen

Average Wage per person per Shift

	Underground (Adults)		Underground (Youths and Boys)		Surface (Adults)		Surface (Youths and Boys)		Total	
	1914	1918	1914	1918	1914	1918	1914	1918	1914	1918
	s. d.	s. d.	s. d.	s. d.	s. d.	s. d.	s. d.	s. d.	s. d.	s. d.
Northumberland	7 4	14 9	3 7	7 4	5 2	10 0	2 1	5 1	6 6	12 1
Durham	7 2	13 7	2 11	6 7	5 6	10 3	2 6	5 5	6 3	12 5
Midland Counties (Notts. and Derby)	7 9	14 7	3 7	7 4	5 2	10 0	2 6	5 3	6 6	12 1
Leicestershire	6 9	14 7	3 8	7 0	4 8	9 8	2 2	4 4	5 11	12 5
Shropshire	6 2	11 8	3 0	5 8	4 4	9 2	1 6	4 0	5 9	9 6
Monmouth and South Wales	7 8	15 7	3 9	7 7	5 8	11 7	3 1	6 9	6 9	13 8
West Yorks.	7 11	14 5	3 6	7 2	5 0	11 2	2 3	5 2	6 6	12 2
North Wales	6 10	13 9	3 5	6 11	4 7	9 6	2 1	5 5	5 10	11 1
North Staffs.	7 3	13 8	3 6	6 7	4 9	9 3	2 5	5 1	5 11	10 8
Warwick	7 3	14 6	3 9	6 7	4 8	9 6	2 5	4 7	6 2	12 0
South Staffs. and East Worcester	6 0	12 6	2 9	6 0	4 3	9 2	2 0	4 9	4 11	9 10
Lancashire and Cheshire	7 3	13 5	3 7	6 11	4 1	9 9	2 4	4 11	6 1	11 3
Cumberland	7 6	15 10	3 6	7 11	4 11	10 8	2 1	5 5	6 2	13 0
Cannock Chase	7 3	13 10	2 11	6 3	4 8	9 0	2 9	5 2	6 2	11 4
South Yorks.	8 9	16 0	3 9	7 6	5 6	11 2	2 5	5 5	7 1	13 0
Somerset	5 2	11 6	3 0	6 5	4 2	9 5	1 8	3 9	4 9	10 7
Forest of Dean	5 10	11 8	3 3	7 2	4 7	9 2	2 2	5 1	5 4	10 6
Bristol	5 5	11 1	2 11	6 9	3 9	8 9	2 0	4 10	4 9	9 10
Notts. and Erewash	8 0	14 7	3 11	7 10	5 7	11 2	2 7	5 7	6 9	12 6
South Derby	7 6	14 4	3 3	6 7	4 7	9 9	1 9	3 11	6 3	12 0
Scotland	7 9	15 3	4 9	9 5	4 9	10 2	2 5	5 6	6 9	13 2
Average	7 7	14 8	3 7	7 4	5 2	10 6	2 5	5 5	6 6	12 5

CHAPTER XI

PRINTING

General levelling up of districts in 1919. Movements of average time rates, 1914–20. Detailed changes in selected towns.

THE following study is confined to the minimum time rates paid to men compositors on jobbing work or weekly news. Composing for evening news is generally paid at a slightly higher rate, while work for morning newspapers and night work are generally paid piece rates. The time rates are the most definite to observe, and no doubt piece rates and time rates for other than hand-setting move in sympathy with them.

Before the War there was no definite system governing the rates in the different towns, which ranged from 39s. in London to 25s. in Folkestone, but on the whole the larger the town the higher the rate. In May 1919 the towns of England and Wales, other than London, were grouped into six grades, the wages falling 3s. from each grade to the next, and subsequent wage-changes were made by adding a uniform sum to all rates, so that the 3s. intervals were preserved. The following table shows the grouping of the towns, grade by grade, in respect of the rates in March 1915. It is clear that a considerable process of levelling has taken place. Further, though the increases in six years have been actually the greater the higher the grade, the percentage increases are considerably the greater in the lower grades. The increase in the average of all compositors' time wages is therefore somewhat greater than that found from the study of selected towns.

A similar grading has taken place in Ireland but not in Scotland.[1]

[1] Grade 1 contains Liverpool and Manchester only. Grade 2 consists of Birmingham, Bradford, Bristol, Cardiff and Barry, Leeds, Newcastle, Rotherham and Sheffield, West Bromwich and Swansea. Grade 3 consists of 75 towns, mainly large or in populous districts. Grades 4, 5, 6 contain respectively 53, 63, and 72 towns, the smaller generally being in the lower grade, but towns in the Home Counties are placed relatively high. On the table, which depends on rates ascertainable in 1915, all grades 1 and 2 are included (except Barry), but only 41, 40, 30, and 15 towns respectively in the lower grades.

TABLE LVII

COMPOSITORS. MINIMUM TIME RATES, JOBBING, AND WEEKLY NEWS.
MARCH 1915 AND DATES SUBSEQUENT TO APRIL 1919

(In nearly all cases the rates were the same in July 1914 and March 1915)

Rates in March 1915	London	Grades arranges in 1919 1	2	3	4	5	6	Totals
s. d.								
39 0	1	—	—	—	—	—	—	1
38 6	—	1	—	—	—	—	—	1
38 0	—	1	—	—	—	—	—	1
37 6	—	—	1	—	—	—	—	1
37 0	—	—	2	1	—	—	—	3
36 6	—	—	1	4	—	—	—	5
36 0	—	—	3	4	—	—	—	7
35 6	—	—	—	1	—	—	—	1
35 0	—	—	2	6	2	—	—	10
34 6	—	—	1	1	—	—	—	2
34 0	—	—	—	12	10	1	—	23
33 6	—	—	—	—	2	—	—	2
33 0	—	—	—	4	4	1	—	9
32 6	—	—	—	5	2	1	—	8
32 0	—	—	—	2	14	5	—	21
31 6	—	—	—	—	1	—	—	1
31 0	—	—	—	1	3	1	—	5
30 0	—	—	—	—	2	8	3	13
29 6	—	—	—	—	—	—	1	1
29 3	—	—	—	—	—	1	—	1
29 0	—	—	—	—	—	3	1	4
28 0	—	—	—	—	—	6	4	10
27 6	—	—	—	—	—	1	—	1
27 0	—	—	—	—	—	1	2	3
26 0	—	—	—	—	—	1	2	3
25 0	—	—	—	—	—	—	2	2
Totals	1	2	10	41	40	30	15	139

	s. d.	s. d.	s. d.	s. d.	s. d.	s. d.	s. d.	s. d.
Average Mar. 1, 1915	39 0	38 3	36 1	34 3	32 8	29 11	27 9	32 5
Uniform rates								
May 1919	77 6[1]	75 0	72 0	69 0	66 0	63 0	60 0	
Nov. 1919		81 0	78 0	75 0	72 0	69 0	66 0	
Jan. 1920	85 0[2]	82 6	79 6	76 6	73 6	70 6	67 6	
June 1920	95 0	92 6	89 6	86 6	83 6	80 6	77 6	
June 1920, increase over average in Mar. 1915	56 0	54 3	53 5	52 2	50 10	50 7	49 9	
Per cent. increase	144	142	148	153	156	169	179	

[1] June 1919.   [2] December 1919.

TABLE LVIII

COMPOSITOR'S TIME RATES (JOBBING AND WEEKLY NEWS) IN CERTAIN TOWNS

	London	Edin-burgh	Man-chester	Shef-field	Birming-ham	Notting-ham	Bristol	Cardiff	Eight towns unweighted Average amount	Percen-tage
July	s. d.	s. d.	s. d.	s. d.	s. d.	s. d.	s. d.	s. d.	s. d.	
1914	39 0	35 0	38 6	36 0	37 6	37 0	35 0	36 0	36 9	100
1915	39 0	35 0	38 6	37 0	37 6	37 0	35 0	36 0	36 10	100
1916	42 0	37 0	40 6	39 0	39 0	39 0	35 0	38 0	38 8	105
1917	49 0	43 0	50 0	42 0	43 0	42 0	37 6	45 6	44 0	120
1918	62 6	56 0	60 0	55 6	59 0	56 0	52 6	57 6	57 4	156
1919	77 6	66 0	75 0	72 0	72 0	69 0	72 0	72 0	71 11	196
1920	95 0	90 6	92 6	89 6	89 6	86 6	89 6	89 6	90 4	246

The effect of the changes in eight towns, London, Edinburgh, and selected towns in grades 1, 2, and 3 is shown in Table LVIII for July of each year. If the percentage changes are compared with those in the building trade (p. 113), it will be seen that the movements of compositors' time rates were, till July 1919, very similar to those of bricklayers', weekly wages, but by July 1920 they had progressed more rapidly (though not so rapidly as the wages of builders' labourers) and had risen in six years very nearly as much as the official index-number of the cost of living. Hours, which before the War were generally 51 in the larger towns in England and Wales and 50 in Scotland, were reduced to 48 throughout the United Kingdom in March 1919.

The details of the changes, so far as they can be ascertained from the *Labour Gazette*, are shown for seventeen towns in the following tables. The towns were selected so as to choose for each grade those in which the wages were the highest, middle, and lowest in 1915, thereby illustrating the process of levelling; but in grade 3 no satisfactory record would be found for the lowest wage, and in grade 6 only Cambridge is included.

TABLE LIX

CHANGES IN TIME RATES IN SELECTED TOWNS, 1914–20, OF COMPOSITORS

(Jobbing and weekly news)
Grade I

	London	s.	d.		Edinburgh	s.	d.		Manchester	s.	d.
1914	July	39	0	1914	July	35	0	1914	July	38	6
1915	Oct.	41	0	1915	Nov.	37	0	1916	May	40	6
1916	Apr.	42	0	1916	Nov.	40	0		Nov.	42	6
	Oct.	45	0	1917	Apr.	43	0	1917	June	50	0
1917	June	49	0		Sept.	47	0	1918	Jan.	60	0
	Nov.	53	0	1918	Jan.	51	0		July	70	0
1918	Jan.	55	0		Apr.	56	0	1919	May	75	0
	Apr.	62	6		Oct.	66	0		Nov.	81	0
	Sept.	72	6	1919	Sept.	73	0	1920	Jan.	82	6
1919	June	77	6	1920	Jan.	80	6		June	92	6
	Dec.	85	0		June	90	6				
1920	June	95	0								

Selected towns in Grade 2

	Birmingham	s.	d.	Sheffield	s.	d.	Cardiff	s.	d.	Bristol	s.	d.	Swansea	s.	d.
1914	July	37	6	July	36	0	July	36	0	July	35	0	July	34	6
1915	—			Jan.	37	0	Dec.	38	0	—			Dec.	37	0
1916	—			Feb.	38	0	—			—			—		
	May	39	0	July	39	0	—			Aug.	37	6	June	37	6
	Oct.	40	0	Dec.	41	0	Nov.	41	6	—			Nov.	41	0
1917	Feb.	43	0	—			Mar.	42	0	—			Jan.	41	6
	Aug.	49	0	July	42	0	June	45	6	—			June	45	0
	—			Oct.	46	0	Dec.	50	0	Sept.	42	6	Nov.	49	0
1918	Feb.	56	6	Jan.	48	0	—			Jan.	44	6	—		
	May	59	0	Apr.	55	6	Apr.	55	0	Mar.	50	0	Apr.	54	0
	—			Oct.	60	0	July	57	6	July	52	6	July	56	6
	Sept.	69	0	Nov.	66	0	—			Sept.	60	0	Sept.	66	6
1919	—			—			—			Jan.	65	0	—		

		s.	d.
	May	72	0
	Nov.	78	0
1920	Jan.	79	6
	June	89	6

1569·34   M

TABLE LIX *(continued)*—CHANGES IN TIME RATES IN SELECTED TOWNS, 1914–20, OF COMPOSITORS

Selected Towns

| | Grade 3 | | | Grade 4 | |
	Nottingham	York	Southport	Plymouth	Dewsbury
	s. d.	s. d.	s. d.	s. d.	s. d.
1914	July 37 0	July 33 0	July 35 0	July 32 0	July 30 0
1915	—	Apr. 34 0	—	—	July 32 0
1916	Apr. 39 0	Dec. 39 0	July 37 0	Aug. 34 6	Sept. 34 0
1917	Mar. 42 0	—	Mar. 40 0	—	Jan. 35 0
	—			July 40 0	July 38 0
	Oct. 47 0	Dec. 45 0	Oct. 46 6	Nov. 42 0	Dec. 45 0
1918	Apr. 52 0	July 52 6	Mar. 55 0	May 47 0	July 52 6
	June 56 0	Oct. 55 0	Sept. 63 6	Aug. 52 0	Oct. 55 0
	Oct. 66 0	Dec. 62 6	—	—	Nov. 62 6
1919	—	—	Jan. 65 0	Jan. 60 0	—

	s. d.		s. d.
May	69 0		66 0
Nov.	75 0		72 0
1920 Jan.	76 6		73 6
June	86 6		83 6

| | Grade 5 | | | Grade 6 Cambridge | |
	Burton-on-Trent	Lincoln	Weston-super-mare	Master Printers' Association	University Press
	s. d.	s. d.	s. d.	s. d.	s. d.
1914	July 33 0	July 30 0	July 26 0	July 28 0	—
1915	Jan. 34 0	Nov. 32 0	—	—	—
1916	—	—	No recognized	July 30 4	38 3
	Sept. 36 0	Dec. 35 0	rate	Oct. 31 5	40 3
1917	—	—	—	Apr. 34 5	41 3
	—	June 38 0	—	Nov. 36 10	45 8
	Oct. 42 0	Oct. 42 0	—	Dec. 40 1	—
1918	Apr. 47 0	Apr. 47 0	—	May 48 9	55 0
	June 51 0	June 51 0	July 37 6	—	—
	Oct. 61 0	Oct. 61 0	Sept. 50 0	Nov. 58 9	60 0
1919	—	—	Jan. 57 6	—	—
	—	—	Mar. 60 0	—	—

	s. d.		
May	63 0		60 0
Nov.	69 0		66 0
1920 Jan.	70 6		67 6
June	80 6		77 6

See p. 97 for comparisons in bonuses paid

CHAPTER XII

RAILWAYS. DOCKS

Railways. Details of changes, 1914–20, and increase of general average.
Dock Labourers. Changes of rates at the principal ports and general average.
The award of the Transport Workers Court of Inquiry in 1920.

Railways. In February 1915 a war bonus was given of 3*s.* to men rated at less than 30*s.* a week, and 2*s.* to other men. This was raised successively to 5*s.* in October 1915 for all men, to 10*s.* in September 1916, to 15*s.* in April 1917; in August 1917 the bonus was converted into a war wage, and raised in November 1917 to 21*s.*, in April 1918 to 25*s.*, in August to 30*s.*, and in November 1918 to 33*s.* From February 1, 1919, an eight hours' day was adopted as standard. No further change took place until August 1919.

In a week in December 1913 the average earnings of all employed by railway companies was 27*s.* 11*d.*[1]; this includes payment for overtime, and also includes men in railway workshops. The average for a normal week was probably about 26*s.* 6*d.*, and therefore the increase of 25*s.* by April 1918 was about 95 per cent., and after November, that of 33*s.*, about 125 per cent.

In August 1919 standard daily rates[2] were arranged for drivers, firemen, and engine cleaners, which, when multiplied by 6 to correspond to a week, are as follows :

	August 1919	Approximate pre-War average
	s.	*s.*
Drivers and Motormen		
First and second year's service	72	
Third and fourth ,,	78	42
Fifth, sixth, and seventh ,,	84	
Eighth and onwards	90	
Firemen and Assistant Motormen		
First and second year's service	57	
Third and fourth ,,	63	26
Fifth and onwards	66	
Engine Cleaners over twenty years	42	—

[1] See *Labour Gazette,* October 1919, p. 416.
[2] A considerable addition to these was granted for long distance journeys.

In the winter of 1919–20, *3s.* was added to these rates to compensate the increased cost of living, and in June 1920 also drivers' wages were increased by *7s.*, firemen's by *4s.*, and cleaners' by *2s.*

The wages of other operatives were unchanged until January 1, 1920, when £1 of back pay was given all round, and the following rates (called abnormal rates because they were to come down to certain minima, 100 per cent. above pre-war wages when the cost of living fell), approximately *38s.* above the pre-war wages, were arranged:

	January 1920	Approximate pre-War average
	s.	*s.*
Guards, passenger and goods		
First and second year's service . .	60	
Third and fourth ,, . .	63	
Fifth, sixth, and seventh ,, . .	66	29
Eighth and onwards . . .	69	
Shunters		
Class I	69	
Class II	66	
Class III	63	26
Class IV	60	
Porters, traffic		
Grade I	60	
Grade II, London . . .	58	22
Other places . .	56	
Goods		
London	61	
Rural stations . . .	57	22
Urban ,, . . .	60	

For signalmen the wages were temporarily fixed at *38s.* above the pre-war rates, until grading was completed (see, however, *Labour Gazette*, July 1920, p. 386).

· The general effect of the changes in August 1919 and January 1920 was to add *38s.* all round, which is about 140 per cent. above the pre-war average, and at the same time to grade, standardize, and level up wages.

At the same time (January 1920) it was arranged that wages should rise or fall *1s.* for every five points that the Cost of Living Index number moved above or below the level in

December 1919 (125 per cent. above the pre-war level), subject to certain provisoes as to a fall. Under this arrangement all wages (excluding those in railway workshops) were raised 3s. in April, 2s. in July 1920, 2s. in October 1920, and 1s. in January 1921.

Finally a general increase was awarded in June 1920 in all traffic grades, as already stated for drivers, &c., varying from 2s. in rural districts, to 7s. 6d. or 8s. 6d. in industrial districts, the larger amount to the larger rates. This tends to restore the pre-war proportions between the wages of the different grades which had been greatly disturbed by the flat rates of increase in the previous five years. Without further information it is not possible to estimate the average increase thus granted; if we take it as 4s. 6d. the whole increase (at least to traffic grades) from July 1914 to August 1920 was about 47s. 6d., which is about 180 per cent. on the presumed pre-war average of 26s. 6d. It is clear that we have not the material to ascertain the average percentage rise at any date accurately; the following table is, however, suggested :

TABLE LX

APPROXIMATE RATES OF WAGES FOR NORMAL WEEK OF RAILWAY OPERATIVES AS PERCENTAGE OF THE PRE-WAR LEVEL

July 1914	.	.	.	100
„ 1915	.	.	.	110
„ 1916	.	.	.	120
„ 1917	.	.	.	155
„ 1918	.	.	.	195
„ 1919	.	.	.	225
„ 1920	.	.	.	280 [1]

This estimate suggests increases in the average throughout very nearly the same as that found for dock labourers.

Dock Labourers. The earnings of dock labourers depend as much on the irregularity of their employment as on the rate

---

[1] According to Sir Hugh Bell (*Contemporary Review*, December 1920) the average annual *earnings* of the whole of the men of all ages of the great railway company in which he is interested were £73 in 1912 and £257 in 1920. This increase is considerably greater than that here shown. Part of the difference may be explained by an increased amount of overtime payments in consequence of the shortened normal week.

of payment. It is not reasonable to assume that a full $5\frac{1}{2}$ days or 6 days is ordinarily worked, but the changes can be studied on the basis of a full day's wage. There are many differences in every port, according not only to the type of work performed, but also according to the status of the employer (the dock authority, shipowners, stevedore, &c.) ; in the tables that follow the lowest ordinary wage is stated, whatever the employer, shipowners' rates being distinguished in London from those paid by the port authority.

Wages generally in the large ports were from 6d. to 8d. an hour before the War. In 1915 they generally advanced 1d., in 1916 and in 1917 2d., and in 1918 $3\frac{1}{2}d.$, i. e. $8\frac{1}{2}d.$ in all. In London, where the advance was given in the form of a daily or weekly bonus, the increase was slightly less.

In April 1919 a uniform 44-hour week (11 half days of 4 hours each) was introduced, in place of the 9, 10, or $10\frac{1}{2}$ hours day formerly worked, and rates were adjusted so that the payment for a full day should be approximately the same before and after the change at each port. No general rise in earnings took place between October 1918 and May 1920. In February 1920 the whole subject of dockers' wages and conditions of employment was investigated by a public Court of Inquiry, and it was recommended that a uniform minimum rate of 8s. a half-day should be paid in all the large ports, and that when wages were thus levelled up the differential rates existing between various ports and between some classes of labour should be merged. In recommending the high rate of 2s. an hour for unskilled work, the court appears to have had in view the inevitable irregularity of labour in the docks, and also to have hoped that the losing of time at the beginning and end of the day would be avoided by better management and goodwill on the part of the men. Effect was given to the recommendation in May 1920, when the minimum rates in all the large ports were raised to 8s. the half day.

If the six daily rates shown in the following tables are averaged, we obtain the following approximate results :

TABLE LXI

AVERAGE OF FULL DAILY RATES AND FULL WEEKLY RATES IN CERTAIN
PORTS OF ORDINARY DOCK LABOURERS

July		Daily			Weekly	
		Amount	Percentage		Amount	Percentage
		s. d.			s. d.	
1914	. .	5 11	100		33 8	100
1915	. .	6 7	111		37 6	111
1916	. .	7 8	130		43 9	130
1917	. .	8 10	150		50 3	150
1918	. .	11 4	193		64 11	193
1919	. .	12 9	216		70 4	209
1920	. .	16 3	276		89 4	266

If these changes are compared with those of bricklayers' labourers (p. 115), it will be seen that dockers had the advantage in 1915, which they maintained until 1918, but that in 1919 and 1920 their increase was slightly lower. By July 1919 the increase in dockers' daily rates (in spite of the reduction of hours) was greater than that shown by the official measure of the cost of living; at earlier dates the increase was less than that shown by the official measure, but nearly equal to that in the modified measure (p. 106).

TABLE LXII

DETAIL OF DOCK LABOURERS' WAGES IN THE PRINCIPAL PORTS

LONDON. *Dock labourers' lowest wages.*

	Paid by Port of London Authority			Paid by Shipowners		
	Hourly rate	Bonus	Full day wage	Hourly rate	Bonus	Full day wage
	d.	s.	s. d.	d.	s. d.	s. d.
July 1914	7	—	5 10	8	—	6 8
Feb. 1915	7	3 weekly	6 4	8	9 daily	7 5
July 1916	7	6 ,,	6 10	8	1 6 ,,	8 2
Apr. 1917	7	12 ,,	7 10	8	2 6 ,,	9 2
May 1917	—	—	—	8	3 0 ,,	9 8
Dec. 1917	7	18 ,,	8 10	—	—	—
Jan. 1918	—	—	—	8	4 0 ,,	10 8
May 1918	9	18 ,,	10 6	15	nil	12 6
Oct. 1918	10½	18 ,,	11 9	16½	nil	13 9
Apr. 1919	{ 44 hours' week introduced, viz. 11 half-days of 4 hours each.					
	—	—	11 8	—	—	13 9
May 1920	—	—	16 0	—	—	17 6

Hours prior to April 1919, 10 daily, except that those employed by shipowners worked only half Saturday.

TABLE LXII (*continued*)—DETAIL OF DOCK LABOURERS' WAGES IN THE
PRINCIPAL PORTS

LIVERPOOL. *Dock porters' wages.*

	s.	d.		
July 1914	4	6		Up to May 1920 shipmen received 6d.,
Feb. 1915	5	6		riggers 1s., and stevedores 2s. 6d. in addi-
July 1916	6	6	For full day	tion to these rates.
Apr. 1917	7	6	of 9 hours.	From May 1920 riggers received 6d., steve-
Sept. 1917	8	6		dores 2s., and shipmen nothing in addition.
May 1918	10	0		
Oct. 1918	11	0		
Apr. 1919	11	8	For full day	
May 1920	16	0	of 8 hours.	

Prior to April 1919 hours were 9 on five days, 8 on Saturdays ; afterwards 8 on five days, 4 on Saturdays.

BRISTOL. *Ordinary labourers.*

	Hourly rate	Full day wage	
	d.	s.	d.
July 1914 . .	7	6	1½
Feb. 1915 . .	8	7	0
Feb. 1916 . .	9	7	10½
Oct. 1916 . .	10	8	9
Apr. 1917 . .	11	9	7½
Oct. 1917 . .	12	10	6
May 1918 . .	14	12	3
Oct. 1918 . .	15½	13	7
Apr. 1919 . .	21	14	0
May 1920 . .	24	16	0

Prior to April 1919 hours were 10½ on five days and 7 on Saturdays. Then the 44-hour week.

HULL. *Ordinary labourers employed by regular traders.*

	Hourly rate	Full day wage	
	d.	s.	d.
July 1914 . .	7½	5	7½
Feb. 1915 . .	8½	6	4½
Oct. 1915 . .	9½	7	1½
Nov. 1916 . .	10	7	6
May 1917 . .	11	8	3
Aug. 1917 . .	12	9	0
Feb. 1918 . .	14	10	6
Oct. 1918 . .	15½	11	7½
Apr. 1919 . .	17½	11	8
May 1920 . .	24	16	0

Prior to April 1919 the hours were 9 on five days and 5 on Saturday in summer, and 8 and 4 in winter. Then the 44-hour week.

GLASGOW. *Ordinary labourers.*

	Hourly rate	Full day wage	
	d.	s.	d.
July 1914 . .	8	6	8
Feb. 1915 . .	9	7	6
Jan. 1916 . .	10	8	4
Nov. 1916 . .	11	9	2
Jan. 1917 . .	12	10	0
Dec. 1917 . .	13	10	10
May 1918 . .	15	12	6
Oct. 1918 . .	16½	13	9
Apr. 1919 . .	21	14	0
May 1920 . .	24	16	0

Prior to April 1919, hours were 10 on five days and 6 on Saturdays. Then the 44-hour week.

CHAPTER XIII

AGRICULTURE

Wages and earnings in 1907. Fixing of minimum rates. Average increases from 1914 to 1920. Wages in Scotland. Detailed statement for all counties in England and Wales, 1914, 1917, 1918, 1919, 1920.

PRIOR to the establishment of minimum wages in 1918 ordinary agricultural labourers in England were paid a weekly cash wage (sometimes a little greater in summer than in winter), and extras and allowances which varied considerably from county to county. The extras were payments at higher rates or by lump sums at hay and corn harvests, the allowances in kind were cottages free or at a cheap rate, with gardens or land, potatoes, milk, bacon, cider or beer, haulage of coals, &c. ; at the same time at some seasons and in some localities, piece rates were paid, which yielded higher earnings than time rates. In fixing the minimum rates the allowances were valued on a definite basis, so that the rate fixed at say 30s. may have been 28s. cash and 2s. value of allowances in kind.

In some districts, especially in the North of England and North Wales, ordinary labourers, and more generally horsemen and cattlemen, were lodged and boarded by the farmer, and the allowances in kind were therefore considerable.

The most complete statement of these allowances and extras is contained in the report of the general inquiry into earnings and hours of labour of workpeople in the United Kingdom, of which Part V (Cd. 5460) deals with agriculture labour. The principal results may be thus summarized.

The Labour Department of the Board of Trade [1] received statements of changes in agricultural cash wages throughout the country, and these are summarized for January 1914 and January 1917 in the *Labour Gazette*, July 1917, p. 239. At the commencement of the War cash wages were on the average for the country about 1s. higher than in January 1907. There

[1] Now transferred to the Ministry of Labour.

was some increase in the latter part of 1914, and a further rise during 1915, so that by April 1915 (*Labour Gazette*, June 1915, p. 200) cash wages were about 2s. higher on the average than in July 1914, and averaged about 17s. 10d. There was a more considerable increase between April 1915 and January 1917, and at the latter date the average was 22s. 3d. To this should be added about 1s. 3d.[1] for the value of allowances at the higher prices of 1914, so that average earnings (without extra payments for harvest or piece work but including allowances) may be estimated at 23s. 6d. in January 1917, as compared with 16s. 10d. in June 1914.[2] The Corn Production Act of 1917 fixed 25s. (including reasonable valuation of allowances other than beer or cider) from August 21, 1917, as the minimum rate for an able-bodied agricultural labourer employed on time work in England and Wales. Table LXVII shows that in the whole of England south of Lincolnshire (except Middlesex) and in the great part of Wales, this minimum was higher than the earnings of January 1917, while the North of England was not affected.

TABLE LXIII

AGRICULTURAL WAGES AND EARNINGS, 1907

	England [3]				Wales [3]
	Ordinary labourers	Horse-men	Cattle-men	Shepherds	All
	s. d.	s. d.	s. d.	s. d.	s. d.
Weekly cash average through the year .	14 9	16 2	16 5	16 0	17 0
Weekly cash earnings .	16 8	17 6	17 7	17 9	—
Value of allowances in kind . . .	10	1 6	1 8	1 10	—
Average weekly earnings	17 6	19 0	19 3	19 7	19 0

In the summer of 1918 minimum rates were fixed separately for all the counties of England and Wales (see Table LXVII), varying from 30s. in the mid-south, south midlands, and eastern counties, to 35s. or 36s. in the northern counties, and 36s. 6d. in Glamorganshire. In May 1919 the lowest rates were increased

---

[1] See Cmd. 76, p. 23.

[2] 14s. 10d. cash in 1907 + 1s. rise to 1914 + 1s. value of allowances in 1914.

[3] Excluding men provided with board or lodging.

by 6s. 6d., so that the minimum in the county was 36s. 6d., while the highest county minimum was 42s. 6d. in Durham and Northumberland. In May 1920 the rates in all counties in which the minimum had been 38s. or less were brought up to 42s., which became the minimum in thirty-five counties, and in sixteen counties 4s. was added, so that the highest minimum became 46s. 6d. (except in Cheshire; see note next page). In August 1920 another 4s. was added all round.

The increases thus obtained in six years varied greatly in England both in absolute amount and in percentage from county to county. There has been a very considerable levelling up of wages.

TABLE LXIV

EARNINGS IN 1914 AND MINIMUM WAGES IN 1920

Counties arranged in ascending order of earnings in 1914	Cash and allowances Jan. 1914		Minimum wage Winter 1920–1		Increase Amount		Per cent.
	s.	d.	s.	d.	s.	d.	
Oxford . . .	13	4	46	0	32	8	245
Suffolk . . .	14	0	46	0	32	0	229
Norfolk . . .	14	4	46	0	31	8	221
Dorset . . .	14	7	46	0	31	5	215
Hunts . . .	14	8	46	0	31	4	214
Wilts . . .	15	0	46	0	31	0	207
Essex . . .	15	1	46	6	31	5	208
Cambridge . .	15	1	46	0	30	11	205
Hants . . .	15	2	46	0	30	10	203
Berks . . .	15	3	46	0	30	9	201
Buckingham . .	15	5	46	0	30	7	199
Bedford . .	15	6	46	0	30	6	197
Northampton . .	15	10	46	0	30	2	191
Hertford . .	15	10	46	6	30	8	194
Sussex . . .	15	10	46	6	30	8	194
Rutland . .	16	0	46	0	30	0	187
Devon . . .	16	1	46	0	29	11	187
Gloucester . .	16	3	46	0	29	9	183
Worcester . .	16	3	46	0	29	9	183
Shropshire . .	16	5	46	0	29	7	180
Warwick . .	16	6	46	0	29	6	179
Lincoln . .	17	1	48	6	31	5	183
Hereford . .	17	2	46	0	28	10	168
Somerset . .	17	4	46	0	28	8	165
Surrey . . .	17	8	47	6	29	10	169
Kent . . .	18	0	47	6	29	6	164
Leicester . .	18	0	46	0	28	0	156

TABLE LXIV *(continued)*—EARNINGS IN 1914 AND MINIMUM WAGES IN 1920

Counties arranged in ascending order of earnings in 1914	Cash and allowances 1914	Minimum wage August 1920	Increase Amount	Per cent.
	s. d.	*s. d.*	*s. d.*	
Cornwall . .	18 3	46 0	27 9	152
Stafford . .	19 0	46 6	27 6	145
Nottingham . .	19 3	46 0	26 9	139
Cheshire . .	19 10	52 0 [1]	32 2 [1]	162 [1]
Yorks. . . .	19 10	49 0	29 2	147
Cumberland [2] . .	20 2	48 0	27 10	138
Middlesex . .	20 7	48 6	27 11	136
Derby . . .	21 4	46 0	24 8	116
Lancs. . . .	21 5	47 6	26 1	122
Durham . . .	23 1	50 6	27 5	119
Northumberland .	23 4	50 6	27 2	116

The average weekly wages (including allowances) in England and Wales of ordinary agricultural wages may be estimated as follows :

TABLE LXV

GENERAL CHANGES IN AGRICULTURAL WAGES, ENGLAND AND WALES

Average weekly wages (including allowances)

	Amount	Percentage
	s. d.	
1914 July . .	16 10	100
1915 Apr. . .	18 10	112
1917 Jan. . .	23 6	140
1918 Aug. . .	31 9	189
1919 May . .	38 0	226
1920 May . .	42 9	254
1920 Aug. . .	46 9	277

This increase is nearly at the same rate as that of builders' labourers. Before the war it was a matter of dispute whether an agricultural labourer gained any real advantage by migrating into a town and earning industrial wages under urban conditions ; on the whole the excess of real wages in the town was probably in September 1920 a definite advantage, if work was regular.

In October 1919 hours of work were reduced through England and Wales to 50 in the summer and 48 in the winter, except in

[1] In Cheshire the hours of work are 54, in other counties they are reduced.

[2] There is no entry for Westmorland in 1914 ; the minimum in 1918 and afterwards is the same as for Cumberland.

Cheshire, where they were 54 throughout the year. Prior to that date hours had generally been 54 in the summer and 48 in the winter.[1] This reduction gives greater facility for over-time, for which 10*d.* to 1*s.* an hour was paid in March 1920, 1*s.* 1*d.* to 1*s.* 2*d.* in June 1920, and 1*s.* 2*d.* to 1*s.* 3½*d.* in September 1920, with 2½*d.* or 3*d.* an hour more for Sunday work. On the other hand the special payments of harvest may perhaps not have increased at the same rate as have weekly wages.

The earnings of shepherds, horsemen, and cattlemen, for which minimum rates above those of ordinary labourers have been fixed, appear to have risen more rapidly than those of ordinary labourers.

In Scotland there is no available published comparison between 1914 and later dates, but a rough estimate of the increase between 1907 and 1919–20 is possible, since for the earlier date estimates are given as for England and Wales (Cd. 5460, pp. xxii seq.), and for the later we have the decisions of the Central Agricultural Wages Committee for Scotland (*Labour Gazette*, June 1919, p. 224, November 1919, p. 463, and September 1920, p. 479).

TABLE LXVI

SCOTLAND, ORDINARY AGRICULTURAL LABOURERS (ORRAMEN)

	1907						1919	1920
							Minimum rates	
	Cash		Allowances		Total		June	Summer
	s.	*d.*	*s.*	*d.*	*s.*	*d.*	*s.*	*s.*
Shetland } Orkney }	7	1	6	9	13	10	{ 37 { 31	46 31
Caithness	9	2	5	0	14	2	30 and 36	35 and 41
Sutherland	12	2	5	7	17	9	30 and 38	40
Ross	12	9	4	0	16	9	27 to 32	27 to 32
Nairn	13	1	4	1	17	2	30	30
Elgin	13	4	4	8	18	0		
Banff	11	4	6	2	17	6		
Aberdeen	11	8	6	7	18	3	35	35
Kincardine	13	8	4	7	18	3		
Forfar	15	9	4	2	19	11	32*s.* 6*d.* and 36*s.*[2]	
Perth	16	1	3	1	19	2	30*s.* to 36*s.*	
Fife	17	5	3	2	20	7	31 and 35[2]	
Kinross	15	1	4	7	19	8		

[1] In Staffordshire, Glamorgan, and Monmouth they had been 57 in the summer, in Notts. 60, in Lancs. 55½, and in Anglesey and Carnarvon 56.

[2] The rates marked thus were decided later than June.

TABLE LXVI (*continued*)—SCOTLAND, ORDINARY AGRICULTURAL LABOURERS (ORRAMEN)

	1907			1919	1920
				Minimum rates	
	Cash	*Allowances*	*Total*	*June*	*Summer*
	s. d.	*s. d.*	*s. d.*	*s.*	*s.*
Edinburgh . .	18 4	2 4	20 8	36	40
Linlithgow . .	14 11	4 6	19 5		
Haddington .	17 6	2 1	19 7		
Peebles . . .	16 9	3 2	19 11		
Berwick . .	16 10	3 6	20 4	30 and 35	37 and 42
Roxburgh . .	16 6	3 9	20 3		
Selkirk . . .	17 2	3 6	20 8		
Dumfries .	14 10	3 3	18 1	33	37s. 4d.
Kirkcudbright .	15 4	2 6	17 10		
Wigtown . .	14 1	4 1	18 2		
Ayr . . .	15 5	3 7	19 0	37	37
Renfrew . .	16 5	3 6	19 11	38	40
Lanark . .	17 3	3 10	21 1		
Dumbarton .	18 6	1 1	19 7		
Stirling . .	16 10	4 3	21 1		
Clackmannan .	17 8	3 8	21 4		
Argyll . . .	14 5	3 5	17 10	30	30
Inverness . .	13 4	3 9	17 1	27 to 32	27 to 32
General average .	15 1	3 10	18 11		

In 1907 the average earnings in Scotland were higher than in England, while in 1920 (even before the general rise of 4s. in England and Wales in September) cash wages were definitely lower ; but in Scotland allowances in kind which are still considerable and estimated as averaging 8s. 3d. in value weekly in the winter 1919–20 are additive to cash wages, and it is stated that more than the minimum was also paid in cash.

The following table is computed from the report of the Committee appointed by the Agricultural Wages Board to inquire into the *Financial Results of the Occupation of Agricultural Land and the Cost of Living of Rural Workers* (Cmd. 76, pp. 21–4 and 57–9), supplemented by official statements of minimum rates in 1919–20.

The cash wages in the summers of 1914 and 1917 are as reported by the investigators of the Board of Agriculture ; the range of wages within some counties is remarkable. The winter rates in these years are taken from the *Labour Gazette*. The estimated value of allowances in 1907 is taken from the Board of Trade Inquiry (Cd. 5460).

TABLE LXVII

RATES OF WAGES OF ORDINARY AGRICULTURAL LABOURERS, ENGLAND AND WALES, 1914, 1917–20

County	1914 Weekly rates of cash wages — Summer	1914 — Winter	Estimated value of allowances in 1907	1917 Weekly rates of cash wages — Summer	1917 — Winter	1918 Summer	Minimum rates [1] 1919 May	1920 May	1920 Aug.
	s. d. s. d.	s. d.	s. d.	s. d. s. d.	s. d.	s. d.	s. d.	s. d.	s. d.
Middlesex	20 0 to 25 0	20 4	3	27 0 to 33 0	27 4	34 0	40 6	44 6	48 6
Essex	14 0 to 22 0	14 8	5	25 0 to 27 0	22 4	32 0			
Hertford	14 0 to 16 0	15 3	7½	25 0	20 5		38 6	42 6	46 6
Surrey	15 0 to 20 0	17 0	8	21 0 to 25 0	22 3	33 0			
Kent	17 6 to 27 0	17 7	5	25 0 to 28 0	23 0		39 6	43 6	47 6
Berkshire	14 0 to 15 0	14 6	9	17 0 to 18 0	19 6	30 0	36 6	42 0	46 0
Sussex	13 0 to 17 0	15 1	9	22 0	21 10	32 0	38 6	42 6	46 6
Hampshire	14 0 to 15 0	14 5	9	20 0	20 2	31 0	37 6	42 0	46 0
Wiltshire	13 0 to 14 0	14 3	9	20 0	20 6				
Dorset	13 0 to 14 0	12 10	9	19 0 to 20 0	17 8	30 0	36 6	42 0	46 0
Somerset	—	15 4	2 0	—	20 5				
Devon	11 0 to 17 6	13 11	2 2	16 6 to 23 0	18 2				
Cornwall	—	16 7	1 8	—	21 1	31 0	37 6	42 0	46 0
Hereford	13 6 to 15 6	15 0	2 2	18 0 to 21 6	19 2	31 0	36 6	42 0	46 0
Gloucester	12 0 to 20 0	15 1	1 2	18 0 to 26 0	20 7				
Oxford	12 0 to 19 0	13 0	4	17 0 to 25 0	19 4				
Buckingham	13 0 to 20 0	14 8	9	18 0 to 28 0	21 3				
Northampton	14 0 to 20 0	15 5	5	20 0 to 27 0	21 1	30 0	36 6	42 0	46 0
Warwick	13 0 to 18 0	15 11	7	22 0 to 25 0	21 11				
Worcester	12 0 to 18 0	15 5	10	16 0 to 26 0	21 6				
Bedford	14 0 to 18 0	15 0	6	22 6 to 25 0	21 3				
Cambridge	13 0 to 16 0	14 8	5	20 0 to 30 0	22 1				
Huntingdon	15 0	14 3	5	24 0 to 25 0	21 9	30 0	36 6	42 0	46 0
Norfolk	14 0 to 18 0	14 0	4	25 0	22 0				
Suffolk	14 0 to 15 0	13 7	5	22 0 to 24 0	20 0				

1 The minimum wage was fixed in Norfolk and Northants in May; in twenty counties in July; in other counties in August or September, except that Lancs. and four counties in N.W. Wales were delayed till October.

TABLE LXVII (continued)—RATES OF WAGES OF ORDINARY AGRICULTURAL LABOURERS, ENGLAND AND WALES, 1914-20

County	1914 Weekly rates of cash wages		Estimated value of allowances in 1907	1917 Weekly rates of cash wages		Minimum rates			
	Summer	Winter		Summer	Winter	1918 Summer[1]	1919 May	1920 May	1920 Avg.
Lincoln	16 6 to 18 0	16 6	7	25 0 to 30 0	24 2	34 0	40 6	44 6	48 6
Rutland	15 6	15 6	6	25 0	22 6				
Leicester	16 0	17 2	10	25 0	25 2	31 0	37 6	42 0	46 0
Derby	16 0 to 21 0	20 1	1 3	25 0 to 30 0	27 3				
Nottingham	16 0	18 3	1 0	26 0	24 7	35 0	38 0	42 0	46 0
Stafford	15 0	17 8	1 4	24 0	23 10	35 0	38 6	42 6	46 6
Shropshire	15 0 to 16 0	15 1	1 4	20 6 to 23 0	21 9	33 0	37 0	42 0	46 0
Cheshire	24 0	18 9	1 1	30 0 to 33 0	25 4	36 0	38 0	48 0¹	52 0
Lancashire[2]	—	20 5	1 0	—	27 7	35 0	39 6	43 6	47 6
Cumberland[2]	18 0 to 30 0	18 11	1 3	24 0 to 30 0	25 1	35 0	40 0	44 0	48 0
Westmorland	18 0 to 21 0	18 6	1 4	18 0 to 21 0	—				
York	—	—	—	—	25 4	35 0	41 0	45 0	49 0
Durham	21 0 to 25 0	20 9	2 4³	32 0 to 34 0	28 10	36 0	42 6	46 6	50 6
Northumberland	—	21 0	2 4³	—	27 5				
	s. d.	*s. d.*		*s. d.*					
Monmouth		17 0		22 6					
Glamorgan		20 2		27 10		36 6	41 6	45 6	50 0
Carmarthan		17 10		23 6					
Cardigan		16 4		20 0		31 0	37 6	42 0	46 0
Pembroke		16 8		21 0					
Brecknock		17 11		23 3					
Radnor		15 0		20 1					
Montgomery		16 8		22 9		30 0	36 0	42 0	46 0
Merioneth		17 9		26 3					
Flint		17 9		26 3					
Denbigh		18 6		25 4					
Carnarvon		20 0		24 8		31 6	36 6	42 0	46 0
Anglesey		—		—					

[1] Cheshire. Wages raised to 42s. 6d. October 1919.
[2] Furness is included with Cumberland.
[3] These figures relate to hinds, the predominant class of weekly paid labourers in these counties.

CHAPTER XIV

COTTON, WOOL

General changes in cotton piece rates. Comparison with earnings. War bonuses in the woollen and worsted industry. The 'cost of living' wage. Comparison of change of rates and earnings. Average earnings month by month.

Cotton. This study is confined to wages in Lancashire, Cheshire, and Yorkshire as far as the movements are the same as in Lancashire.

The rates of earnings of the great bulk of the operatives in the cotton industry are governed by standard piece lists, and changes are arranged by adding a percentage to the standards. Though various lists are in operation, there has been a tendency to uniformity in recent years, and the same percentages have been awarded throughout the great part of the cotton district for preparing operations and spinning on the one hand and for weaving on the other.

In July 1914 the rates both for spinning and for weaving were 5 per cent. above the standard. Subsequent changes up to February 1921 have been as follows :

TABLE LXVIII

GENERAL CHANGES IN COTTON PIECE RATES

| | | Preparing and spinning | | Weaving | |
		Percentage increase on standard	Resulting rates. Standard = 100	Percentage increase on standard	Resulting rates. Standard = 100
1914	July	—	105	—	105
1915	June	5	110	—	—
1916	January	—	—	5	110
	June	5	115	—	—
1917	January	—	—	5	115
	February	10	125	—	—
	July	—	—	10	125
	December	15	140	15	140
1918	June	25	165	25	165
	December	50	215	50	215
1919	July	30	245	30	245
1920	May	70	315	70	315

Till July 1917 the increases on the weaving lists were granted six months after those on the spinning lists. From December 1917 the dates of award were the same in the two branches.

In July 1919 weekly hours of work were reduced from $55\frac{1}{2}$ to 48. If the output per hour was unchanged, the increase of 30 per cent. on the standard arranged at the same date would have resulted in a slight reduction of earnings, viz. $245 \times 48 \div 55\frac{1}{2}$ $=212$, instead of 215 as before, and the final rate, 315 for 48 hours, would be equivalent to 273 for $55\frac{1}{2}$ hours. It is remarkable that no increase in rates took place (when the reduction of hours is thus brought into reckoning) between December 1918 and May 1920. A bonus was, however, given in the first three months of 1920 of £9 to men and £6 to women in spinning, £4 to men and women in weaving, and smaller sums to young persons and children (*Labour Gazette*, February 1920, p. 86).

It is never safe to assume that changes in piece rates are proportional to changes in resulting earnings, both because gradual changes in machinery and methods of production may facilitate output, and, on the other hand, because the operatives may make less effort when rates are higher, being content with their former earnings. We have the means of testing in part such reactions, since every month there is published in the *Labour Gazette* a statement of the numbers employed and the total wages paid by a large number of firms at the last pay day of the previous months; the firms who make returns vary a little from month to month, but little error seems to be introduced from this cause. Earnings reckoned depend, of course, not only on rates of payment, but on the amount of time worked, and are reduced if the operatives paid have not had a full week's work, but they are not affected by any change in the number employed. The falling off in earnings shown in the following table in the latter part of 1914 and since May 1920 is attributable to short time. The earnings stated are the total for all operations, men, women, boys, and girls, and as the War continued the number of men was relatively smaller, and average earnings might be expected to fall for this reason. Even the comparison between 1914 and the latter part of 1919 is not altogether free from this difficulty. The following table shows the average earnings as computed from these returns :

TABLE LXIX

COTTON INDUSTRY

AVERAGE WEEKLY EARNINGS OF ALL OPERATIVES EMPLOYED BY CERTAIN FIRMS

Last week of	1914 £	1915 £	1916 £	1917 £	1918 £	1919 £	1920 £
January .	0·98	0·94	1·11	1·17	1·42	2·15	2·35
February .	1·00	0·98	1·10	1·21	1·42	2·12	2·37
March .	1·00	0·99	1·10	1·21	1·43	2·11	2·39
April . .	1·00	1·03	1·12	1·23	1·43	2·00	2·39
May . .	1·01	1·04	1·12	1·23	1·45	2·17	3·10
June . .	1·00	1·04	1·12	1·22	1·43	2·11	3·02
July . .	0·98	1·06	1·16	1·27	1·46	2·20	3·03
August .	0·68	1·06	1·15	1·28	1·56	2·28	2·96
September .	0·79	1·05	1·14	1·26	1·60	2·32	—
October .	0·78	1·07	1·16	1·28	1·65	2·31	—
November .	0·83	1·06	1·15	1·28	1·57	2·35	—
December .	0·89	1·06	1·14	1·44	Strike	2·33	—

The figures in this table may be compared with the changes in rates as follows :

TABLE LXX

COMPARISON OF CHANGES IN COTTON PIECE RATES AND EARNINGS

			Piece rates July 1914=100		Earnings June 1914=100
1914	June .	.	100		100
1916	February	.	105		110
1917	February	.	110		121
	August .	.	119		128
	November	.	119		128
	December	.	133		144
1918	January .	.	133		142
	May .	.	133		145
	June .	.	157		143
	July .	.	157		146
	August .	.	157		156
	November	.	157		157
	December	.	205		—
1919	January .	.	205		215
	June .	.	205		211
	July .	.	202	233 [1]	220
	August .	.	202	233 [1]	228
1920	April .	.	202	233 [1]	239
	May .	.	259	300 [1]	310
	June .	.	259	300 [1]	302

[1] Not allowing for reduction in hours. Some classes of operatives had special increases in 1920.

In the summer of 1918 many of the mills worked short time, and consequently the increase in piece rates was not immediately reflected in earnings.

In June 1914 trade was only moderately good, and there was some room for improvement in earnings without any change in rates. After allowance is made for this it still appears that earnings have increased more rapidly than rates, and that in particular the reduction of hours in July 1919 did not result in a reduction in the weeks' output.

Prior to the increase in December 1918 rates in the cotton industry lagged far behind the increase in the cost of living however reckoned; whether the ground was made good in 1919 depends on which measurement of cost of living and which of rates or earnings ought to be taken. The rise in May 1920 brought the increase of rates and earnings definitely above the increase in the cost of living in the six years.

Wool and worsted, Yorkshire. It is much more difficult to deal generally with wages in the woollen and worsted industry than with those in cotton, for the different branches of the trade are numerous and localized, and wages and methods of adjusting wages vary from place to place and from occupation to occupation; also a smaller proportion are on piece rates than in the cotton industry, and therefore wages do not move together on a definite percentage. From June 1917, however, wage movements have been made on a uniform basis in all the woollen and worsted mills in Yorkshire [1]; prior to this date wages in the Huddersfield district (for which the information is fairly complete) are taken as probably typical. The following analysis exhibits the changes of wages of woollen and worsted operatives in the Huddersfield district; the first change named was estimated to affect 50,000 persons.

[1] Excluding overlookers and operatives in dyeing, combing, and some other classes of mills and factories.

War bonuses, Huddersfield

	Apr. 1915	Jan. 1916	Apr. 1916	Oct. 1916	Jan. 1917	Total
	s. d.	d.	d.	s. d.	s. d.	s. d.
All earning 10s. or under .	6	6	1 0	1 0	6	3 6
Women, earning 10s. to 15s.	1 0	6	1 6	1 6	6	5 0
15s. or more . .	1 0	6	1 6	1 6	2 0	6 6
Men, earning 10s. to 15s. .	1 0	6	1 6	1 6	6	5 0
15s. to 20s. .	1 0	6	1 6	1 6	2 0	6 6
20s. to 30s. . .	2 6	6	2 0	2 0	3 0	10 0
30s. to 40s. . .	2 0	6 1	2 0	2 0	3 6	10 0

In June 1917 and afterwards percentage increases were given throughout Yorkshire, the percentages being reckoned on the earnings on which the war bonuses had been given, and these war bonuses were cancelled. The increases were as follows :

Resulting percentages on basic earnings

	June 1917	Oct. 1917	Mar. 1918	Aug. 1918	Nov. 1918	Feb. 1919
Time workers . . .	50	60	72½	81½	104¾	107
Subject to maximum increase for						
Men . . .	—	—	21s. 9d. }	24s. 6d.	31s. 5d.	32s. 1d.
Women . . .	—	—	— }			
Piece workers						
Men . . .	40	48	58	65½	83¾	85¼
Women . . .	42½	51	61¼	69½	89	91

The increases to piece workers were thus $\frac{16}{20}$ and $\frac{17}{20}$ (for men and women respectively) of those to time workers.

In August 1919 the basic rates on which the percentages were calculated were raised 10 per cent., except for operatives in worsted spinning-mills whose rates had been adjusted in April. In September 1919 it was agreed to relate the percentage increases for time workers every month to the index-numbers of the Cost of Living (Food, Rent, Clothing, &c.) published in the *Labour Gazette*,[2] subject to a maximum increase of 3s. for every 10 points in the index-number, a limitation which affects only the men whose basic wage was more than 30s., who were probably some 25 per cent. of all men. These percentages were to be applied to the basic rates as before August 1919, but in

[1] 1s. to piece workers.

[2] More exactly the increase was to be 105, 115, 125, &c. (with no intermediate numbers), when the index-number reached one of these figures.

August 1920 the basic rate was raised another 5 per cent., and the subsequent percentages applied to the raised rates. Some other additions have been made to the basic rates in other cases, so that the percentages shown below are an under-estimate.

		Cost of living. Increase on basic rates	Time workers	Increase on original basic rates	
				Piece workers	
				Men	Women
1919	September	115	125	102	107¾
	December	125	135	110	116¼
1920	May	135	145	118	124¾
	July	145 .	155	126	133¼
	September	155	193¼	162¼	170
	December	175	216¼	181¼	190
1921	February	165	204¾	171¾	180

It is not easy to compute the average movement of earnings from these data, but an attempt has been made from the information relating to the numbers of men and of women on time and piece rates contained in the average wage census of 1906 (Cd. 4545), with the following results :

TABLE LXXI

WOOL AND WORSTED INDUSTRIES

Comparison of Changes of Nominal Rates and of Earnings

				Calculated percentages 1914=100	1914=£0·85	Average earnings from 'Labour Gazette' records
					£	£
1914	July	.	.	100	0·85	0·85
1915	April	.	.	115	0·98	0·98
1916	January	.	.	124	1·05	1·03
	April	.	.	126	1·07	1·07
	October	.	.	134	1·14	1·14
1917	January	.	.	138	1·17	1·17
	June	.	.	144	1·22	1·22
	October	.	.	152	1·30	1·33
1918	March	.	.	164	1·39	1·45
	August	.	.	172	1·46	1·67
	November	.	.	193	1·64	1·83
1919	February	.	.	196	1·66	1·82
	September	.	.	212	1·80	2·10
	December	.	.	221	1·88	2·35
1920	May	.	.	230	1·95	2·44
	July	.	.	239	2·03	2·59

The wage returns in the last column are on the same basis as described above (p. 178) under cotton, and are subject to the same qualifications as to the lost time and to improvement in processes. The averages agree exactly with those computed from the wage changes till June 1917; from that date they show a continually greater increase, which becomes marked from the summer of 1918. This increase is due to the great prosperity of these industries. Overtime and night-work have been common, and in several months a shortage of labour was reported. In 1917, on the other hand, work was reduced owing to the shortage of wool.

TABLE LXXII

WOOLLEN AND WORSTED INDUSTRY

Average Weekly Earnings of all Operatives Employed by certain Firms

Last week in	1914 £	1915 £	1916 £	1917 £	1918 £	1919 £	1920 £
January	0·83	0·90	1·03	1·17	1·41	1·82	2·25
February	0·86	0·93	1·05	1·24	1·44	1·82	2·36
March	0·87	0·95	1·06	1·26	1·45	1·91	2·41
April	0·87	0·98	1·07	1·29	1·49	1·94	2·40
May	0·88	0·99	1·08	1·30	1·53	1·95	2·44
June	0·87	0·98	1·10	1·22	1·58	2·00	2·51
July	0·85	1·00	1·10	1·26	1·60	2·04	2·59
August	0·52	1·00	1·09	1·25	1·67	1·95	2·53
September	0·80	1·02	1·11	1·34	1·70	2·10	2·78
October	0·88	1·01	1·14	1·33	1·70	2·19	2·34
November	0·91	1·00	1·17	1·42	1·83	2·25	2·30
December	0·91	1·01	1·18	1·42	1·86	2·35	2·31

Normal hours were reduced from 55½ to 48 weekly in March 1919; time rates were unchanged and piece rates increased 15 per cent. (quite apart from the changes already shown) to equalize the week's earnings for the same output.

If the changes in the rates are compared with the index-numbers of the cost of living (p. 106), it will be seen that they lagged behind both measures till the beginning of 1918, and were only brought up to the official measure by the arrangement of August 1919. Since that date the increase in wages for the (reduced) normal week have kept pace with the official measure, and are above the modified measure. If regularity of earnings and overtime are taken into account, it is clear that up to the summer of 1920 the operatives in these industries had increased their earnings (expressed in commodities) by some 20 per cent. After July 1920, however, earnings fell considerably, though rates of wages increased.

CHAPTER XV

WOMEN'S WAGES. WAGES UNDER THE TRADE BOARDS ACT

Increase of number of women in industry during the war. Orders regulating wages. Increase in earnings by 1918 and increase in nominal wages. Earnings in selected industries.

Minimum wages and their changes, 1914–20.

WOMEN'S WAGES

THOUGH the wages of women are included in the previous sections on Cotton, Wool, and Minimum Wages, they need also separate treatment, both because these trades do not include the majority of women workers, and because women's wages were subject to special regulation in connexion with munitions work. A sufficient account of these is given in the Report of the War Cabinet Committee on Women in Industry (Cmd. 135) up to the end of 1918, and an interesting summary is contained in a paper by Dorothea M. Barton in the *Journal of the Royal Statistical Society*, 1919, pp. 508 seq. To these two sources the writer is specially indebted.

The following tables (computed from Cmd. 135, pp. 80–1) indicate the magnitude and direction of the change and increase of women's employment for wages in the four years ending July 1918:

TABLE LXXIII

NUMBERS OF WOMEN AND GIRLS OCCUPIED IN 1914 AND 1918

	In July 1914	In July 1918
	000's	000's
Number of women and girls working		
In industry	2,179	2,971
,, domestic service	1,658	1,258
,, commerce, &c.	505	934
,, national and local government, including education	262	460
,, agriculture	190	228
,, employment of hotels, public houses, theatres, &c.	181	220
,, transport	18	117
Other occupied women and girls, including employers, home workers, workers on their own account	973	1,123
	5,966	7,311
Not in paid occupations, nor included above	12,946	12,496
Total women and girls over 10 years	18,912	19,807

The increase in the number occupied is partly due to an estimated increase of nearly 900,000 in the number of women and girls in the United Kingdom, and partly to an increase in the number occupied from about 32 to about 37 per cent. of all women and girls. The numbers in these tables are, in fact, rather rough estimates, for there has been no means of obtaining exact records at either date.

The increase of nearly 800,000 in industry is analysed as follows :

TABLE LXXIV

WOMEN AND GIRLS IN INDUSTRY, 1914 AND 1918

Industries	July 1914	July 1918	Differ-ence	Estimated number directly replacing men or boys in January 1918
	000's	000's	000's	000's
Metal	170	594	+ 424	195
Chemical	40	104	+ 64	35
Textile	863	827	− 36	64
Clothing	612	568	− 44	43
Food, drink, and tobacco .	196	235	+ 39	60
Paper and printing . .	148	142	− 6	21
Wood	44	79	+ 35	23
Government establishments	2	225	+ 223	197
Other	104	197	+ 93	62
Totals .	2,179	2,971	+ 792	704 [1]

It was the flow of women into occupations of an entirely new character, and into those which had formerly been followed by men and boys only, that gave rise to difficulties in fixing rates of wages.

Orders regulating wages were issued from time to time by the Ministry of Munitions. These extended over National Factories, operated directly for the Government, and at first as recommendations and later as instructions to all controlled establishments, that is factories coming under control in respect of production, costs, profits, &c. They had great influence on women's wages in similar occupations in uncontrolled factories, and indirectly they tended to set the standard for women's

[1] So stated. The total of the column is 700,000.

wages in general. It is said that 46 orders were issued between February 1916 and September 1918[1]; the following extracts show the principal regulations.

Order of October 1915 for National Factories, recommended to controlled establishments; enforced on controlled establishments February 28, 1916.

Clause 1. 'Women of 18 years and over employed on time, on work customarily done by men, shall be rated at £1 per week, reckoned on the usual working hours of the district in question for men in the engineering establishments. This, however, shall not apply in the case of women employed on work customarily done by fully skilled men, in which case the women shall be paid the time-rates of the tradesmen whose work they undertake.'

Clause 4. 'Where women are employed on piece-work, they shall be paid the same piece-work prices as are customarily paid to men for the job.'

In November 1915 an agreement was made between the Midland Employers' Federation and the Workers' Union to regulate the wages of female munition workers not covered by the above order, by which time rates for women over 21 years were fixed at 16*s.* in place of 12*s.* before the War. If the new rate gave no advance (since war bonuses had already been awarded) the minimum increase was to be 2*s.* on current rates.

Orders of July 1916. All women's wages in National Factories and controlled establishments were to be at least 4½*d.* an hour for time workers and 4*d.* an hour for piece workers. At fifty-three hours this gave women £1 weekly whether they were employed on men's work or not. This was a substantial increase on the wages agreed eight months before in the Midlands. In danger zones and on woodwork process in aircraft manufacture the rate was ½*d.* an hour more.

Order of December 1916. For women on men's work the £1 rate already fixed was made to apply to a forty-eight hours week (5*d.* an hour); an additional rate of 6*d.* an hour was payable for hours in excess of forty-eight up to fifty-four, when overtime rates were payable. Clause 1 of the order of October

---

[1] Barton, *loc. cit.*, p. 539.

1915 was modified to allow of reductions where women were not sufficiently trained or did not carry out the work of the men they replaced without extra cost to the employer. No one was, however, to receive less than £1.

Up to March 1917 women doing fully-skilled men's work had received the same advances as artisans in engineering trades (p. 126). After that date the advances to women were regulated separately.

Order of April 1917. The wages of women on fully-skilled men's work were advanced 4s. on the rates payable under the order of December 1916. The time rates for other women on men's work were also advanced 4s. to 24s. for forty-eight hours or less ; for further hours up to fifty-four the rate remained at 6d. The time rates for women on women's work were advanced to 5½d.

Order of August 1917. All earnings of women in munitions work were advanced 2s. 6d. a week. ' The scope of this order was far wider than any single previous statutory Order and the " munitions advance " was in fact very widely applied among women, whether strictly on munitions work or not ' (War Cabinet Committee, p. 118).

Advances on a similar basis were given in December 1917 (3s. 6d.), in September 1918 (5s.), and in January 1919 (5s.). As munitions work ceased these rates became applicable only in the engineering trade. The minimum for women on men's work after the last advance was 40s. for forty-seven hours.[1]

From the preceding paragraphs it is seen that the minimum rates for women in munition industries doing men's work was :

		s.	d.	
February 1916	. . .	20	0	for about 53 hours.
April 1917	. . .	24	0	for 48 hours or less.
August 1917	. . .	26	6	,, ,,
December 1917	. . .	30	0	,, ,,
September 1918	. . .	35	0	for 47 hours.
January 1919	. . .	40	0	,,

These rates should be compared with those of men in the engineering trades (pp. 125 seq.).

[1] A further advance of 3s. 6d. took place in December 1919.

Average earnings were considerably higher than these
minimum rates.   In April 1918 the average rates of women in a
number of National Factories were found to be 32s. 8d. (Shell),
34s. 8d. (Projectile), while the average earnings were 42s. 4d.
and 56s. 8d. respectively (ibid., p. 121).

It is stated (ibid., p. 124) that ' the actual average of women's
wages in the metal and munition trades as a result of the Orders
was increased rather more than threefold '.   It may be added
that the minimum rate for women on men's work was in January
1919 about three times the general average of women's wages
before the War.   A considerable part of this increase was, of
course, due to the movement to more skilled occupations and to
war conditions of demand.   The general increase in women's
wages was considerably less.

In 1906 the averages of the wages in a normal week in those
industries covered by the so-called wage census of that date,
which related principally to workpeople in factories and
excluded domestic service and most home work, were approximately 13s. 6d. for women over 18 and 7s. 3d. for girls.[1]   This is
approximately 3d. an hour for women.   The occupations omitted
would probably have shown a lower average, but on the other
hand there was a general tendency to an increase of wages (but
slight on modern standards) till 1914, so that the average of all
women over 18 employed in manual work at the beginning of the
War was approximately 3d. with a margin of doubt of perhaps
10 per cent.   The Cabinet Committee report ' It is probable that
the average of women's earnings over the whole field of industry
proper were (sic) towards the end of the war nearer 35s. than 30s.
weekly ' (p. 150).   This estimate of course includes the effect on
earnings of the stepping upward of women into men's occupations and into new occupations and includes also earnings for
overtime.   Before the War it is probable that broken time was
more prevalent than overtime, but not in all industries.   On
this basis women's earnings in industry as a whole were in
the autumn of 1918 about two and a half times their average
earnings in 1914.

[1] Bowley, *The Division of the Product of Industry*, 1919, p. 29.

In support of their estimate the Committee give details as follows (p. 151 of Report) :

' According to the estimates of witnesses, the average earnings of women at present may thus be graded roughly according to occupation :

Earning under 25s. weekly :
>   Dressmakers, milliners (first five years), laundry workers, pottery workers (most grades), knife girls and kitchen hands in refreshment houses.

Earning between 25s. and 30s. weekly :
>   Cutlery workers, soap and candle makers (unskilled), corner tenters (cotton), woollen and worsted weavers, backwashers (Scotch tweed), dyers and cleaners, biscuit makers, cigarette makers, pottery workers (certain grades), waitresses in refreshment dépôts.

Earning between 30s. and 35s. weekly :
>   Ammunition makers (women's work), chainmakers, salt packers, fine chemical workers, soap makers (most operations), card-room operatives (cotton), clothing machinists, workers in grain-milling and brewing, cigar makers, shop assistants (co-operative).

Earning between 35s. and 40s. weekly :
>   Workers in the light casting trade, chemical labourers, big tenters and ring-spinners (cotton), wool-combers, tailoring fitters and cutters, boot operatives, bakery workers, jigger women in potteries, tanners, shop assistants (large stores).

Earning between 40s. and 45s. weekly :
>   Workers in engineering, chemicals (shift work), and explosives ; textile dyers, tobacco machinists, motor drivers (for shop), railway carriage cleaners, telephonists, railway clerks.

Earning between 45s. and 50s. weekly :
>   Cloth lookers (cotton), hosiery machinists, web dyers, gas index-readers and lamplighters, railway porters, ticket collectors, telegraphists.

Earning between 50s. and 60s. weekly :
>   Ledger clerks, Civil Service clerks (Class I).

Earning over 60s. :
>   Women on skilled men's work in engineering, omnibus conductors (London), gas workers (heavy work for South Metropolitan Gas Co.).

The two lowest grades represent mainly feminine occupations, the three highest are almost entirely men's work, and the middle grades represent mainly occupations in which both sexes are engaged.'

The very important occupation of cotton-weaving, in which women's average earnings were estimated at 40s. at that date (p. 130), is omitted from the list, and it seems probable that wool-combers entered at 35s. to 40s. are those who replaced men, while others would be in the same grade as worsted weavers.

For women on women's work the average was no doubt lower than for all women, but these rough statements suggest that it can hardly have been below 30s. for a normal week, so that the rise during rather more than four years was in the neighbourhood of 120 per cent. In cotton we have seen that in June 1918 the rise in piece rates was 57 per cent. on the 1914 level and 105 per cent. in December 1918. In wool and worsted it was in November 1918 105 per cent. for time workers and 89 per cent. for piece workers.

A further partial review can be made for the summer of 1919 after the general reduction of hours to forty-eight. By this date munitions work was over, pressure for overtime was removed, and men had to a considerable extent replaced the women who had stepped into their occupations, so that a measure of stability had been reached. Cotton piece rates after July 1919 were 133 per cent. above the pre-war level, in the woollen and worsted industries in September 1919 time rates and piece rates for women were respectively 125 and 108 per cent. up, and minimum rates under the Trade Boards Act had in all cases doubled by the end of the year. It appears that on the whole after the reduction of hours women's wages for a normal week were definitely rather more than double the corresponding rates before the War. At the end of five years the general increase was little, if at all, more than the increase in the cost of living on the official measurement. The following extracts from a table given by Mrs. Barton (loc. cit., pp. 540 seq.) confirm this view. Industries included in the Trade Boards Section are omitted.

TABLE LXXV

MISCELLANEOUS STATEMENTS OF WOMEN'S WAGES

		1914 Usually 51½ to 55 hours	1918–19 Usually 48 hours
Sewing			
Dressmaking (bodice hand)			
London	. .	15*s*. to 22*s*.	April 1919, minimum 28*s*.
Birmingham	. .	15*s*. to 18*s*.	„ „ „
Millinery			
Bespoke, London	.	Competent, 12*s*. to 18*s*.	January 1919, minimum 24*s*.
Underclothing			
London	. .	15*s*. to 20*s*.	April 1919, minimum 28*s*.
Northampton	. .	14*s*.	„ „ „
Upholstery			
London	. .	12*s*. to 18*s*.	May 1919, minimum 52*s*. for french polishers, 44*s*. for upholsterers.
Leather			
Boot and shoe			
Bristol	. . .	14*s*. to 18*s*.	March 1919, minimum 30*s*.
Tobacco			
London			
Cigar making, hand		20*s*. to 30*s*.	May 1919, proposed minimum for Great Britain 35*s*.
„ mould		15*s*. to 25*s*.	
Stripping	. .	12*s*. to 14*s*.	
Printing and bookbinding			
London	. . .	Minimum 16*s*.	September 1918. Time workers 37*s*. Piece workers, increase of 100 to 120 per cent.
Brushmaking			
London	. . .	9*s*. to 12*s*.	August 1918, war bonus of 8*d*. in 1*s*.
Potteries			
Warehouse-women	.	12*s*.	May 1919, minimum 26*s*. 4*d*.
Fire-brick makers			
Stourbridge	. .	10*s*.	November 1918, war wage of 8*s*.
Metal trades			
Needles, &c.	. .	12*s*. 10*d*.	March 1919, minimum 22*s*. 11*d*. 50 hours.

In the figures quoted above (p. 179 and p. 183) for actual average earnings in certain industries men, women, boys, and girls are taken all together. The Department of Labour Statistics in 1916 persuaded a proportion cf the employers to state separately the earnings of women and girls, and some of the resulting figures are given in the Report of the Women's

Employment Committee (Cd. 9239, app. iv, p. 82); those for the cotton and woollen and worsted industries and the total are as follows:

TABLE LXXVI

AVERAGE WEEKLY EARNINGS OF WOMEN AND GIRLS REPORTED
BY EMPLOYERS

		Cotton		Woollen and worsted		All industries included		Percentages of 1906 level
		s.	d.	s.	d.	s.	d.	
1906	Wage Census							
	Averages . .	16	2	12	1	12	8	100
1915	May to Aug. .	17	1	15	3	14	9	116
	Sept. to Dec. .	17	0	15	6	14	10	117
1916	Jan. to Apr. .	17	11	16	1	15	4	121
	May to Aug. .	18	4	16	8	15	10	125
	Sept. to Dec. .	18	9	17	11	16	8	132
1917	Jan. to Apr. .	19	7	19	8	17	8	140
	May to Aug. .	20	7	19	9	19	1	151
	Sept. to Dec. .	21	5	21	9	20	5	161
1918	Jan. to Apr. .	23	3	22	8	21	10	172
	May to Aug. .	24	1	25	3	23	6	185
	Sept. to Nov. .	—		—		25	4 [1]	200
1919	Sept. . . .	—		—		30	2	238
	Oct. . . .	—		—		30	5	240
	Nov. . . .	—		—		31	2	247
	Dec. . . .	—		—		32	0	253

The industries included are Cotton, Woollen, Worsted, Linen, Jute, Hosiery, Lace, Silk, Carpet, Bleaching, &c., Boot and Shoe, Shirt and Collar, Ready-made Clothing, Printing, Book-binding, Pottery, Glass, and Food preparation; but the numbers included are not exactly proportional to the whole numbers employed.

It is not easy to continue to trace exactly the general movement from the end of 1918 to the summer of 1920, but there are data relating to particular industries which enable some judgement to be formed. In most cases in this period hours were reduced to forty-eight weekly, and the figures that follow compare the wages in the normal week of 51 to 55 hours in 1918 with that of 47 or 48 hours in 1920.

Cotton. At the end of 1918 the piece rates were 105 per

---

[1] This and subsequent figures have been furnished by the Ministry of Labour.

cent. above 1914; in June 1920 they were 159 per cent. above (p. 179).

Wool and Worsted. Time rates rose from 104¾ to 155 and women's piece rates from 89 to 133¼ per cent. above the basic rates of 1914 (p. 182).

Industries regulated, the Trade Boards Acts. Minimum rates rose from about 26s. (in some cases with a war bonus in addition) to 32s. or 34s. (pp. 194 seq.).

Hosiery. Leicestershire and neighbourhood. In December 1918 a bonus of 6½d. was paid on every 1s. earned on the pre-war scale, making an increase for the same work of 54 per cent. Earnings had, however, increased much more rapidly than this and were estimated to average 30s. apart from the bonus (Cabinet Committee, p. 133). In December 1919 there was a general increase of 6s. weekly, which may be estimated as raising wages for the same work to 90 or 95 per cent. above the pre-war level.

Jute and Linen. In Dundee women on women's work were receiving a bonus of 13s. a week and 2s. a week for keeping full time. This was raised to 18s. + 2s. in December 1919 and 21s. + 2s. in January 1920. Wages before the war averaged probably under 15s., so that they were more than doubled by the end of 1918, and were 150 per cent. above the pre-war level in 1920. The minimum rate in August 1920 was 32s.

Linen. In Belfast the war bonus had reached 18s. for females by December 1919, when hours were reduced to forty-eight weekly, and a further 5s. was added in May 1920.

These examples all support the general view that women's weekly rates were at the end of 1918 rather more than double the pre-war level, while their earnings had increased (owing to overtime, to undertaking men's work, or to temporary bonuses) more than this, while by the summer of 1920 the excess of earnings above rates had tended to disappear, and weekly rates were 2½ times those before the War. Average hourly rates of course rose more, from about 3d. to some amount between 8d. and 9d.

Note. In the *Tobacco* industry in Great Britain a minimum
of 35*s.* for forty-eight hours for women was agreed on by
employers and work people in May 1919, and under the Trade
Boards Act was raised to 38*s.* 6*d.* and made obligatory in July
1920. In 1906 the average was 12*s.*

In the *Cocoa and Chocolate* manufacture minimum rates
for women were arranged at 36*s.* in January 1920 and raised
to 42*s.* in August 1920.

In the Staffordshire *Potteries* rates, with a bonus on earnings,
were 80 per cent. above the pre-war level in March 1920 and
raised to + 100 per cent. in April and + 108⅓ in September 1920.

⚹ MINIMUM WAGES UNDER THE TRADE BOARDS ACT

Prior to the War statutory minimum wages had been
established under the Trade Boards Act of 1909 in the Chain-
making, Ready-made tailoring, Paper box, and Lace finishing
industries, and in 1915 and 1916 four other industries were
included. These industries were estimated to include about
320,000 women and 80,000 men in 1914. The general system
has been to fix minimum hourly rates for adults, without any
legal definite number of hours per week; since many of the
workers are paid piece rates, it is ordered that the piece rates
must be adequate to yield, in the circumstances of the case, to
an ordinary worker at least as much money as the minimum
time rate. Since 1918, however, most of the trades have fixed
a piece-work basis which is higher than the ordinary time rate,
and therefore many workers have benefited more than is shown
by the movement in minimum time rates. On pp. 198–9 are
shown for illustration the rates in the sugar and food-preserving
trades in 1915 and 1920.

The table on pp. 196–7 shows all the changes from July 1914
to July 1920 in the eight industries for which rates were established in or before 1916, and on p. 198 are shown the percentages
that the rates in July of each year bore to the starting rate.
It is noticeable that the movement was very slow from 1914 to
1917 and that the rise even by July 1918 was much slower than

in most of the industries dealt with in the previous chapters. These rates, however, are minimum and there was nothing to prevent an employer paying higher wages, and in some cases in 1918 there was a definite war bonus which was subsequently merged in the considerable increments granted in 1919 and 1920. It is noticeable that the statutory minimum time rates in the Chain trade have moved seldom and little, but ' according to the evidence of the Chain Manufacturers' Association, piece-work prices were advanced by negotiation with the Unions, so that women earned 140 per cent. over pre-war rates and not less than 25s. and up to 35s. a week ' (War Cabinet Committee on Women in Industry, Cmd. 135, p. 125). Similarly, in the Tin Box industry the large firms, ' in which the bulk of the work-people are employed, were covered by the earlier Orders of the Ministry of Munitions requiring advances of 6s. per week ' (ibid.), in addition to the advances in the statutory minimum. In 1919 hours were generally reduced to forty-eight and over-time rates were payable when this number was passed. Even if we suppose that in fact only forty-eight hours were generally worked after the shorter normal week was fixed, the increase during six years in the women's rates is on the whole about the same as in the industries included on p. 106 above. Men's rates in most cases increased more in pence per hour but less relatively. In 1914 they were about twice the women's rates, while in 1920 they were (except in chain-making) only 50 to 70 per cent. above.

The movement in these rates tends to reflect the general increase in the lowest rates paid for relatively unskilled women's work. In 1914 3¼d. was the highest rate, in 1920 7½d. was the lowest.

TABLE LXXVII

MINIMUM HOURLY RATES FIXED UNDER THE TRADE BOARDS ACT OF 1909
IN CERTAIN INDUSTRIES

| | Chain-making | | Paper box | | Tailoring ready-made | | Lace-finishing |
	Men	Women	Men	Women	Men	Women	Women
1914	*d.*	*d.*	*d.*	*d.*	*d.*	*d.*	*d.*
July	5·5 to 7·7	2¾	6	3	6	3¼	2¾
1915							
June	,,	,,	,,	,,	··	··	,,
July	,,	,,	,,	,,	,,	3½	,,
Nov.	,,	,,	,,	,,	,,	,,	··
Dec.	,,	,,	,,	3¼	,,	,,	··
1916							
Jan.	,,	,,	,,	,,	,,	,,	,,
Aug.	,,	,,	,,	,,	,,	,,	··
1917							
Feb.	,,	,,	,,	··	7	4	,,
Mar.	,,	,,	,,	,,	,,	,,	,,
May	,,	··	,,	,,	,,	,,	,,
July	,,	,,	··	,,	,,	,,	,,
Aug.	,,	,,	7	4	,,	,,	3½
Oct.	,,	··	,,	,,	,,	,,	,,
Nov.	,,	··	,,	,,	8	4½	,,
1918							
Jan.	,,	,,	8	4¾	,,	,,	,,
Mar.	6½ to 10	4	,,	,,	,,	5	,,
June	,,	,,	,,	,,	,,	,,	4
Sept.	,,	,,	,,	,,	,,	,,	,,
Nov.	,,	,,	,,	,,	,,	,,	,,
Dec.	,,	,,	9	5¾	,,	,,	,,
1919							
Feb.	,,	,,	,,	,,	,,	,,	4½
June	,,	,,	,,	,,	,,	,,	5½
Oct.	,,	,,	,,	··	,,	,,	,,
Nov.	17 to 23½	7½	13¾	8	,,	,,	,,
Dec.	,,	,,	,,	,,	13	8½	,,
1920							
Jan.	,,	,,	,,	,,	,,	,,	··
Feb.	,,	,,	,,	,,	,,	,,	7
June	,,	,,	,,	,,	,,	,,	,,
July	,,	,,	,,	,,	,,	,,	,,

The dates given are those in which the rates came into limited operation. During 6 months after the date employers could by agreement with their

TABLE LXXVII

MINIMUM HOURLY RATES FIXED UNDER THE TRADE BOARDS ACT OF 1909
IN CERTAIN INDUSTRIES

| | Sugar, confectionery and food preserving | | Hollow ware | | Tin box | | Shirt-making |
	Men	Women	Men	Women	Men	Women	Women
	d.	d.	d.	d.	d.	d.	d.
1914							
July	—	—	—	—	—	·—	—
1915							
June	6	3	—	—	—	—	—
July	,,	,,	—	—	—	—	3½
Nov.	,,	,,	—	—	6	3¼	,,
Dec.	,,	,,	—	—	,,	,,	,,
1916							
Jan.	,,	,,	5½	3	,,	,,	,,
Aug.	,,	3¼	,,	,,	,,	,,	,,
1917							
Feb.	,,	,,	,,	,,	,,	,,	4
Mar.	,,	,,	,,	,,	7	3¾	,,
May	7	3¾	,,	,,	,,	,,	,,
July	,,	,,	6½	3½	,,	,,	,,
Aug.	,,	,,	,,	,,	,,	,,	,,
Oct.	8	4½	,,	·,	8	4½	4½
Nov.	,,	,,	,,	,,	,,	,,	,,
1918							
Jan.	,,	,,	,,	4	,,	,,	,,
Mar.	,,	,,	,,	,,	,,	,,	5
June	,,	,,	,,	,,	,,	,,	,,
Sept.	,,	5	,,	,,	,,	,,	,,
Nov.	,,	,,	,,	,,	,,	,,	6
Dec.	,,	,,	,,	,,	9	5½	,,
1919							
Feb.	11	6½	,,	,,	,,	,,	,,
June	,,	,,	,,	,,	,,	,,	,,
Oct.	,,	,,	,,	7·85 [1]	,,	,,	,,
Nov.	,,	,,	,,	,,	12	7½	8
Dec.	,,	,,	,,	,,	,,	,,	,,
1920							
Jan.	,,	,,	13½	,,	·,,	,,	,,
Feb.	13½	7½	,,	,,	,,	,,	,,
June	,,	,,	,,	,,	15	9	,,
July	14½	8½	15 [2]	8¾ [2]	,,	,,	,,

employees pay less, but in fact very few did. In 1918 this arrangement was abolished, and 7 weeks allowed for complete application.

[1] 30s. 9d. for 47 hours.
[2] 58s. 6d. for 47 hours men, 34s. 3d. women.

TABLE LXXVIII

INDUSTRIES UNDER THE TRADE BOARDS ACTS

MEN

Hourly rates as percentages of rates in July 1914, 1915, 1916

	Chain-making		Paper box	Tailor-ing	Sugar &c.	Hollow ware	Tin box
	Highest	Lowest					
July 1914 . .	100	100	100	100	—	—	—
1915 . .	100	100	100	100	100	—	—
1916 . .	100.	100	100	100	100	100	100
1917 . .	100	100	100	117	117	118	117
1918 . .	130	118	133	133	133	118	133
1919 . .	130	118	150	133	183	118	150
1920 . .	305	309	229	217	241	273	250
Weekly rates July 1920 as percentages of weekly rates July 1914	—	—	210	208	223	236	231

WOMEN

Hourly Rates as Percentages of Rates in July 1914, 1915, or 1916

	Chain	Paper box	Tailor-ing	Lace	Sugar, &c.	Hollow ware	Tin box	Shirts
July 1914 . .	100	100	100	100	—	—	—	—
1915 . .	100	100	108	100	100	—	—	100
1916 . .	100	108	108	100	100	100	100	100
1917 . .	100	108	123	127	125	117	115	114
1918 . .	145	158	154	145	150	133	138	143
1919 . .	145	192	154	200	217	262	169	171
1920 . .	273	267	262	255	283	292	277	229
Weekly rates July 1920 as percentages of weekly rates July 1914	—	246	251	232	262	254	256	219

Towards the end of the War there were additional bonuses in some cases, but these were all consolidated with subsequent increases of the standard minima.

The Sugar Confectionery and Food Preserving Trade Board (Great Britain).

The rates fixed, to come into limited operation in June 1915, were as follows :

Male workers, other than learners 6d. an hour.
Female workers, ,, ,, 3d. ,,

Male learners, ranging from 6s. a week for those under 15 years of age.

to 23s.   ,,   ,,   of 21 and under 22 years.

Female learners, ranging from 6s. a week for those under 15 years of age.

to 11s.   ,,   ,,   of 17 and under 18 years.

Male workers over 22 years, with no previous experience 23s. weekly for 12 months.

Female workers over 18 years, with no previous experience 11s. weekly for 12 months.

The normal week was fifty-two hours.

These rates were raised from time to time (see p. 197) till in December 1918 they stood at $9d$. for males and $5\frac{1}{2}d$. for females.

In June 1919 the normal week was fixed at forty-eight hours and overtime rates were payable for hours in excess. In November 1919 the rates were raised to $12d$. and $7\frac{1}{2}d$.

In February 1920 (*Labour Gazette*, March 1920, pp. 154-5) females employed on certain processes were given the same rates as males. For learners these rates varied from 12s. for those under fifteen years to 50s. for those of twenty-three and under twenty-four years, increasing generally 4s. each year. For those over twenty-four years the rate was 1s. $1\frac{1}{2}d$. an hour, that is 54s. for a normal week of forty-eight hours.

Other female workers were to receive the same rates as males if under eighteen years, but if over eighteen a uniform minimum of $7\frac{1}{2}d$. an hour or 30s. a week.

Piece workers were rated so as to give a minimum of 1s. 4d. an hour for males and females on the special processes and 9d. for other females.

Overtime rates were double time on Sundays and holidays, and after nine hours on any ordinary day or five hours on Saturday time-and-a-quarter for first two hours and time-and-a-half afterwards.

APPENDIX I

WHOLESALE PRICES FROM THE ECONOMIST, 'MAINLY IN LONDON AND MANCHESTER'

GROUP I. CEREALS AND MEAT

Beginning of month	WHEAT North Manitoba No. 1 Quarter	WHEAT British Gazette Quarter	FLOUR Town Households 280 lb.	BARLEY British Gazette Quarter	OATS British Gazette Quarter	POTATOES Good English Ton	RICE Rangoon Cwt.	BEEF Inf. mid. to Prime large 8 lb.	MUTTON Inf. mid. to Prime 8 lb.	PORK 8 lb.
	s. d.	s. d.	s. d.	s. d.	s. d.	s. d.	s. d.	s. d.	s. d.	s. d.
1914										
Jan.	35 3	31 0	28 0	25 10	18 4	70 0	7 7½	3 10 to 5 6	5 2 to 7 6	4 4
Apr.	36 9	31 6	28 3	25 6	18 5	65 0	7 7½	3 6 to 5 2	4 2 to 7 6	4 5
July	36 9	34 1	28 6	25 4	20 0	—	7 0	3 8 to 5 4	4 0 to 6 8	3 7
Oct.	42 6	37 0	36 0	29 1	22 9	67 6	nom.	3 6 to 5 6	4 10 to 7 2	5 0
1915										
Jan.	54 3	43 3	41 0	29 10	26 6	77 6	12 6	3 4 to 6 2	4 8 to 6 8	4 11
Apr.	67 9	55 3	51 0	31 11	30 6	97 6	12 1½	3 10 to 6 4	6 0 to 8 2	6 0
July	58 0	52 0	44 0	35 3	31 1	80 0	12 10½	5 6 to 7 10	5 8 to 7 4	5 10
Oct.	60 0	43 5	43 0	40 4	26 5	77 6	14 4½	4 4 to 7 4	5 4 to 7 8	6 9
1916										
Jan.	66 4½	53 11	50 0	47 5	30 10	100 0	14 7½	4 6 to 6 6	5 6 to 7 6	6 10
Apr.	66 6	55 11	49 0	44 6	31 4	100 0	16 9	4 8 to 7 2	7 4 to 9 6	6 10
July	54 9	46 3	42 0	49 1	30 10	280 0	16 0	6 6 to 9 2	7 6 to 9 2	7 2
Oct.	77 6	58 10	57 0	54 1	31 1	145 0	17 0	6 2 to 7 10	6 8 to 8 10	7 11
1917				G. R.						
Jan.	90 0	74 10	59 0	67 5	47 4	240 0	20 0	6 8 to 10 0	8 6 to 11 4	7 4
Apr.	nom.	80 3	60 0	69 11	55 1	240 0	26 6	8 0 to 10 4	8 10 to 11 4	8 1
July	nom.	78 1	nom.	69 5	55 2	nom.	26 3	9 0 to 11 8	10 0 to 12 8	8 10
Oct.	75 6	70 8	44 3	57 9	44 9	140 0	26 3	7 10 to 10 0	9 2 to 11 0	9 6

								First grade cwt. s. d.		
1918 Jan.	77 6	71 2	44 3	58 0	45 5	140 0	26 3	72 6	12 0 to 14 0	9 6
Apr.	81 6	72 4	44 3	56 7	48 10	135 0	26 3	72 6	9 6	10 8
July	82 6	74 4	44 3	67 10	46 4	260 0	26 3	73 6	9 6	10 8
Oct.	82 6	72 7	44 3	60 3	50 3	150 0	26 3	73 6	9 6	10 8
1919 Jan.	84 1½	72 3	44 3	62 3	50 6	198 0	26 3	73 6	9 6	12 0
Apr.	—	72 6	44 3	62 8	46 11	212 6	26 3	78 6	9 6	10 8
July	—	73 4	44 3	62 4	49 0	165 0	29 0	79 6	9 6	10 1
Oct.	63 6	73 4	44 3	94 4	59 6	200 0	27 0	79 0	9 6	10 1
1920 Jan.	—	72 6	44 3	107 1	57 8	220 0	33 0	79 6 *8 lb.*	10 0	10 7
Apr.	95 0	72 8	63 6	91 8	56 5	225 0	32 0	9 4	10 0	10 7
July	95 0	78 9	63 6	87 2	64 7	237 6	28 0	9 4	10 0	10 6
Oct.	94 0	90 5	86 0	80 2	55 5	190 0	27 0	9 5	10 2	10 10
1921 Jan.	102 0	84 11	80 0	73 5	41 5	180 0	20 0	9 4	9 10	8 4

NOTE.—The figures in this table are compiled from various issues of the *Economist* during the years 1914-21. They are not in all cases the numbers on which The *Economist* Index-number is based; these were not published till the issue of February 19, 1921 (pp. 407 seq.), and there the exact descriptions of the commodities are not given throughout the period.

GROUP II. OTHER FOOD PRODUCTS, ETC.

	TEA	COFFEE	SUGAR		BUTTER	TOBACCO
	Congou Mid. com. to med. gd. lb.	Jamaica Ord. to Fine ord. cwt.	Cane West India Syrups cwt.	Beet German cwt.	Danish cwt.	Virginia leaf in bond lb.
1914	d. d.	s. d.	s. d.	s. d.	£ s. d.	d. d.
Jan.	5 to 7½	59 0	11 6	9 0	6 11 0	5½ to 18
Apr.	5 to 7¼	56 6	11 3	9 2	6 3 0	5½ to 18
July	6⅛ to 8¼	57 0	11 3	9 2½	6 1 0	5½ to 18
Oct.	8⅜ to 9¾	55 0	18 3	—	7 0 0	5½ to 18
1915						
Jan.	8⅜ to 9¾	59 0	14 7	—	7 12 0	5½ to 18
Apr.	9¼ to 11¼	54 0	14 9	—	7 0 0	5½ to 18
July	8½ to 11¼	52 6	16 0	—	7 12 0	5½ to 18
Oct.	8¾ to 11¼	49 0	22 0	—	10 0 6	5½ to 18
1916						
Jan.	7¾ to 11¼	53 0	27 9	—	7 13 0	5½ to 18
			Granulated			
April	7 to 12	56 6	37 0	—	8 12 0	5½ to 18
July	8½ to 12	63 0	41 10½	—	8 14 0	8 to 18
Oct.	8½ to 12	64 0	41 10½	—	10 11 0	8 to 18
1917						
Jan.	8½ to 12	64 0	41 10½	—	10 18 0	8 to 18
	Broken and fannings					
Apr.	15 to 18	nom.	41 10½	—	10 10 0	8 to 18
July	nom.	,,	46 9	—	10 10 0	9 to 21
Oct.	18 to 24	,,	46 9	—	nom.	9 to 21
1918						
Jan.	12 to 18	,,	46 9	—	,,	12 to 24
Apr.	nom.	,,	46 9	—	,,	12 to 24
July	16	,,	57 9	—	,,	18 to 30
Oct.	16	,,	57 9	—	,,	18 to 30
		East India, Fine ord. and Santos	*West Indian Syrups*			
1919		s. d.	s. d.			
Jan.	16	142 9	55 6	—	,,	18 to 30
Apr.	16	142 9	55 6	—	,,	24
July	15½	143 0	55 6	—	,,	24
Oct.	18½	151 6	55 6	—	,,	24
1920						
Jan.	20½	152 6	63 6	—	,,	24
Apr.	19½	158 9	71 9	—	13 16 0	24
July	12½	152 6	95 9	—	13 6 0	24
Oct.	11¼	134 9	95 9	—	16 14 0	24
1921						
Jan.	11½	131 9	62 0	—	16 16 0	24

In many cases prices fluctuated so rapidly that a good deal depends on what day of the month prices are quoted.

GROUP III. TEXTILES

	Silk	Hemp	Flax	Jute	Wool		Cotton			
							Raw		Yarn	Cloth
	Blue elephant lb.	*Manila ton*	*Riga Z K ton*	*Native firsts ton*	*English 240 lb.*	*Good Victoria lb.*	*Middling American lb.*	*Egypt Good fair brown lb.*	*32's twist lb.*	*37½ yards 16 by 15 39 in. shirtings 8¼ lb.*
1914	*s. d.*	*£ s.*	*£ s.*	*£ s.*	*£ s.*	*s. d.*	*d.*	*d.*	*d.*	*s. d.*
Jan.	11 4½	26 15	32 15	35 15	15 4	1 11	7·14	9·65	10¼	8 1
Apr.	11 7½	26 15	28 10	34 5	15 15	2 0½	7·22	8·80	9 15/16	7 10
July	11 7½	26 0	30 15	26 15	15 15	2 0½	7·53	8·75	10	7 10
Oct.	11 4½	27 5	nom.	35 5	14 15	2 0½	5·30	7·35	8½	7 1
1915										
Jan.	10 1½	26 0	,,	18 5	17 15	1 9	4·58	6·05	7⅛	6 5½
Apr.	10 1½	41 0	,,	22 15	19 15	2 1	5·48	7·50	8¼	7 0½
July	9 4½	41 0	,,	21 15	21 5	2 3	5·22	7·20	8⅜	6 10
Oct.	9 7½	41 0	,,	25 10	22 5	2 2	6·85	9·35	10⅛	7 9
					South Down ewes and wethers lb.					
1916					*s. d.*					
Jan.	12 9	47 0	,,	27 15	1 11¼	2 5½	7·75	9·80	12	8 9
Apr.	14 9	56 0	,,	34 0	2 0½	2 7	7·83	10·63	12⅜	8 10
July	15 9	54 0	,,	30 0	1 11¾	2 10½	8·21	11·4	12¾	9 2½
Oct.	17 3	53 0	91 0	33 0	2 0	3 1½	9·95	14·45	14⅝	10 5
1917										
Jan.	18 0	60 0	94 0	43 5	2 4½	4 4½	10·88	19·95	17¼	12 0
Apr.	19 3	96 0	100 0	nom.	2 4	4 6	12·69	26·25	17¼	12 0
July	20 6	85 0	152 0	,,	2 4½	4 10½	19·10	29·10	24½	16 1½
Oct.	25 0	85 0	152 0	,,	2 4½	4 10½	20·37	33·0	27	18 3

GROUP III (*continued*). TEXTILES

	SILK	HEMP	FLAX	JUTE	WOOL		COTTON			
							Raw			
	Blue elephant	*Manila*	*Riga Z K*	*Native firsts*	*South Down ewes and wethers*	*Good Victoria*	*Middling American*	*Egypt Fully good fair*	*Yarn 32's twist*	*Cloth 37½ yards 16 by 15 39 in. shirtings 8¼ lb.*
	lb.	*ton*	*ton*	*ton*	*lb.*	*lb.*	*lb.*	*lb.*	*lb.*	*8¼ lb.*
1918	*s. d.*	*£ s.*	*£ s.*	*£ s.*	*s. d.*	*s. d.*	*d.*	*d.*	*d.*	*s. d.*
Jan.	25 0	85 0	147 0	nom.	2 4½	4 10½	23·52	31·40	38¼	25 0
				Coir yarn good to fine						
Apr.	25 0	100 0	147 0	25 0	—	—	25·16	30·56	43	28 0
July	26 0	100 0	147 0	25 0	—	—	22·92	28·82	49¾	30 6
Oct.	27 6	100 0	147 0	nom.	—	—	25·24	29·40	56¾	36 3
1919										
Jan.	23 6	100 0	177 0	,,	—	—	22·20	27·30	41¼	32 3
Apr.	20 6	58 0	177 0	,,	—	—	16·16	26·59	26	23 0
						Victorian Australian scoured good				
July	27 0	55 0	177 0	56 15	2 4½	—	19·64	27·09	39½	29 0
Oct.	33 0	49 10	230 0	70 0	2 4½	6 6	20·02	30	42¼	30 6
1920	*Canton*									
Jan.	48 6	60 0	230 0	61 0	2 4½	6 10	30·75	54	55½	40 6
Apr.	57 6	68 10	362 10	57 0	2 7	8 2	29·01	83	62	45 0
July	28 0	59 0	382 10	45 0	2 4	7 4	26·62	62	54½	42 6
Oct.	31 6	69 10	382 10	56 10	2 1½	6 0	20·90	54	47	34 0
1921										
Jan.	24 0	58 0	150 0	38 10	1 8	3 8	10·27	23	24½	21 0

GROUP IV. MINERALS

	Pig Iron	Steel	Iron Bars	Coal	Lead	Tin	Copper
	Middlesbro' good marked Bars ton	Heavy Rails ton	Welsh Ports ton	Best Yorkshire Silkstone House ton	English Pig ton	English Bars ton	Standard ton
	£ s. d.	£ s. d.	£ s. d.	s. d.	£ s. d.	£ s. d.	£ s. d.
1914							
Jan.	2 10 6	6 10 0	7 15 0	17 6	18 15 0	171 0 0	64 0 0
Apr.	2 11 9	6 10 0	7 15 0	17 6	18 10 0	171 10 0	65 15 0
July	2 11 3	6 0 0	7 15 0	16 6	19 10 0	145 0 0	61 12 6
Oct.	2 11 3	6 15 0	7 15 0	16 6	19 5 0	135 0 0	57 0 0
1915							
Jan.	2 14 3	6 7 6	8 0 0	14 0	19 15 0	146 10 0	56 12 6
Apr.	3 7 3	7 10 0	7 15 0	18 0	24 0 0	177 10 0	69 2 6
July	3 7 0	8 0 0	7 15 0	17 3	26 0 0	173 0 0	78 2 6
Oct.	3 5 3	9 0 0	7 15 0	17 3	25 10 9	151 5 0	73 0 0
1916							
Jan.	3 18 0	11 0 0	7 15 0	18 3	30 0 3	169 0 0	86 2 6
			Middlesbro'				
Apr.	4 2 6	10 17 6	13 10 0	18 3	nom.	202 0 0	116 0 0
July	4 7 6	11 5 0	13 15 0	18 3	30 5 0	179 10 0	103 10 0
Oct.	4 7 6	11 5 0	14 17 6	18 6	32 5 0	180 10 0	120 10 0
1917							
Jan.	4 7 6	11 5 0	15 0 0	18 6	32 5 0	184 0 0	133 5 0
Apr.	4 12 6	10 17 6	15 0 0	19 0	nom.	224 10 0	136 5 0
July	4 12 6	11 5 0	15 0 0	19 0	—	251 0 0	130 5 0
Oct.	4 12 6	11 5 0	15 0 0	18 3	—	246 0 0	110 5 0
1918							
Jan.	4 15 0	10 17 6	13 15 0	20 6	—	283 10 0	110 5 0
Apr.	4 15 0	10 17 6	13 15 0	21 3	nom.	322 10 0	110 5 0
July	4 15 0	10 17 6	13 17 6	20 6	,,	345 0 0	122 5 0
Oct.	4 15 0	10 17 6	14 15 0	24 0	,,	338 10 0	122 5 0
1919							
Jan.	4 15 0	10 17 6	15 10 0	24 0	,,	237 0 0	112 0 0
Apr.	4 15 0	13 10 0	17 15 0	24 0	28 10 0	236 12 6	78 5 0
July	8 0 0	16 0 0	20 10 0	24 0	23 10 0	240 10 0	91 0 0
Oct.	8 0 0	16 10 0	22 0 0	30 0	26 0 0	278 5 0	103 7 6
				Best House, Forest of Dean			
1920							
Jan.	8 0 0	17 10 0	22 10 0	21 6	46 10 0	347 12 6	116 2 6
Apr.	10 0 0	21 0 0	26 0 0	26 6	45 0 0	348 5 0	107 7 6
July	10 17 6	23 0 0	30 0 0	40 0	36 10 0	260 5 0	89 17 6
Oct.	11 5 0	25 0 0	30 0 0	40 0	34 15 0	271 12 6	94 7 6
1921							
Jan.	11 5 0	25 10 0	27 10 0	40 0	25 10 0	205 15 0	71 17 6

GROUP V. MISCELLANEOUS

	Timber	Leather	Petroleum	Oil		Seeds		Tallow	Indigo	Crystals	India-Rubber
	Dantzic and Memel load	Mixed Tannage. Butts or Bends lb.	(Water-white) 8 lb.	Seal-Pale 252 galls.	Palm (Lagos) tun	Linseed ton	English Rape casks	Town cwt.	Bengal (good red violet) lb.	(Soda-Bi-Carbonate) ton	Paru (Fine hard) lb.
1914	£ s. d.	s. d.	s. d.	£ s.	£ s.	£ s. d.	£ s.	£ s. d.	s. d.	£ s. d.	s. d.
Jan.	4 10 0	2 2	9½	nom.	35 0	24 17 6	32 0	1 14 0	3 3	2 7 6	3 1½
Apr.	4 10 0	2 2	9	25 10	36 0	26 0 0	24 5	1 13 6	3 3	2 7 6	2 11½
July	4 10 0	2 2	8¼	25 10	31 10	25 3 9	32 0	1 10 9	3 3	2 7 6	2 9½
Oct.	4 10 0	2 8	nom.	nom.	nom.	25 10 0	35 10	1 9 0	9 9	5 16 0	2 9½
1915											
Jan.	4 15 0	2 3	8¼	,,	33 0	23 18 9	34 10	1 10 6	13 6	5 16 3	2 10½
Apr.	5 10 0	2 6	9½	,,	39 0	36 0 0	41 10	1 17 6	14 3	5 16 3	2 5½
July	7 0 0	2 7½	9¾	,,	31 0	27 7 6	39 0	1 12 3	13 6	5 16 9	2 7¼
Oct.	7 0 0	2 5	10½	,,	29 10	27 2 6	37 15	1 14 9	13 6	5 16 9	2 4½
1916											
Jan.	7 0 0	2 3½	11	,,	43 0	41 5 0	50 15	2 4 6	14 0	6 17 6	3 9
Apr.	11 15 0	2 5½	1 0	,,	49 0	39 6 0	55 6	2 8 6	14 9	6 17 6	3 0¼
	Pitch Pine										
July	13 0 0	2 7½	1 1	,,	40 0	33 10 0	49 0	2 5 0	14 9	6 17 6	2 8
Oct.	13 0 0	2 7½	1 2½	,,	38 0	38 15 0	49 0	2 2 6	14 0	6 17 6	3 3
1917											
Jan.	13 0 0	2 6	1 2½	56 0	51 0	50 10 0	58 0	2 10 6	13 9	7 12 6	3 3½
		English shoulders									
Apr.	17 10 0	2 3	1 3	nom.	49 0	53 15 0	69 0	2 17 6	12 10½	7 5 0	3 1½
July	17 10 0	2 4½	1 3½	—	44 0	58 0 0	71 0	2 18 6	12 9	7 5 0	3 0
Oct.	17 10 0	2 0	1 9½	—	47 0	56 0 0	76 0	3 10 6	11 3	7 15 0	3 4½

1918											
Jan.	17 10 0	2 1	1 8½	—	47 0	58 0 0	76 0	3 10 6	10 3	7 15 0	2 9½
		Sole bends 6-10 lb.									
Apr.	17 10 0	2 9	1 8½	—	45 0	58 0 0	nom.	nom.	9 6	8 2 6	3 1
July	17 10 0	2 10	1 10½	—	45 0	75 0 0	,,	4 8 6	9 6	7 15 0	3 0¾
Oct.	nom.	2 10	1 11½	—	45 0	75 0 0	,,	4 8 6	10 6	6 15 0	3 2
1919											
Jan.	,,	2 10	1 5½	—	—	—	—	4 8 6	10 6	6 15 0	2 7½
Apr.	,,	2 10½	1 5½	—	44 0	58 0 0	76 0	3 15 0	10 6	5 15 0	2 5
July	,,	3 6	1 5½	—	84 0	125 0 0	108 0	3 5 0	10 0	5 15 0	2 5
Oct.	,,	3 8½	1 7½	—	78 0	81 0 0	105 0	3 5 0	9 0	5 15 0	2 6
				Mean		*Mean*					
1920				£ *s.* *d.*		£ *s.*					
Jan.	,,	3 10	1 10	75 12 6		109 0		3 5 0	12 6	5 15 0	2 7
Apr.	,,	3 2	2 1¾	98 17 6		122 0		3 4 0	14 9	12 10 0	2 4
July	,,	2 10	2 1¾	83 5 0		80 10		2 6 0	14 9	12 10 0	1 11½
Oct.	17 10 0	2 8	2 1¾	87 17 6		82 10		2 7 0	14 9	10 0 0	1 7
1921											
Jan.	13 0 0	2 6	2 3¼	64 7 6		59 10		2 2 0	12 0	10 0 0	1 0½

APPENDIX II

MAXIMUM FOOD RETAIL PRICES

SUMMARY OF MAXIMUM FOOD RETAIL PRICES, SEPTEMBER 1917 TO MARCH 1920

CEREALS, &c.

Bread. From September 17, 1917, 4 lb. loaf, 9*d.*; 2 lb. loaf, 4½*d.*; 1 lb. loaf (if 2 lb. is on sale), 2½*d.* Unchanged till September 1919, when ½*d.* and ¼*d.* were added to the price of the 4 lb. and 2 lb. loaves. Unchanged till after March 1920.

Flour. From September 17, 1917, Sack (280 lb.) or half sack at 50*s.* per sack; 7 lb. to 140 lb. at 2*s.* 8*d.* per 14 lb.; quartern (3½ lb.), 8½*d.*; half quartern, 4¼*d.*, 1 lb., 2½*d.* Self-raising, 3½*d.* Unchanged till after March 1920.

Oatmeal and Oats (rolled, flaked, and like products). September 1917, England, 5*d.*, Scotland, 4½*d.* per lb.; January 1, 1918, 7 lb., 2*s.* (Scotland), 2*s.* 3*d.* (Rest of United Kingdom), 1 lb., 3½*d.* and 4*d.*, oat-flour, ½*d.* per lb. more. February 21, 1918, 7 lb., 2*s.* 3½*d.* (Scotland and Ireland), 2*s.* 6½*d.* (England and Wales), 1 lb., 4*d.* and 4½*d.* Unchanged till May 1919, after which date no maximum price.

Maize. Flour, flakes, semolina. September 1917, 3½*d.* per lb., raised to 4*d.* September 1918, unchanged till March 1919, after which no maximum price.

Rice. Maximum price first fixed in February 1918 at 4*d.* per lb., some grades higher if rice at 4*d.* is also on sale. Unchanged till after March 1920.

Beans, Peas, Lentils. September 1917 : beans, coloured haricot, 5½*d.* per lb., white haricot, 6*d.*, large butter, 8*d.* ; peas, blue and green (whole or split), 9*d.*, yellow (split), 6*d.* ; lentils, large manufactured, 8*d.*, small manufactured, 7*d.* Unchanged till after March 1920.

Potatoes. September 1917 ; according to buyer's price, generally at 7*d.* for 7 lb. Unchanged till summer of 1918, and then no maximum price. Reimposed in December 1918 on a slightly higher scale till September 1919, then dropped.

DAIRY PRODUCTS AND MARGARINE

Cheese. September 1917, United States, Canadian, Australian, and New Zealand cheese, 1*s.* 4*d.* per lb. November 1917, retailer's profit on British cheese limited to 2½*d.* per lb., and limitation continued on cheese not controlled in distribution till January 1920, when restrictions on price were removed.

The Government acquired and distributed cheese from June 1917. The retail price in August 1918 was 1s. 8d. per lb., in March 1919 it was lowered to 1s. 6d., and raised again to 1s. 8d. in December 1919, at which price it remained till after March 1920.

Milk. The winter maximum prices for 1917–18 were fixed at 7d. per quart in October 1917, 8d. November to March inclusive, prices in rural districts being 1d. less. Summer maximum prices were first fixed at 2s. 8d. for April 1918, and at 2s. for the next three months, but subsequently they were raised to 2s. 4d. for June and July, and 2s. 8d. for August and September. The maximum prices for the winter of 1918–19 were 9d. in October and November and 10d. from November 22, 1918, till April 30, 1919, subject to variation by Local Committees (as were the summer prices of 1918). The summer maximum prices in 1919 were fixed for England and Wales [1] at 7d. in May and June, 8d. in July and August, and 9d. in September. The subsequent winter maximum prices were October 11d., and November and December 1s. Control was removed in January 1920. An idea of the extent to which these maxima were realized can be obtained from a study of the figures on pp. 42–6 and 54.

The maximum prices of *condensed milk* were fixed in May 1918 and at subsequent dates altered as follows :

		May 1918	July 1918	Feb. 1919	Aug. 1919	Nov. 1919	Jan. 1920
		s. d.	s. d.	s. d.	s. d.	s. d.	
Full Cream sweetened	14 oz. net	1 2½	1 2½	1 1	1 2½	1 3	Maximum
„ „ evaporated	16 „ „	1 1	11½	10	1 0	1 0	prices
„ „ unsweetened	12 „ „	1 0½	11½	10	11	11	sus-
Machine skimmed	16 „ gross	1 1	1 1	1 0	1 0	1 0	pended.

Butter. In September 1917 the retailer was restricted to a profit of 2½d. per lb. From November 1917 home and imported butter were blended together ('Government butter') and sold at 2s. 3d. to 2s. 5d. Subsequent prices were December 1917, 2s. 6d., June 1918, 2s. 4d., September 1918, 2s. 6d., February 1920, 2s. 8d., March 1920, 3s. Home-produced butter was decontrolled January 31, 1920.

Margarine. The prices were first fixed in November 1917 at 1s. per lb. for margarine, 1s. 4d. for oleo-margarine. In February 1918 Dutch margarine was sold at 1s. 2d. In March or April 1918 all margarine was sold at 1s. ; in July 1918 the price was raised to 1s. 2d., in November lowered to 1s., at which price it remained till May 1919, after which no maximum price was enforced.

[1] In Scotland, 8d. in May, 7d. in June and July, 8d. in August, 9d. in September.

MEAT, BACON, AND FISH

Meat. From August 29, 1917, retailers were limited to charging not more than 2½d., or 20 per cent. (whichever was less) in excess of the prices they paid to the wholesalers. In March 1918 a scale of maximum retail prices was prescribed for London and the Home Counties and another for the rest of England and Wales. This was amended from time to time and is too complicated for exhibition at every change, but since it is important as illustrating how detailed such regulations must be the scale for London and the Home Counties is given at six monthly intervals.

Uniform scale for London and Home Counties

	In force Aug. 14, 1918	Jan. 22, 1919	Aug. 13, 1919	Jan. 14, 1920 Home killed	Imported
	s. d.	*s. d.*	*s. d.*	*s. d.*	*s. d.*
Beef Joints per lb.					
Topside of Round . . .	1 8	1 10	1 8	1 10	1 7
,, (best cut) boneless .	1 10	2 0	1 10	2 0	1 9
Silverside with bone .	1 6	1 8	1 6	1 8	1 5
,, boneless . .	1 9	1 11	1 9	1 11	1 8
Thick flank . . .	1 7	1 9	1 7	1 10	1 7
,, ,, best cut .	1 8	1 10	1 8	1 11	1 8
,, ,, knuckle end .	1 6	1 8	1 6	1 9	1 6
Aitch bone . . .	1 0	1 2	1 0	1 2	11
,, ,, boneless .	1 5	1 7	1 5	1 7	1 4
Sirloin	1 7	1 9	1 7	1 9	1 6
,, cuts . . .	1 8½	1 10½	1 8½	1 10	1 7
,, rolled boneless .	1 11	2 1	1 11	2 1	1 10
Thin flank . . .	1 0	1 2	1 0	1 2	11
,, ,, rolled boneless .	1 4	1 6	1 4	1 6	1 3
Leg and shin whole. .	8	10	8	10	7
,, ,, boneless .	1 4	1 6	1 4	1 6	1 3
Suet	1 6	1 8	1 6	1 8	1 5
Fore ribs . . .	1 6	1 8	1 6	1 8	1 5
,, boneless . .	1 9	1 11	1 9	1 11	1 8
Wing ribs 4 bones . .	1 8	1 10	1 8	1 10	1 7
Long ribs . . .	1 4	1 6	1 4	1 7	1 4
,, ,, rolled boneless .	1 9	1 11	1 9	1 11	1 8
Back ribs . . .	1 3	1 5	1 3	1 6	1 3
,, ,, boneless . .	1 7	1 9	1 7	1 9	1 6
Top ribs . . .	1 3	1 5	1 3	1 6	1 3
,, ,, boneless . .	1 7	1 9	1 7	1 9	1 6
Brisket	1 0	1 2	1 0	1 2	11
,, boneless . .	1 4	1 6	1 4	1 6	1 3
Clod and sticking with bone .	1 0	1 2	1 0	1 2	11
,, ,, boneless	1 4	1 6	1 4	1 6	1 3
Rump	1 8½	1 10½	1 8½	1 11	1 8
,, steak (boneless) .	2 2	2 4	2 2	2 4	2 1

	In force Aug. 14, 1918	Jan. 22, 1919	Aug. 13, 1919	Jan. 14, 1920 Home killed	Imported

Beef Joints per lb.

	s. d.	s. d.	s. d.	s. d.	s. d.
Fillet steak	2 2	2 4	2 2	2 4	2 1
Buttock steak (boneless)	2 0	2 2	2 0	2 2	1 11
Thick flank steak	1 10	2 0	1 10	2 0	1 9
Chuck steak	1 8	1 10	1 8	1 10	1 7
Gravy beef	1 4	1 6	1 4	1 6	1 3
Minced beef	1 6	1 8	1 6	1 8	1 5
Sausage to contain not less than 50 per cent. of meat	1 3	1 4	1 2	1 3	1 3
Sausage to contain not less than 67 per cent. of meat	1 6	1 7	1 5	1 6	1 6
Sausage meat to contain not less than 50 per cent. of meat	1 1	1 2	1 0	1 1	1 1
Sausage meat to contain not less than 67 per cent. of meat	1 4	1 5	1 3	1 4	1 4
Sausage and sausage meat containing less than 50 per cent. meat to be sold at a price not exceeding	10	—	—	—	—
Bones	2	2	2	2	2

Mutton and Lamb Joints per lb.

	s. d.	s. d.	s. d.	s. d.	s. d.
Leg whole	1 7	1 9	1 7	1 9	1 4
„ cut, Fillet	1 7½	1 9½	1 7½	1 9½	1 4½
„ „ Shank	1 7½	1 9½	1 7½	1 9½	1 4½
„ „ Middle	1 10	2 0	1 10	—	
Loin, whole	1 5	1 7	1 5	1 7	1 2
„ Best end	1 8	1 10	1 8	1 10	1 5
„ Chump end	1 5	1 7	1 5	1 6	1 1
Loin chops (not to be trimmed)	1 10	2 0	1 10	2 0	1 7
Saddles	1 5	1 7	1 5	1 7	1 2
Shoulders, whole	1 5	1 7	1 5	1 8	1 3
„ cut knuckle end	1 5	1 7	1 5	1 8½	1 3½
„ Blade side	1 5	1 7	1 5	1 8½	1 3½
„ Middle	1 6	1 8	1 6	—	—
Neck, whole	1 2	1 4	1 2	1 4	11
„ Best end	1 6	1 8	1 6	1 8	1 3
„ Middle	1 2	1 4	1 2	1 4	11
„ Scrag	11	1 1	11	1 1	8
Best Neck Chops	1 8	1 10	1 8	1 10	1 5
Breasts, whole	11	1 1	11	1 1	8
„ cut, Best end	1 0	1 2	1 0	1 2	9
„ „ Fat end	10	1 0	10	1 0	7
„ „ Sliced	1 2	1 4	1 2	1 4	11
Suet	1 2	1 4	1 2	1 4	11

	In force Aug. 14, 1918	Jan. 22, 1919	Aug. 13, 1919	Jan. 14, 1920 Home killed	Imported
Pork Joints per lb.	s. d.	s. d.	s. d.	s. d.	s. d.
Leg, whole	1 8	1 8	1 8	1 8	1 6
,, cut knuckle end	1 6	1 6	1 6	1 6	1 4
,, Middle	1 11	1 11	1 11	1 11	1 9
,, Fillet	1 10	1 10	1 10	1 10	1 8
Hind Loin, whole	1 10	1 10	1 10	1 10	1 8
,, ,, Chump end	1 9	1 9	1 9	1 9	1 7 '
,, ,, Best end	1 11	1 11	1 11	1 11	1 9
Fore Loin or Griskin, or Spare Rib, without Blade bone	1 10	1 10	1 10	1 10	1 8
Hand with Foot	1 4	1 4	1 4	1 4	1 2
Loin, excluding Back fat	1 10	1 10	1 10	1 10	1 8
,, Best end	1 11	1 11	1 11	1 11	1 9
Neck end	1 8	1 8	1 8	1 8	1 6
Shoulder without Hock	1 7	1 7	1 7	1 7	1 5
Blade Bone	1 7	1 7	1 7	1 7	1 5
Belly	1 8	1 8	1 8	1 8	1 6
,, Best or Rib end	1 9	1 9	1 9	1 9	1 7
,, in slices	1 9	1 9	1 9	1 9	1 7
,, thin end	1 7	1 7	1 7	1 5	1 5
Flare or Leaf	1 5	1 5	1 5	1 5	1 3
Back fat	1 2	1 2	1 2	1 2	1 0
Chops or Steaks	2 0	2 0	2 0	2 0	1 10
Heads, including Tongue	11	11	11	11	9
,, excluding Tongue	10	10	10	10	8
Tongues	1 6	1 6	1 6	1 4	1 4
Eye Piece or Face	5	5	5	5	5
Chops	1 4	1 4	1 4	1 4	1 4
Hocks	10	10	10	10	10
Feet	5	5	5	5	5
Tenderloin, without bone	2 0	2 0	2 0	2 0	2 0
Pork bones, excluding Factory bone	5	5	5	5	5
Sausages to contain not less than 67 per cent. Pork	1 7	1 7	1 7	1 7	1 7
Sausages to contain not less than 50 per cent. Pork	1 5	1 5	1 5	1 5	1 5
Blood sausage and Black Pudding	—	1 0	1 0	1 0	1 0

OFFALS

Cattle Offal (Home killed)

	s. d.		s. d.	s. d.	s. d.
Head, excluding tongue	4		5	3	3
Tongue, fresh or pickled	1 1		1 4	1 4	1 4
Hearts, whole	11		1 1	10	10
,, cuts of	1 2		1 3	1 0	1 0

	In force Aug. 14, 1918		Jan. 22, 1919		Aug. 13, 1919		Jan. 14, 1920	

Cattle Offal (Home killed)

	s.	d.	s.	d.	s.	d.	s.	d.
Liver, whole	1	0	1	1	1	0	1	0
,, cuts of . . .	1	2	1	4	1	2	1	2
Lights, per set . . .	1	6	1	6	1	6	1	6
Melt		4		4		4		4
Tripe, dressed . . .	1	0		—	1	0	1	0
Feet, scalded		4		5		3½		3½
Tail	1	4	1	4	1	2	1	2
Heart and throat bread .	1	4	2	4	1	4	1	4
Gut breads . . .		6		6		6		6
Skirt and Kidney . .	1	4	1 4 or 1	6	1	4	1	4
Cheek, boneless . .	1	2	1	3		11		11
Brains		6		6		6		6

Sheep Offal (Home killed)

	s.	d.	s.	d.	s.	d.	s.	d.
Heads, without Horns .		4		5		4		4
Tongues . . .	1	0	1	1	1	0	1	0
Brains	1	0	1	1	1	0	1	0
Kidneys . . .	2	6	2	6	2	6	2	6
Sweetbreads . . .	2	0	2	6	2	6	2	6
Trotters, raw, cleaned, and excluding hoof each . .		2		2		2		2
Heart	1	4	1	4	1	2	1	2
Liver	1	6	1	6	1	6	1	6
Lights per set . . .		4		5		4		4

Calves Offal (Home killed)

	s.	d.	s.	d.	s.	d.	s.	d.
Head, scalded . . .		10		10		—		8
Sweetbreads . . .	2	6	2	6		—	2	6
Feet		6		6		—		6
Heart	1	2	1	2		—	1	2
Liver	1	9	1	9		—	1	9
Lights per set . . .		6		6		—		6

Pigs Offal (Home killed)

	s.	d.	s.	d.	s.	d.	s.	d.
Plucks or plucks and fats .		10		11		11		11
Inwards or Chitterlings .	1	0	1	2	1	2	1	2
Liver and fats . . .	1	4	1	4	1	4	1	4
Heart	1	2	1	2	1	2	1	2
Lights per set . . .		4		4		5		5

There are some slight additions to the list in the later tables. Prices are also given for veal and for imported offals.

Bacon, Ham, and Lard. In November 1917 the retailer's profit was limited to an average of 3*d.* per lb. for bacon and hams and 2*d.* for lard over the cost of the goods to him. In July–August 1918 a schedule of prices was prescribed, which remained in force till April 1919, at which date it was simplified. In August 1919 a detailed schedule at highei prices for some cuts was fixed and was not changed till after March 1920. The schedule may be abbreviated as follows :

	August 1918 per lb.	August 1919 per lb.
Pale, dried, or smoked Bacon, or Ham (uncooked)	s. d.	s. d.
Back, middle, rolled or boneless Bacon or Ham, best cut of Ham or Gammon	2 4	2 6
Streak	2 4	2 4
Shoulder meat and collar without bone . . .	2 0	2 0 or 2 2
Shoulder meat with bone, Gammon or Ham Hock .	1 8	1 9
Flank, Fore Hock	1 4	1 4
Trimmings without bone	1 0	1 0
Shanks, Sheet Ribs	8	8
Bones	2	2

Green Bacon or Ham 1½d. per lb. less in Aug. 1918, 1d. less in Aug. 1919.

From April to August 1919 the only maxima prescribed for the cuts named above were 2s. 4d. for pale dried and smoked and 2s. 2½d. for other, i.e. the same as those already current for the best cuts ; it was apparently left to the retailer to sell the inferior cuts at any price he could.

Fish. Maximum prices were prescribed in March 1918. The following table shows those for some of the principal kinds :

	Aug. 1918	Oct. 1918 to Mar. 1919	Mar. 1919	Aug. 1919	Dec. 1919	Jan. 1920	Feb. to May 1920
	s. d.	s. d.	s. d.	s. d.	s. d.	s. d.	s. d.
Fresh Fish							
Cod . per lb.	1 1	1 0	—	—	9	9	11
Haddocks . .	1 1	1 0	—	—	9	9	11
Hake . . .	1 1	1 0	—	—	10½	1 0	1 1½
Mackerel . .	8	8	8	8	8	8	8½
Plaice . . .	1 8	1 6	—	—	1 4	1 4	1 6
Salmon . . .	3 0	3 0	3 0	3 0	[1]	[1]	[1]
Soles (lemon) . .	1 11	1 9	1 9	—	1 6	1 6	1 8½
Whiting . .	1 1	1 0	—	—	9	9	11
Smoked and Cured							
Cod . . .	1 9	1 7	—	—	1 4	1 4	1 6
Haddock . .	1 9	1 7	—	—	1 4	1 4	1 6
Kippers . . .	11	11	11	11	11	11	10
Bloaters . .	9	9	9	9	9	9	8

From March to December 1919 the prices were decontrolled in the cases where no entry is made. All fish prices were decontrolled after May 1920.

[1] No maximum price stated.

MISCELLANEOUS

Tea. In May 1917 a uniform retail price of 2*s.* 4*d.* per lb. was fixed for 40 per cent. of the tea liberated from bond ; this order was almost immediately modified to 2*s.* 4*d.* for 30 per cent., 2*s.* 8*d.* for 35 per cent., 3*s.* for 25 per cent., while the remaining 10 per cent. was free of restriction. After some modifications it was found that this scheme led to abuse, and in March 1918 ' National Control ' tea was sold at 2*s.* 8*d.* It remained at this price till March 1919, when restrictions were removed.

Sugar. Maximum prices were not fixed in the same way as with other foods, the whole supply being in the hands of the Sugar Commission from the beginning of the War, who determined the prices at which various grades ought to be retailed. Price movements are shown sufficiently in pp. 42–6.

In September 1917 the maximum price for *chocolate* was 3*d.* per oz., and for other sweetmeats 2*d.* per oz. These prices remained till the part of the order referring to them was revoked in March 1919.

In August 1918 the list of maximum prices contained, besides the foods already named, Beehive Sections, Beer, Canned Meat, Cocoa Butter and Powder, Coco-nut desiccated, Coffee, Damaged Grain, Dried Fruit, Dripping, Jam, Poultry and Game, Rabbits, Spirits, and Strawberries. That for November 1918 contained also Apples, Crystallized and Glacé Fruits, Eggs, Grape Nuts, Onions, Oranges and Lemons, Shredded Suet, Vegetarian Butter and Lard, and Vegetable Marrows.

APPENDIX III

REDUCTION IN HOURS OF WORK

(From the *Labour Gazette*, August 1919, pp. 345–6.)

The following table gives particulars of the principal reductions in recognized hours of labour in the various industries of the United Kingdom since the beginning of the present year [viz: 1919].

As regards the adjustments in rates of wages, which accompanied the reductions in hours, in cases where the piece rates have either remained unaltered, or have been increased by definite percentages, the fact is noted in the last column of the table. In other cases the letters (*a*), (*b*), or (*c*) are used to denote respectively adjustments of the following characters :

  (*a*) In trades where workers are paid at weekly, daily, or shift rates, no reduction made in such rates; in other cases, rates increased so as to give weekly wages not less than those previously paid.

  (*b*) Base rates and methods of payment revised to compensate for the shorter hours.

  (*c*) The reduction in hours was accompanied by new minimum weekly rates, and a provision that piece rates are to be increased so as to enable the average worker to earn 25 per cent. above such minimum rates.

PRINCIPAL REDUCTIONS IN RECOGNIZED HOURS OF LABOUR DURING 1919

Industry [1]	District	Hours of Labour in a full ordinary week at		Particulars (see Note, p. 215) of Wage Adjustments	
		December 31, 1918	July 31, 1919	Time Rates of Wages	Piece Rates of Wages
BUILDING AND ALLIED TRADES					
Building trade operatives	Certain towns in Yorkshire, Lancashire, Cheshire, and North Wales	48½ to 55½ [2]	46½ [2]	(a)	—
Building trade operatives	Scotland	50 [2] (generally)	44	(a)	—
Electricians (maintenance work)	United Kingdom	48 to 56	47	(a)	—
MINING AND QUARRYING					
Coal mining, &c.:					
Underground workers	Great Britain	8 per shift [3]	7 per shift [3]	(a)	(a)
Surface workers	Great Britain	51 to 58 [4]	46½	(a)	—
Ironstone mining:					
Underground workers	Cleveland and Ayrshire	8 per shift [3]	7 per shift [3]	(a)	(a)
Surface workers	Cleveland and Ayrshire	Various	46	(a)	—
China-clay mining	South Devon and Mid-Cornwall	46	42	(a)	(a)
Shale mining, &c.:					
Surface workers and oil workers	Scotland	50 to 54	49	(a)	—
Limestone quarrying	West and South Durham	48	46½	(a)	—
Slate quarrying	North Wales	52½ to 55 [2]	47 and 47½ [2]	(a)	—
METAL, ENGINEERING, AND SHIPBUILDING TRADES					
Pig-iron and iron and steel manufacture:					
Shift workers	North of England, Midlands, South Wales, and Scotland	8 or 12 per shift	8 per shift	(b)	(b)
Day workers		Various	47 and 48	(a)	—

Engineering, boilermaking, and ship-building trades	United Kingdom	58 or 54 [5]	47	(a)	No change.[6]
Timplate manufacture:					
Shift workers on alternate day and night shifts	South Wales and Monmouthshire	8 to 12 per shift	8 per shift	(a)	No change.
Other shift workers		6 to 8 per shift	6 per shift [7]	(a)	—
Day workers			47	(a)	—
Ammunition making, brass-working, bridge-building, nut, bolt, nail, screw, rivet, hollow-ware, tube, sheet metal, spring, anvil and vice, wagon building, wire rope, tank, &c., making	Midland Counties	53 (generally) 53 or 54	47	(a)	No change.
Light castings manufacture	England and Scotland	50 to 54	47	(a)	No change.
Lock and latch making	Wolverhampton, Wednesbury and district	54	47	(a)	Increased 10%
Tube manufacture	Glasgow, Airdrie, and Coatbridge	54 to 59	47	(a)	No change.
Heating and domestic engineering	England and Wales	52½ to 54	47	(a)	—
	Sheffield	Various	47	(a)	No change.
Edge tool manufacture	Birmingham and Wolverhampton districts	54	47 and 48	(a)	No change.
Jewellery, silver, and electroplate working	Sheffield and Birmingham	49 to 55	47	(a)	Increased 5%

1 Except where otherwise stated the particulars given apply to the operatives generally in the industry specified.

2 The hours quoted are those for the summer months; in winter the weekly hours are less.

3 The length of the shift is defined as the period between the times at which the last man in the shift leaves the surface and the first man in the shift returns to the surface.

4 Except in Northumberland and Durham, where, in some cases, the hours were longer.

5 In certain districts and at certain firms the hours were less.

6 Where a workman is not able to earn on piece work his previous remuneration on the same job, suitable adjustments are made in the piece-work price for that job.

7 Subject to the reservation that no extra mills shall be started in individual works until all mills now working in those works are on 6-hour shifts; but no mills to be stopped in order to change from 8- to 6-hour shifts.

PRINCIPAL REDUCTIONS IN RECOGNIZED HOURS OF LABOUR DURING 1919 (continued)

Industry[1]	District	Hours of Labour in a full ordinary week at		Particulars (see Note, p. 215) of Wage Adjustments	
		December 31, 1918	July 31, 1919	Time Rates of Wages	Piece Rates of Wages
METAL, ENGINEERING, AND SHIPBUILDING TRADES (continued)					
Spelter manufacture:					
Daymen	Swansea	54 (generally)	47	(a)	(a)
Shift workers	Swansea	Various	8 per shift	(a)	—
Bobbin and shuttle making	Cumberland, Westmorland, Yorkshire, Lancashire, and Nottinghamshire	Various	48	(a)	(a)
Farriery	London, Yorkshire, Lancashire, Glasgow, Edinburgh, and other districts	51 to 55	47 and 48	(a)	—
TEXTILE TRADES					
Cotton industry	Lancashire, Cheshire, and adjoining counties	55½	48	(a)	Increased 30% on list prices.[2]
Woollen and worsted industry	England and Wales	55½ (generally)	48	(a)	(a)
	Various districts in Scotland	49¼	48	(a)	(a)
	Yorkshire	54 to 55½	48	(a)	(a)
Textile bleaching, printing, dyeing, &c., trades	Lancashire, Cheshire, and Derbyshire	55½ to 56 (day) 50 to 52½ (night)	48 (day) 43¾ (night)	(a) (a)	Increased 13 to 15%
	Scotland	55 to 56	48	(a)	(a)
Silk industry	Leek, Macclesfield, Congleton, Brighouse, and Braintree districts	49½ to 56	49	(a)	No change.
Linen, bleaching, dyeing, and finishing	Belfast and North of Ireland	Various	49½	(a)	(a)

Trade	District	Previous hours	Present hours		
Carpet manufacture	Kidderminster and various districts in Yorkshire and Lancashire	55 and 55½	48	(a)	Increased 15%
Hosiery manufacture	Various districts in Scotland	49 to 56	48	(a)	Increased 15%
Dyeing and finishing	Leicester and Loughborough districts	Various	48	(a)	Increased 7½%
		56	48	(a)	Increased 10%
CLOTHING TRADES					
Boot and shoe manufacture	United Kingdom	52¼[1] (generally)	48	(o)	(c)
Tailoring (ladies' trade)	London (West End)	50	48	(a)	(a)
Dressmaking and millinery (retail)	Scotland	Various	44	(a)	—
Tailoring (bespoke trade)	Scotland	51 (average)	47¾	(a)	(a)
Felt-hat making	Bury, Denton, Hyde, and Stockport districts	55¼	46½	(a)	(a)
Laundries	London, Newcastle, Sunderland, Hull, Bristol, and other districts	Various	48	(a)	(a)
TRANSPORT TRADES					
Railway service (traffic section)	United Kingdom	Various	48	(a)	—
Carting, motor driving, stable and garage work, &c.	Great Britain	55½ to 68	48	(a)	—
Tramways (except tradesmen, &c.)	Great Britain	49½ to 61¾	48	(a)	—
Dock labour	Principal ports	Various	44[3] (Belfast 46)	(a)	(a)
Motor omnibus service (drivers and conductors)	London	63 and 64	48	(a)	—
Furniture removing and warehousing	United Kingdom	60 (generally)	48	(a)	(a)

1 Except where otherwise stated the particulars given apply to the operatives generally in the industry specified,
2 Equivalent to about 14 per cent. on current rates.
3 The hours of work are 4 per half-day (i.e. 44 per week), but men are required to be booked a quarter of an hour before starting time for each half-day's work.

PRINCIPAL REDUCTIONS IN RECOGNIZED HOURS OF LABOUR DURING 1919 (continued)

Industry[1]	District	Hours of Labour in a full ordinary week at		Particulars (see Note, p. 215) of Wage Adjustments	
		December 31, 1918	July 31, 1919	Time Rates of Wages	Piece Rates of Wages
OTHER TRADES					
Printing and allied trades	United Kingdom	50 or 51 (generally)	48	(a)	(a)
Pottery manufacture	North Staffordshire	52	47	(a)	(a)
Cement making	United Kingdom	54 to 56½	48	(a)	(a)
Chemical manufacture	England and Wales	53 or 54 (generally)	47	(a)	—
Explosives manufacture	Great Britain	50 to 53	47	(a)	
Furniture manufacture	Principal centres in England and Wales	48 to 53	44 to 48	(a)	(a)
Vehicle building	Principal districts in Great Britain, and Belfast	50 to 54	47	(a)	—
Packing-case making	London, Manchester, Sheffield, and other districts	48 to 54	47	(a)	
Saw-milling	United Kingdom	49 to 58½	47	(a)	(a)
Breweries	Burton-on-Trent	54	48	(a)	—
Wholesale textile warehouses	London	Various	44	(a)	
Cocoa, chocolate, sugar confectionery, &c., manufacture:					
Time workers	Great Britain	Various	47	(a)	(a)
Shift workers			44	(a)	(a)

	District				
Flour milling:					
Shift workers	Great Britain and various districts in Ireland	56 (generally) {	44	(a)	—
Day workers			47	(a)	—
Saddlery, harness, portmanteau, bag and fancy leather trades (except horse-collar makers and saddlers in the Midlands)	Great Britain	50 to 54	48	(a)	Increased 12½%
Leather tanning, &c.	London, Northampton, Walsall, Yorkshire, and Scotland	50 to 54	48	(a)	(a)

PUBLIC UTILITY SERVICES

	District				
Electrical undertakings:					
Shift workers	London and suburbs	56	48	(a)	—
Day workers		54	47	(a)	—
Gas undertakings:					
Shift workers	Great Britain	Various	8 per shift	(a)	—
Day workers		Various	47	(a)	—
Tramways (see under Transport)					

¹ Except where otherwise stated the particulars given apply to the operatives generally in the industry specified.

PRINCIPAL REDUCTIONS IN HOURS OF LABOUR IN THE VARIOUS INDUSTRIES IN THE UNITED KINGDOM BETWEEN AUGUST 1919 AND OCTOBER 1920

[In continuation of the Table published on pp. 345-6 of the *Labour Gazette* for August 1919.]

(Communicated by the Intelligence and Statistical Department of the Ministry of Labour.)

Industry	District	Hours of Labour in a full ordinary week at		Particulars (see Note, p. 215) of Wage Adjustments	
		December 31, 1918	October 31, 1920	Time Rates of Wages	Piece Rates of Wages
BUILDING AND ALLIED TRADES					
Building . .	United Kingdom generally .	48¼ to 55½	44	(a)	—
MINING AND QUARRYING					
Shale mining:					
Underground workers.	Scotland	8 per day	7 per day	(a)	(a)
Surface workers		Various	46½	(a)	—
Oil workers		Various	48	(a)	—
TEXTILE TRADES					
Cotton industry (firemen, engineers, &c.)	Lancashire and Cheshire with Glossop	55½	48	(a)	—
Silk industry	Brighouse, Leek, and Macclesfield	49¼ to 56	48	(a)	No change.
Linen industry.	Belfast and North of Ireland .	Various	48	(a)	(a)
Linen and jute industry	Dundee, Carnoustie, Perth, Tayport, Forfar, and Kirriemuir	55	48	(a)	(a)
Textile, Dyeing, Bleaching, &c.	Dundee and District	50	48	(a)	Increased 4%
Jute industry (mechanics and other tradesmen, &c.)	Dundee	55	47	(a)	(a)

CLOTHING

Trade	Country				
Glove manufacture:					
Males	England	Various	47	(a)	(a)
Females		Various	44	(a)	(a)
Wholesale clothing trade	Great Britain	Various	48	(a)	(a)
Shirt and collar making	Great Britain	Various	48	(a)	(a)

OTHER TRADES

Trade	Country				
Paper manufacture:					
Dayworkers	United Kingdom	Various	48	(a)	|
Shiftworkers		Various	44	(a)	|
Paper-bag manufacture	Great Britain	Various	48	(a)	|
Coopering	United Kingdom	Various	47	(a)	|
Baking	England and Wales	48 to 60	48	(a)	|
	Scotland	48 to 55	44	(a)	|
Incandescent mantle manufacturing industry	Great Britain	Various	48	(a)	(a)
Leather trade	England and Wales	Various	48	(a)	(a)

INDEX

OUTLINE OF PLAN

FOR THE

ECONOMIC AND SOCIAL HISTORY OF THE WORLD WAR

I

EDITORIAL BOARDS
(Further arrangements to be announced later.)

GREAT BRITAIN

Sir William Beveridge, K.C.B., *Chairman.*
Mr. H. W. C. Davis, C.B.E.
Professor E. C. K. Gonner, C.B.E., M.A., Litt.D.
Mr. Thomas Jones.
Mr. J. M. Keynes, C.B.
Mr. F. W. Hirst.
Professor W. R. Scott.
Professor James T. Shotwell, *ex officio.*

FRANCE

Professor Charles Gide, *Chairman.*
M. Arthur Fontaine, *Vice-Chairman.*
Professor Henri Hauser, *Secretary.*
Professor Charles Rist.
Professor James T. Shotwell, *ex officio.*

BELGIUM

Dr. H. Pirenne, Belgian Editor.

AUSTRIA-HUNGARY

Professor James T. Shotwell, *ex officio, Chairman.*
Professor Dr. Friedrich von Wieser, *Honorary Secretary.*
Professor Dr. Clemens von Pirquet, *Honorary Treasurer.*
Dr. Gustav Gratz.
Dr. Richard Riedl.
Dr. Richard Schüller.

ITALY

Professor Luigi Einaudi, *Chairman.*
Professor Pasquale Jannaccone.
Professor Umberto Ricci.
Professor James T. Shotwell, *ex officio.*

THE BALTIC COUNTRIES

Professor Harald Westergaard (Denmark), *Chairman.*
Professor Eli Heckscher (Sweden).
Mr. N. Rygg (Norway).
Professor James T. Shotwell, *ex officio.*

THE NETHERLANDS

Professor H. B. Greven, Editor for the Netherlands.

MONOGRAPHS IN COURSE OF PREPARATION

(This list includes only those at present in course of preparation, and will be added to from time to time.)

GREAT BRITAIN

British Archives in Peace and War, by Dr. Hubert Hall.
Manual of Archival Administration, by Captain Hilary Jenkinson.
Bibliographical Survey, by Dr. M. E. Bulkley.
The War Government of Great Britain and Ireland with special reference to its economic aspects, by Professor W. G. S. Adams, C.B.
War Government in the Dominions, by Professor A. B. Keith, D.C.L.
The Mechanism of Certain State Controls, by Mr. E. M. H. Lloyd.
Rationing and Food Supply, by Sir William Beveridge, K.C.B., and Professor E. C. K. Gonner, C.B.E.
Prices and Wages in the United Kingdom during the War, by Professor A. L. Bowley.
Food Statistics of the War Period, by Professor E. C. K. Gonner, C.B.E.
Taxation during the War, by Sir J. C. Stamp, K.B.E.
The General History of British Shipping during the War, by Mr. E. Ernest Fayle.
Allied Shipping Control; an Experiment in International Administration, by Mr. J. A. Salter, C.B.
The British Coal Industry during the War, by Sir Richard Redmayne, K.C.B.
The British Iron and Steel Industries during the War, by Mr. W. T. Layton, C.H., C.B.E.
The Wool Trade during the War, by Mr. E. F. Hitchcock.

The Cotton Control Board, by Mr. H. D. Henderson.
Food Production, by Sir Thomas Middleton, K.B.E.
English Fisheries during the War, by Professor W. A. Herdman, C.B.E.
The Labour Unions; Transport trade unions (excluding railways), Mining trade unions, Workshop organization, Railway trade unions, Relation of skilled and unskilled workpeople; by the Labour Research Department (Mr. G. D. H. Cole).
Labour Supply and Regulation, by Mr. Humbert Wolfe, C.B.E.
The Agricultural Labourer during the War, by Mr. Arthur Ashby.
The Health of the Civilian Population during the War, by Dr. A. W. J. Macfadden, C.B.
The Clyde Valley during the War, by Professor W. R. Scott and Mr. J. Cunnison.
Scottish Agriculture during the War, by Mr. H. M. Conacher.
Scottish Fisheries during the War, by Mr. D. T. Jones.
Scottish Textiles (jute) during the War, by Dr. J. P. Day and Dr. R. C. Rawlley.
Source Materials of Relief Organizations in Scotland, by Miss N. Scott.
The Effects of the War on the Economic and Industrial Development of Ireland, by Professor Charles H. Oldham.

FRANCE

Bibliographical Guide to the Literature concerning France for the Economic History of the War, by Dr. Camille Bloch.
Administrative and Constitutional Changes caused by the Economics of the War in France, by M. Chardon.
French Industry during the War, by M. Arthur Fontaine.
The Organization of War Industries, by M. Albert Thomas.
Government Control—National and International, by M. Etienne Clementel.
Rationing and Food Control, by M. Adolphe Pichon.
Price Fixing, by Professor Charles Gide.
Statistical Study of Prices during the War, by M. March.
French Commercial Policy during the War, by Professor Henri Hauser.
The Blockade, by M. Denys-Cochin.
Changes in French Commerce during the War, by Professor Charles Rist.
French Merchant Shipping during the War, by M. Paul Grunebaum-Ballin.
Internal Waterways, Freight Traffic, by M. Pocard de Kerviler.
Reorganization of French Ports, by M. Georges Hersent.
French Railroads during the War, by M. Marcel Peschaud.
Supply of Coal and Petroleum, by M. Peyerimhof.
Metallurgy and Mining, by M. Pinot.
The Chemical Industries, by M. Mauclère.
Aeronautic Industries, by Colonel Dhé.

The Development of Hydraulic Power, by Professor Raoul Blanchard.

Forestry and the Timber Industry during the War, by General Chevalier.

French Agriculture during the War, by M. Augé-Laribé.

Labour during the War, by MM. Oualid and Picquenard.

Unemployment during the War, by M. Crehange.

Women in Industry under War Conditions, by M. Frois.

Syndicalism, by M. Roger Picard.

Foreign and Colonial Labourers in France, by M. Nogaro.

Problem of Housing during the War, by M. Sellier.

Statistics of Population, by M. Huber.

The Cost of the War to France, by Professor Charles Gide.

War Costs : Direct Expenses, by Professor C. Jeze.

War Finances, by M. Truchy.

The Money Market and French Banks, by M. Aupetit.

The Movement of Exchange, by M. Decamps.

Questions of Public Health and Hygiene, by Professor Leon Bernard.

The Economic Redivision of France (Regionalism), by Professor Henri Hauser.

The Invaded Territory of France, by M. Demangeon.

The Refugees, by M. P. Caron.

The Organization of Labour in the Invaded Territories, by M. Boulin.

The Economic History of French Cities during the War, by MM. Sellier (Paris), Herriot (Lyon), Brenier (Marseille), Levainville (Rouen), etc.

The Colonies, by M. Giraud.

Northern Africa, by M. Aug. Bernard.

The Allied Armies in France, by M. Dolleans.

Alsace-Lorraine, by G. Delahache.

BELGIUM

The History of Belgium after the Armistice, by Dr. H. Pirenne.

The Deportation of Belgian Workmen and the Forced Labour of the Civilian Population during the German Occupation of Belgium, by M. Fernand Passelecq.

The Food Supply of Belgium during the German Occupation, by M. Albert Henri.

German Legislation with Reference to the Occupation of Belgium, by M. M. Vauthier and M. J. Pirenne.

Unemployment in Belgium during the German Occupation, by Professor Ernest Mahaim.

The Social History of Belgium during the German Occupation, by M. J. Pirenne.

Destruction of Belgian Industry by the Germans, by Count Kerchove.

AUSTRIA-HUNGARY

Austria-Hungary :

Bibliography of Printed Materials, by Dr. Othmar Spann.

Survey of the Economic Situation in Austria at the Outbreak of the War, by Dr. Richard Schüller.

War Government in Austria-Hungary, by Professor Dr. Joseph Redlich.

The Economic Use of Occupied Territories : Russia and Roumania, by Dr. Gustav Gratz and Dr. Richard Schüller.

The Economic Use of Occupied Territories : Serbia, Montenegro, Albania, by General Kerchnawe.

'Mittel-Europa': the Preparation of a new Joint Economy, by Dr. Gratz and Dr. Schüller.

The Exhaustion and Disorganization of the Hapsburg Monarchy, by Professor Dr. Friedrich von Wieser.

The Break-up of the Monarchy, by Dr. Richard Schüller.

Empire of Austria :

The Economic Situation of Austria before the War, by Dr. G. Stolper.

Regulation of Industry in Austria during the War, by Dr. Richard Riedl.

Food Control and Agriculture in Austria during the War, by Dr. H. Löwen-feld-Russ.

Kingdom of Hungary :

General History of the War Economics of Hungary, by Dr. Gustav Gratz.

Public Health and the War in Austria-Hungary :

General Survey, by Professor Dr. Clemens von Pirquet.

Military Survey, by Colonel Georg Veith.

(Others to follow.)

THE UNITED STATES

Guide to American Sources for the Economic History of the War, by Mr. Waldo G. Leland and Dr. N. D. Mereness.

Cornell University Library

HB 235.G7B78

Prices and wages in the United Kingdom,

3 1924 002 583 205

This volume from the
Cornell University Library's
print collections was scanned on an
APT BookScan and converted
to JPEG 2000 format
by Kirtas Technologies, Inc.,
Victor, New York.
Color images scanned as 300 dpi
(uninterpolated), 24 bit image capture
and grayscale/bitonal scanned
at 300 dpi 24 bit color images
and converted to 300 dpi
(uninterpolated), 8 bit image capture.
All titles scanned cover to
cover and pages may include
marks, notations and other
marginalia present in the
original volume.

The original volume was digitized
with the generous support of the
Microsoft Corporation
in cooperation with the
Cornell University Library.

Cover design by Lou Robinson,
Nightwood Design.

14272169R00159

Printed in Poland
by Amazon Fulfillment
Poland Sp. z o.o., Wrocław